THE SIXTIES AT 40

Leaders and Activists Remember and Look Forward

Ben Agger

Paradigm Publishers
Boulder • London

For Kreg Viestenz and all the others

Copyright © 2009 Paradigm Publishers

Published in the United States by Paradigm Publishers, 3360 Mitchell Lane Suite E, Boulder, CO 80301 USA.

Paradigm Publishers is the trade name of Birkenkamp & Company, LLC, Dean Birkenkamp, President and Publisher.

Library of Congress Cataloging-in-Publication Data
Agger, Ben.
    The sixties at 40 : leaders and activists remember and look forward / Ben Agger.
        p. cm.
    Includes bibliographical references and index.
    ISBN 978-1-59451-691-7 (hardcover : alk. paper)—ISBN 978-1-59451-692-4 (pbk. : alk. paper)
    1. Protest movements—United States—History—20th century.   2. Peace movements—United States—History—20th century.   3. Civil rights—United States—History—20th century.   4. Political activists—United States—History—20th century.   5. United States—History—1961–1969. 6. United States—Politics and government—1961–1963.   7. United States—Politics and government—1963–1969.   8. Nineteen sixties—History. I. Title.
    HN59.A533 2009
    303.6'6097309046—dc22

                                    2009015324

Printed and bound in the United States of America on acid-free paper that meets the standards of the American National Standard for Permanence of Paper for Printed Library Materials.

Designed and Typeset by Mulberry Tree Enterprises.

13   12   11   10   09   1   2   3   4   5

Contents

Preface

The sixties would not have brought such significant gains on many fronts without the enormous courage of so many people. This was physical courage: You could get killed. It was emotional courage: People stood up for what they believed in, and they broke ranks with comfortable consensus and risked ostracism. Today, people hew to the center because that is safe. It is easy to forget the courage of earlier generations, or perhaps people do not know of it. This book presents profiles in courage.

At the end of this book, I speak of walking the Oregon coast in 1968 after Lyndon Baines Johnson announced that he would not seek a second term as president. Bobby Kennedy, who threw his hat in, could not have known that he would die shortly because of that decision. The rough Oregon surf was a metaphor of the sixties. It boiled with the blood of those who sacrificed or were simply innocent. Occasionally, treasures would be disgorged from the pounding, blood-stained surf: civil rights legislation, an end to the war, the empowering of a generation. I have not been back to that beach—perhaps my generation's Omaha Beach—but I would find it still roiling and crimson. The blood of the Vietnamese and civil rights workers would have been replaced with that of Iraqis and Afghans and, as always, of our own soldiers, who never seemed to have a chance. But this time the prized Japanese glass floats deposited onshore from faraway fishing nets would be called Barack Obama—born of the sixties and of our struggles then. Watching Jesse Jackson cry on election eve in November 2008 made me aware of the connections that tie us to that era, when courage animated great and enduring deeds. These were tears of joy. He had shed different, sorrowful tears forty years earlier when he watched Martin Luther King die. I want to remember the sixties by crying tears of joy, but also by mourning those many who gave their lives and liberty to the movement. Those like me who were privileged and avoided war have an obligation to tell these stories, so that we can put an end to war and death and injustice.

Acknowledgments

I could not have written this book without the help and support of my fourteen interview subjects—the people who helped make the sixties. Of course, it is their book because these are their words. Others offered invaluable assistance, editorial and intellectual. The manuscript was read by Lionel Lewis, Tim Luke, Steve Dandaneau, Roxanne Dunbar-Ortiz, Tom Hayden, Steve Maizlish, Ken Philp, Jeremy Varon, Kevin Wehr, and Becky Thompson. Assistance was provided by Chesa Boudin, Naomi Jaffe, and Sam Greene. Gary Mack of the Sixth Floor Museum in Dallas clarified crucial issues for me about the JFK assassination. Dean Birkenkamp advised me patiently to rethink the first version and restructure the second version. I resisted, but, to quote Charles Lemert, "Dean is always right!" Finally, finally, we got to the finish line with this version. In retrospect, I was trying to solve the riddle of the sphinx: how I belong to the sixties and how they belong to me. Sharon Daugherty of Paradigm performed the exhausting and exhaustive photo research and secured permissions, helping the book become available to a multimedia generation of readers. She and I know that the book would have been delayed a decade had I tried to do that skilled work!

Invaluable assistance was provided by a number of Eugeneans. Heather Briston and Lesli Larson of the University of Oregon archives opened the vault of images and memories. President David Frohnmayer of the University of Oregon provided the key to the vault. Fred Tepfer took a number of important photos and was unfailingly helpful and cheerful. Freddy, as we knew him then, was a partner in crime at South Eugene High School those many years ago. Dan Goldrich helped me look for something that probably does not exist! Caroline Imbert, an adopted Eugenean, offered me many wonderful photos of Eugene and Oregon, one of which I use toward the end of this book. Adrian Vaaler, Kerry Viestenz, and Kathleen Allison provided indispensable background information.

Like it or not, we live in interesting times.
—Robert Kennedy

✌ One ✌

Time It Was:
Telling the Sixties Politically

If you can remember anything about the sixties, you weren't really there.

—Paul Kantner

By now, the subject of "the sixties" should have been laid to rest. There have been many books, articles, films, and songs about that tumultuous decade. I am a baby boomer, raised "in modest comfort," as Tom Hayden said of our middle-class generation at the beginning of Students for a Democratic Society's (SDS) 1962 Port Huron Statement, which launched the New Left. We baby boomers are obsessed with ourselves, including our own pasts. But my interests are neither nostalgic nor antiquarian. This is not a definitive history. Rather, I look forward by looking back, learning from that time forty years ago in order to grapple with our present difficulties and opportunities. In particular, I want to "tell" the sixties to young people for whom the sixties are but a rumor of marijuana and album rock. They need to know that we were young once.

The decade is becoming clear to me only long after the fact, which is perhaps the way it always is when people living in turbulent times fail to understand the convergence of their personal histories with history itself, adolescence blurring with activism. I want to sort this out, but in a way that offers insights to kids today, to whom history seemed closed off until Obama.

A book like this should begin with true confessions that disclose the author's perspective on the past and the present. Although I fondly remember certain things about the sixties—civil rights, early

1

SDS, my first kiss, concerts—I have come to realize, as I did research for this book, that I did not particularly like the sixties. There was too much pain and too many casualties, on all sides. But there is something I dislike more than the sixties, and that is the dominance of the Right, today and yesterday. The Right blames the sixties for all that is wrong and uses this blaming to push back the significant gains of civil rights and equal opportunity achieved in that decade. In addition, and this comes out more clearly when I discuss the unraveling of the sixties into "revolutionary" politics, the Right was challenged by a Left in its image—violent, dogmatic, closed. What I remember most vividly about my last years in high school is how people on both sides used derogatory terms such as "gook," "pig," and "nigger." People's complex humanity was reduced to slogans that dehumanized. I am hopeful that Barack Obama's recent election will move us beyond race, which was always the way to go. As a parent, I realize that kids do not see "color" and they are the future.

The issue here is not whether I personally like or dislike the sixties but why I came to this project with fondness and nostalgia for those events and experiences and yet ended with a more somber perspective. This nostalgia afflicts many of us who wear peace buttons and listen to sixties music on our car radios or CD players. We want to relive and revive those exciting times, and with good reason: The politics was more progressive and people were freer—to challenge authority, think outside the box, experiment. This is all good. However, in succumbing to nostalgia, we repress what really happened: The Klan murdered black and white people; millions died in Vietnam, at "our" hand; police beat nonviolent protesters. The Right consolidated its turf and toehold in power by decade's end. The sixties were a decade of defeat, a decade of death.

I plan to teach this book because "telling" the sixties can keep the good parts alive. I will recommend background reading and videos that capture those times. I recommend a book, long out of print, called *Diana: The Making of a Terrorist*, by Thomas Power (1971). The book was first published only a year after some radicals called Weatherman (colloquially known as the Weathermen) blew themselves up in a Manhattan townhouse as they made bombs to kill American soldiers. The heartbreaking story is about a nice privileged girl from the Midwest who got caught up in "the movement," who was in way over her head. It was almost as if trouble chose Diana Oughton, poisoning her good intentions to help people. There were many Dianas who lost their way as the decade went bad, which it may have done nearly at the beginning.

During that decade, pathology coexisted with perspective. Sometimes young people were more mature than their parents and adult decisionmakers. People were willing to speak truth to power, to be passionate and genuine. Members of my generation lacked pretense and valued commitment. But some went over the top, perhaps driven there by events that seemed lunatic. I realize that the sixties I liked lasted only a few years, from about 1960, with the emergence of the civil rights movement (in an outfit called the Student Non-Violent Coordinating Committee, or SNCC); to the assassination of President John Kennedy in 1963, to a famous civil rights march originating in Selma, Alabama, in 1965. In between was the Port Huron Statement, about which I speak later. After Kennedy was gone, the Vietnam War escalated irretrievably. And even before Martin Luther King Jr. was assassinated in 1968, the civil rights movement was moving toward Black Power. We saw that, for example, in the Black Panthers, who read from the same militant and military script as Weatherman. They wanted to fight, but the odds were against them. They were also macho, which is an important part of the sixties story. A major difference between the Panthers and Weatherman was that the Panthers were interested in self-defense: Blacks had been brutalized during the early years of SNCC (1960–1965), and the Panthers took up the gun in order to protect their communities. No one was assaulting the privileged young white kids who made up Weatherman. They chose violence as a strategy, even if there were underlying issues of male self-identity in play (as there also were for the Panthers).

WHY THE SIXTIES?

There are many good books about the sixties. Jim Miller's (1987) *"Democracy Is in the Streets": From Port Huron to the Siege of Chicago* and Todd Gitlin's (1987) *The Sixties: Years of Hope, Days of Rage* are important contributions. Kirkpatrick Sale (1973) wrote a detailed book about SDS with that title. Tom Hayden's (1988) *Reunion: A Memoir* is a searching account of his own participation in that fascinating decade. Wini Breines (1982) analyzed the early SDS and student movement in her *Community and Organization in the New Left, 1962–1968*. Perhaps above all, Cleveland Sellers's (1990) autobiographical work, *River of No Return: The Autobiography of a Black Militant and the Life and Death of SNCC*, eloquently interweaves a public account of important events, such as the Orangeburg shootings in South Carolina during 1968, and his own participation in them. And I recently received another book in my mail about the legacy of the sixties, suggesting that these are not settled issues. Or perhaps we baby boomers and ex–New Left activists have not settled our score with the sixties, which may amount to the same thing.

Why offer another book on the sixties, so long after that decade's end? The first reason is both sociological and demographic: The sixties are still with us; they are all around us in their consequences; and they are in us, people formed by the sixties and their children, who were raised by sixties parents. Although we baby boomers are highly diverse, populating and influencing both "blue" and "red" states, many of us are sixties people—progressive, introspective, antiauthoritarian, sometimes hubristic. The sixties consequences include the enduring dominance of the Right, which was made possible by President Richard Nixon and FBI director J. Edgar Hoover's counterrevolution against the New Left and the Black Panthers. The Right's dominance connects then and now, making a study of the sixties in effect a study of today's dangerous world.

A second reason for writing this book is that there are dramatic parallels, as well as connections, between the 1960s and the present: We are mired in a foreign war; conservatives have controlled the political agenda for most of the last forty years; conflict abounds on the domestic front; patriotism amounts to a loyalty oath.

A third reason is this: We can learn from the sixties about the role young people might play in dramatic social change. Perhaps young people today lack examples of kids who made a difference, another reason to "tell" them the sixties.

Although this book will resonate with the children of the sixties, who are now parents, it is also intended for the "children of the children," the postboomers who struggle to make sense of their world and who seek community electronically. Many of the events discussed are familiar to people born between about 1946 and 1960, the official span of the baby boom. I explore these events for younger readers, teasing out their significance for the world we inhabit and for the possibility of future activism. Not all young people are on the sidelines. Many made up Barack Obama's cyberarmy of supporters, organizers, and donors in his successful 2008 bid for the presidency.

In spite of the impressive literature on the sixties written by scholars of social movements and contemporary American history, misconceptions about the sixties abound among the general public and even the media. Many remembrances of the sixties emphasize cultural experiences and expressions over political movements and conflict. This is a decade redolent of sweet-smelling incense, with a background sound track containing familiar golden oldies. The book I received in the mail, *Prime Green: Remembering the Sixties* (Stone 2007), suggests that the sixties were a distant, dreamy time, an Age of Aquarius. Other histories emphasize a uniform decade, with common experiences and a gradually building narrative, such that we can even talk about a moment called "the sixties."

And then there is what Garrison Keillor calls "The Great Crusade Against the Sixties." The Right's version of the decade stresses excess and extremism and lays contemporary problems at the feet of sixties radicals, who are now asked to repent for their sins forty years ago (see Ellis 2000). This story blames professors, educated during the sixties and now in their sixties, for the moral drift of the country, even, astonishingly, for the events of 9/11 (see D'Souza 2007). Participants in the so-called culture wars struggle to define not only the present but also our past. The remarkably progressive gains of the sixties—think of civil rights and the antiwar movement—are reinterpreted as the causes of today's dysfunctional entitlement programs, welfare cheaters, and the demise of the family supposedly brought about by gay marriage. Keillor makes it clear that the issue of our past is not of idle academic interest. It is a matter of public interest at a time when we waste lives in Iraq, have tortured prisoners of war, and permit domestic repression in the name of nation. He is heartbroken about the Right's betrayal of democracy.

I challenge the nostalgic and neocon versions of the sixties by offering a distinctive perspective on the decade. Jeremy Varon, an astute historian of the decade, reminds me that historians already know many of these things. However, I am telling this story not for academics but for the young who have not heard this before and for their sixties parents, who are still wondering what to make of their formative years. And the story I tell has archival value because much of my narrative flows through the voices of sixties leaders and activists whom I asked to reflect on these times and their implication for the present and future.

My discussion with the leaders I interviewed focused on six broad issues, highlighted in the following list. These issues help structure the book.

- *The sixties were a decade of discontinuity and a gradual dispiriting unraveling.* The sixties started well, with civil rights, Kennedy, and SDS's participatory democracy, but they ended badly, with Nixon's domestic repression, Weatherman, and the escalation of the tragic Vietnam War. These shifts make a seamless narrative of that decade impossible.

- Against many retrospectives of the times, *I emphasize politics over cultures and countercultures* in my account of the decade, even though I acknowledge their intersection. Everyone listened to rock, but fewer participated in what was called "the movement," which was the really interesting thing about the sixties.

- *There are parallels between Nixon/Bush and Vietnam/Iraq as well as connections*, with the Right's triumph by the end of the sixties making way for Ronald Reagan and Bush Jr.'s militarization of foreign policy, aggressive unilateralism, and intolerant patriotism. Central to the Right's continuing dominance is the idea of American manifest destiny.

- *I stress the role of youth, mere twenty-year-olds like Hayden, who changed the world based on reading they did in their college courses and their prodigious political energy and will*, which they channeled into the movement. Until the Obama phenomenon, young people have been understandably turned off politics, but they search for community using unconventional means such as the Internet and text messaging.

- *There was a tendency in the late sixties male Left, both white and black, to become like their enemy*, the Right, which controlled state power and the means of domestic repression. Weatherman tried to fight fire with fire, which was never the way to go, given both overwhelming odds and the tendency of the "revolutionary" Left to resemble the Right in its dogma. Indeed, the Black Panthers tried to protect their community by taking up the gun.

- *The origins of sixties social movements can be traced to the civil rights movement, which began long before 1960.* SDS patterned itself on SNCC, which set the standard for radical nonviolence. The civil rights movement succeeded in bringing about important federal civil rights legislation, but, like SDS, it lost momentum as it abandoned nonviolence in favor of armed self-defense. It was pushed in this direction by the police and the Klan, which inflicted death and destruction on black communities in the South and North. The civil rights movement evolved into a poor people's movement under Martin Luther King's leadership. With King's assassination, the possibility of post–World War II democratic socialism in the United States disappeared.

Many of the people I discuss were real heroes—the civil rights workers in the murderous South, those who burned their draft cards and would not serve, even the poor young men who went to

Vietnam against their will. They were heroes in the way that New York City firemen and policemen were on September 11, 2001. They risked everything in order to do the right thing. However, heroism is often defeated in a "media culture" the likes of which Hayden, early SDS, and the civil rights workers could not have imagined, accustomed as they were to learning about the world through pulp means and perhaps via low-resolution black-and-white televisions. Had SDS's Port Huron Statement been posted on the Internet, it might have floated off into cyberspace, yet another niche Web page with little impact. Or it could have changed everything, given its accessibility. Books, let alone speeches and demonstrations, do not have the impact they once did, which is part of the problem.

Indeed, one of my theses is that the cultural sixties, commercialized by and for graying boomers who buy sixties rock on the installment plan, undercut the sixties told as a story of radical politics and transforming energy. Although countercultural expressions and experiences flavored the times, with rock refracting resistance, sixties cultural commodities have been ripped out of context and sold, like lava lamps and jewelry shaped like a peace symbol, as postmodern artifacts. Bob Dylan shills for iPod, and Jefferson Airplane's "Volunteers" is the anthem of an advertisement for a brokerage house. In an earlier era, that song inspired the Weathermen. Many of us attended concerts and hippie be-ins, and some smoked dope and experimented with hallucinogens. And some still do these things. But the sixties I narrate are largely political, from civil rights to Vietnam to Nixon's repression of the New Left and the Black Panthers. The political sixties are more interesting to me than the cultural sixties because New Left politics held so much promise for a new world, even though this politics was largely defeated by the well-organized Right. The cultural sixties are readily co-opted by the culture industry; think of FM stations devoted to sixties rock. Reexamining the political sixties offers insight about how to deal with the Right today, and it may even provide a powerful "imaginary" of progressive social change, as we adapt SDS's Port Huron Statement, which stressed "participatory democracy," to the current global circumstance.

But, as I explore later, we cannot ignore cultures and countercultures in our political account. The San Francisco bands were antiwar and antiestablishment. Building on black blues and rock, the British bands, such as the Beatles and Rolling Stones, imaginatively criticized middle American materialism. The Doors offered anthems of protest and existential angst. Everyone was steeped in the music, and many attended concerts, which were communal events— gatherings, communities. And politics and pot intermingled. Indeed, one of the major initiatives of the Right beginning at the end of the decade was the "war on drugs," as President Richard Nixon first called it in 1971. The Right believed that getting high could have political implications as young people escaped into a world of yellow submarines and strawberry fields.

An organized program named COINTELPRO, which dates from the McCarthy period, was used to keep track of and persecute New Left radicals. When we talk about organized state repression, we are not using abstractions. The U.S. government tormented people who disagreed with official policy. Here, we have a page from the released FBI file of that notorious radical John Lennon, of Beatles fame, in which the FBI is trying to arrest Lennon for possessing "downers" (a depressant drug) in order to have the Immigration and Naturalization Service (INS) deport him to England. By 1972,

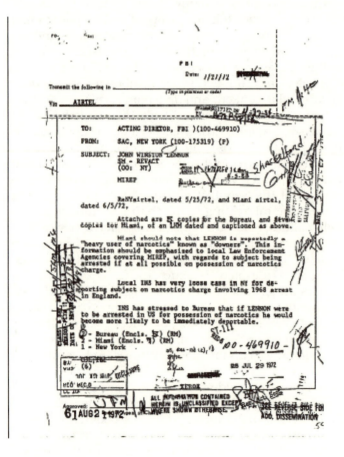

Dangerous John Lennon. (FBI file)

the FBI wanted Lennon, who was against the war in Vietnam, out of sight and out of mind. Lennon's most seditious recommendation was that we give peace a chance.

Organized state repression during the sixties was not confined to the federal government. Here is an image of a memorandum found in the files of the University of Texas at Austin's campus police department. The memo addresses the doings of the SDS chapter on campus, and it cites Tom Hayden, who is described as "the

MEMORANDUM FOR INFORMATION

October 2, 1968

RE:SDS

The SDS held "an educational" meeting October 1, 1968 in Garrison Hall Room 1. Approximately 200 were in attendance at beginning of meeting. DICK HOWARD a former leader in SDS is back in Austin and appeared to be in charge. A representative of the Austin Police Department and a representative of the Texas Department of Public Safety were asked to leave the meeting before HOWARD would talk about the student revolt in France. HOWARD supposedly was in France during the revolt. The officers asked for a vote by those present as to whether they should leave. The majority were in favor of the officers as well as the press being asked to leave. The officers and the press did leave the meeting and about one-fourth of those present walked out with the officers and press. DAVE CLAYTON from Columbia University spoke about how satisfying the riot was at Columbia to those who participated and made a statement which suggested that a similar act be tried here (University of Texas at Austin), CLAYTON received a standing ovation. Consensus is that such an act will not materialize because the leaders alienated too many present. BOB PARDUN is reported to be the "key" man in local SDS as far as National SDS policy. TOM HAYDEN also reported to be the"power" behind National SDS.

Other local leaders noted at meeting were ALAN LOCKLEAR, PHIL RUSSELL, CARLOS ASOCAR and GREG CALVERT. L. CAROLINE, MARIANN VIZARD, and DICK REAVIS not observed at meeting.

Consensus is SDS will likely be more militant than in past and University Committee To End the War in Vietnam less militant.

UT-Austin police department memo about SDS in Austin, Texas, Oct. 2, 1968. (This document was found in the files of former University of Texas campus police chief Allen Hamilton. The document was first revealed to the public in an article by Thorne Dreyer titled "The Spies of Texas," which appeared in the Nov. 17, 2006, issue of the Texas Observer.)

'power' behind National SDS." The memo concludes with the prediction that campus "SDS will be more militant than in past." The campus police were keeping track of radicals. One would have thought that the United States was at war against a foreign force called SDS.

Telling the sixties politically is not a soothing boomer bedtime story. It could produce nightmares. Many lives were wasted in political conflict. However, the decade opened and continued with an idealism largely missing from today's political discourse. Indeed, this idealism preceded the decade, perhaps requiring us to conclude that the sixties began in the fifties, with Rosa Parks's refusal to move to the back of the bus and the Little Rock school desegregation, and continued into the seventies and even beyond, with the legacy of Nixon's domestic repression of dissenters. The four young men who attempted to desegregate a lunch counter in Greensboro, North Carolina, in 1960; the 1961 Freedom Riders; the Port Huron campers in 1962; and the courageous black and white civil rights workers who participated in Freedom Summer in 1964 were the real idealists of the decade, putting their bodies and liberty on the line for social justice. I know that Hayden admired the Kennedys, and I agree with him that if Jack had not been assassinated and then Bobby, the Democrats would probably have won the 1964 and 1968 presidential elections. However, the Kennedys were interested in power. This set them apart from the largely youthful activists. Hayden knows all this, and he responds that the Kennedys could be moved to do the right thing by the protest movement that he helped start. Unlike Nixon, who was impervious, they were in touch with public sentiment and they could be influenced.

To tease out the implications of the political sixties, I interviewed fourteen leaders of the New Left for this study. I sought a diverse group, with multiple perspectives. Some are famous, others less well-known. The interviews were conducted between 2004 and 2009, spanning the campaign that led to Bush's second term as president and, later, Obama's election.

Quotes from black, white, Hispanic, male, and female leaders form the backbone of this book. I explore their agreements and disagreements. I place their debates in historical and sociological context. In our discussions, we explored the New Left, particularly SDS's Port Huron Statement; the impact of a late 1960s faction that took over SDS and promoted a campaign of "exemplary violence" that might today be called terrorism; the relevance of national identity and patriotism for progressive social change; who "won" the sixties, the Right or the Left, and the legacy of that outcome; the origins of the antiwar and women's movements in the civil rights movement; and, finally, their views of the future, which are quite optimistic, even "Pollyannaish," as Dick Flacks describes himself.

The method of this study is largely remembrance and storytelling; call it generational archaeology—a search for both history and identity. Our retelling of the sixties is bound up with our personal experiences of coming of age and our generation's collective experience of major change. There is no other vantage on the sixties, no objective truth apart from perspective. My data are memories, which, as ex-Weatherman Bill Ayers remarks, can twist and distort. The point is the use to which we put our remembering—what we learn about ourselves and what advice we give our children. People's identities are framed by their common life experiences—where they were during epochal events making them who they were and are.

The protagonists in my oral history, founders and leaders of the New Left, had a major impact on our society. Hayden, who authored SDS's Port Huron Statement, perhaps had the most impact. Bob Moses rivaled his influence in early civil rights work. The interviews reveal that all of the activists have reckoned with the sixties and their roles in it; there is very little rationalization or excuse making here, but rather a learning from experience. One of them, David Gilbert, is still in prison for his deeds.

In Chapter 2, I present a chronological outline of the sixties, focusing on the ways in which the optimism early in the decade faded into the despair of the 1968–1970 period, from the assassinations of Robert Kennedy and Martin Luther King to Kent State and Weatherman. Any account of the sixties cannot erase the biases of the author who participated in, and grew up during, that decade. My own memories merely provide context and establish the perspective from which my sixties unfold. There are other sixties and I call for them. They will enrich and correct mine. Because total objectivity is unattainable, I do not erase my own fingerprints; I acknowledge my involvement in the subject matter that I discuss. Confounding the issue is that for many of us, growing up and participating in the sixties movements and moments were inseparable processes. Only some forty years later can I begin to separate the two as I reconstruct my identity as a "sixties person." I grew up in Eugene, Oregon, a college town with its share of antiwar and civil rights politics, and Eugene plays a role in my telling of the sixties.

Chapters 3 through 8 draw heavily from the interviews I conducted. Each of these chapters begins with a stage setting that puts the discussions in context. I conclude the book, in Chapter 9, by considering how my account of the sixties reexamines the parallel between how we grew up during the sixties and how the linear history of events unfolded. For me and many others, the end of the sixties deposited us on the shores of young adulthood. We brought the sixties forward with us. Events imprinted themselves on us, and in our own small ways we affected events. Sometimes we made a difference just by being alive and witnessing what was happening, standing on the periphery of demonstrations and protests. We lent our presence to the huge crowds that, by the decade's close, congregated everywhere to end a war that would not end.

In my interviews with the New Left leaders and activists, there are surprising revelations, interesting disagreements, passion, even contradictions. We learn that Mark Rudd will never fly the American flag. Todd Gitlin is not ashamed to be a patriot, of a certain nonmessianic sort. Flacks confesses his humanist Marxism, whereas Hayden denies his (and they were coauthors of the single most powerful document of the sixties, the Port Huron Statement). Roxanne Dunbar-Ortiz views Martin Luther King in retrospect as a revolutionary. The former activists are learned and self-confident, and they speak at length without hesitation. They are charismatic. Above all, many of them are optimistic, even in these times. I wish I shared their optimism, but perhaps that is why I am an academic, outside the fray, and they are activists. These qualities help explain why they were such successful leaders and organizers some forty years ago. I never had the feeling that these New Left political leaders were telling me what I wanted to hear. They were candid, and, to use a phrase from that era, it was easy to see how they were willing to "speak truth to power." By the time I completed my writing, Obama had been elected president, perhaps vindicating their optimism.

As I refresh my memories, I am surprised by the intermingling of the personal and political that I repressed. Perhaps their connection is the counterculture. Two rock concerts I attended (Jefferson Airplane and the Doors) are sandwiched around two intense political events, the brutal attack on Dick Flacks at the University of Chicago and Weatherman's takeover of SDS, all of which occurred in 1969. I kissed a girl at a Eugene McCarthy rock concert fund-raiser two weeks after King's assassination. I remember both 1968 events clearly, but have no memory that they occurred at nearly the same time.

And yet many sixties veterans, probably older than I was at the time, report that the decade was so unusual because, on occasion, they realized that personal experience had far-reaching historical implications: Attending demonstrations, for civil rights and against Vietnam, produced the experience of *citizenship*, which is often lacking today. We saw the rebirth of citizenship during the recent presidential campaign, which produced a huge turnout. Perhaps this was how the patriots at Concord or the Bolsheviks at the Winter Palace experienced their immersion in history— moments when the present opened directly to the future. As young people grow up today, few have the experience of channeling history, as many of us did then. But that could change, especially if we show them recent examples of children's movements that changed the world. They may already have found their way in their support of Obama.

DRAMATIS PERSONAE

Tom Hayden

Tom helped start SDS in the early 1960s and coauthored the Port Huron Statement. He became a state legislator in California, where he sponsored progressive legislation. Having been term-limited out of office, Tom teaches, writes, and organizes for worthy progressive causes, such as the antisweatshop movement. His memoir *Reunion* remains an essential source for scholars of the sixties.

Tom Hayden, still an activist. (Photo courtesy of City Lights Books/Tom Hayden)

Richard Flacks

Dick was one of SDS's early intellectuals; he grounded the New Left in European debates about socialism. He became a sociologist and recently retired from the University of California at Santa Barbara. He and his wife, Mickey, are involved in progressive politics in Santa Barbara County.

Mark Rudd

Mark was a leader of the Columbia uprising and then helped form the Weathermen. He teaches math at a community college in Albuquerque. His memoir is *Underground* (2009).

Todd Gitlin

Todd was an early SDS president who became critical of Weatherman. He teaches in the journalism school at Columbia. He authored *The Sixties*, an indispensable account of the movement.

Roxanne Dunbar-Ortiz

Roxanne was active in the late sixties radical women's liberation movement. Unlike many of the other activists, she came from hardscrabble roots in rural Oklahoma. She is professor emerita of ethnic studies at Cal State Hayward. Her book *Outlaw Woman: A Memoir of the War Years, 1960–1975* (Dunbar-Ortiz 2002) describes her life during the sixties.

Bob Moses

Bob was a charismatic leader of early SNCC who orchestrated the summer project in 1964. A philosopher by training, he empowers poor kids by teaching them algebra. His Algebra Project could be viewed as an extension of the 1964 Mississippi Summer Project, which he spearheaded.

Casey Hayden

Casey was one of the few high-profile activists who was equally at home in SDS and in SNCC. She wrote influential early papers about how women were second-class citizens in New Left organizations. She is involved in environmental efforts and Buddhism in Tucson.

Frances Beal. (Photo
courtesy of Ruth Morgan)

Frances Beal

Fran, one of the first sixties feminists, was active in SNCC, and she helped unify the concerns of black people and women's liberation. She remains active in the progressive movement and writes and lectures widely, making her home in the San Francisco Bay Area.

Carl Oglesby

Carl was SDS president during the mid-1960s. He parted company with SDS over Weatherman and became a noted student of the JFK assassination. A resident of Amherst, Massachusetts, he recently issued his memoir of the sixties, *Ravens in the Storm: A Personal History of the 1960s Antiwar Movement* (Oglesby 2008).

Cleveland Sellers

Cleve was an important SNCC leader as the organization moved from civil rights to Black Power. He was nearly killed in Orangeburg, South Carolina, in 1968. His young son, Bakari, is a South Carolina state legislator who organized for Obama. Cleve is now president of the historically black Voorhees College, after having taught for years at the University of South Carolina.

Jaja (Tommy Anderson) Nkrumah. (Photo courtesy of Jaja Nkrumah)

Tommy Anderson (now Jaja Nkrumah)

Tommy was a leader of the Eugene, Oregon, Black Panthers, and a close friend and student of my father, Robert Agger. He teaches junior high school in Oakland, California.

David Gilbert

David, a former Weatherman, is serving a life sentence in a New York State prison for a 1981 action in which a robbery to provide funds for the revolution went wrong and law officers were killed.

José Angel Gutiérrez

José Angel is the founder of the Raza Unida Party, an important Mexican American social movement. He teaches political science at the University of Texas at Arlington, where he founded the Center for Mexican American Studies.

Kenneth L. Johnson

Ken was one of the first black jurists in the U.S. military and later a circuit court judge. In his youth, he participated in the Baton Rouge civil rights movement. Retired and residing in Atlanta, Ken publishes political commentary in newspapers and is completing his memoir on an "unfinished America."

‮ Two ‭

Timeline of the Sixties

(Which Begin Earlier)

The chaos of events is tamed by putting them in order, giving the impression of great intensity and turmoil as the movement lurched from battle to battle, foe to foe. This chapter offers a chronology of the decade for readers who do not remember or never knew. The decade seemed to build to a crescendo, after which people lost their energy and their way. Now we are trying to find a way back to the sixties in order to learn from them about issues and opportunities that have many contemporary parallels. This is an attempt to teach the children, who wonder about those heady and desperate times but who mistrust adult nostalgia, perhaps not understanding fully that we were young once. Although linear histories risk imposing order or pattern where none existed, my story of the sixties is aided by a timeline that tracks the gains and defeats of the movement.

Ella Baker (b. 1903)

One could argue that the sixties started just after the turn of the century when Ella Baker was born. Baker was instrumental in starting the Student Non-Violent Coordinating Committee (SNCC) in 1960 after she grew frustrated with the top-down leadership of Martin Luther King's Southern Christian Leadership Conference (SCLC). (See Box 2.1.)

Carl Oglesby (b. 1935)

Elected president of Students for a Democratic Society (SDS) in 1965, Oglesby became a serious student of the assassination of

----------- ⁊ᴐ **Box 2.1** **Ella Baker** ᴄ᙮ -----------

Ella Baker was born in 1903, the granddaughter of a slave. Although she was born in Virginia, she spent much of her adult life in New York as a community organizer and civil rights activist. Between about 1941 and 1946, she worked in the National Association for the Advancement of Colored People (NAACP), but after the Montgomery bus boycotts, she joined with Martin Luther King Jr. and others to form the Southern Christian Leadership Conference (SCLC), of which she was an interim director for a year. She found that King preferred a top-down organization modeled on the black church, but she was inclined toward a more grassroots, bottom-up approach to political organizing. She felt that organizations needed empowered activists more than powerful leaders, a sentiment that defined her political involvements. After four courageous young black men attempted to desegregate a lunch counter in Greensboro, North Carolina, in early 1960, she helped organize the Student Non-Violent Coordinating Committee (SNCC). This organization reflected her grassroots approach, and it also allowed women to play more active roles than in either NAACP or SCLC.

As Tom Hayden indicates in the interviews in this book, there would have been no Students for a Democratic Society (SDS) if there had been no SNCC on which to model it. SDS and SNCC were young men's—and, sometimes, young women's—organizations. Although their leaders, such as Hayden, Bob Moses, and Stokely Carmichael, were charismatic, their organizational cultures stressed consensus formation based on free-flowing discussion. The New Left offered "new" and decentralized models of organization and leadership.

Ella Baker helps found SNCC. (AP Photo/Jack Harris)

Ella's story instructs us that progressive change, although always hard-won, emerges from domination and defeat. She joined and helped organized the civil rights movement as a response to slavery and racism. Her early involvement in those organizations convinced her that they were too top-down and did not allow women to play major roles. She helped form a new type of organization, SNCC, that was attentive to these issues. Of course, SNCC, too, as we see later in this book, had its own issues with sexism. Out of Ella's struggles and the struggles of other progressive women like her, black, white, Chicana, Asian, and American Indian, the women's movement was born. This is the dialectic at work: push, pull, negation, synthesis. Although I cannot interview Ella Baker (she passed away in 1986), I explore her legacy in this book as I talk to the young people she influenced about the types of change and organization for which they all worked.

----------- ᴄ᙮ -----------

John Fitzgerald Kennedy and of the Watergate scandal, which led to President Richard Nixon's resignation. He was the first of his family to work at a white-collar job, and he came to the New Left when he was already in his thirties.

Buddy Holly (1936–1959)

Holly is widely viewed as the first white rocker, whose songs, such as "Peggy Sue," got a younger generation bopping to the beat.

Richard Flacks (b. 1938)

Flacks was one of the prime movers of SDS. He collaborated with Tom Hayden on improving Hayden's draft of the Port Huron Statement. He is now an emeritus sociology professor at the University of California, Santa Barbara.

Tom Hayden (b. 1939)

Hayden, a student at the University of Michigan, became active in the fledgling SDS and authored the first draft of the Port Huron Statement, a document calling for participatory democracy in America; he remained active in the civil rights and antiwar movements during the decade and later spent twenty years as a legislator in California. Here is an image of Hayden, a twenty-two-year-old civil rights worker, being beaten up in Mississippi in 1961.

Hayden getting beaten in McComb, Mississippi, 1961. (Bettmann/Corbis)

Bernardine Dohrn (b. 1942)

A radical lawyer during the sixties, Dohrn helped organize and lead the Weatherman faction of SDS, which took over the organization in 1969. Weatherman bombed key buildings with symbolic importance in order to "bring the war [in Vietnam] home." Dohrn and others went underground as police pursued them, changing the name of their organization from Weatherman to the Weather Underground.

Todd Gitlin (b. 1943)

An early president of SDS while a Harvard student, Gitlin played an active role in the movement, especially offering intellectual contributions. He was also involved in the 1968–1969 San Francisco State action as an "outside agitator." (At San Francisco State, university president S. I. Hayakawa took a hard line against student protesters who went on strike to protest university and national politics.) Todd is now a professor at Columbia who speaks out against the Weather Underground and is somewhat circumspect about the radicalism of the sixties movement.

Bill Ayers (b. 1944)

With Dohrn, Ayers was a founding participant in the Weather movement. He is now Dohrn's life partner and a professor of education at the University of Chicago. His memoir *Fugitive Days* (Ayers 2001) is rather unapologetic about his Weather days. Barack Obama, during his recent presidential campaign, was linked to this notorious radical, who lives in Obama's Chicago neighborhood.

First Indochina War (1946–1954)

France held Indochina, now Vietnam, in colonial status. The Vietnamese attempted to expel the French and fought a nearly decade-long war to accomplish this, which they finally did. This led to U.S. involvement in Vietnam as the Vietnam regime appeared to be Marxist-Leninist. The U.S. government, involved in a cold war with the Soviet Union, did not want to see Soviet or Chinese influence spread. Both the Soviet Union and China were organized along the lines of Marxism-Leninism, with dictatorial rule by the communist party.

Mark Rudd (b. 1947)

Rudd organized the student takeover of Columbia University in 1968, spearheaded by SDS's "action faction." That faction later became a major force in Weatherman, which Rudd joined.

Baby Boom (1947–1960)

Demographers debate the causes of the baby boom, which produced an average of four kids per family, instead of the usual two. Abstinence from fertility during World War II is one explanation. Another is the post–World War II economic recovery, which allowed men to reclaim their jobs from the women who had taken over for them in factories during the war. These women then went home to suburbia and began to have kids in record numbers.

Levittown (1947)

This was the first suburban community built in America, on Long Island, New York. The creation of Levittown began middle-class people's flight from the city to these homogeneous planned communities.

Jackie Robinson Broke into the Major Leagues (April 15, 1947)

Jackie Robinson broke the "color line" when he became the first black professional baseball player to be allowed to play in white-only leagues. Arguably, this event began the civil rights movement as whites realized that blacks could "play" and blacks realized that they, too, could enjoy the fruits of integration.

McCarthy Era (1950–1954)

Senator Joe McCarthy spearheaded the "red scare," which identified and persecuted alleged communists and sympathizers in Hollywood, academia, the government, and even the army. This period caused such fear that leading American intellectuals such as Richard Wright moved to Europe.

First Bus Boycott and Desegregation Effort Staged in Baton Rouge, Louisiana (June 20, 1953)

The first black bus boycott and effort to desegregate public buses was staged in Baton Rouge, Louisiana. This precursor action to the civil rights movement (the beginnings of the sixties found deep in the fifties) was closely monitored by Rosa Parks in Montgomery, Alabama.

U.S. Supreme Court Decision in *Brown v. Board of Education* (May 17, 1954)

In *Brown* the Court held that school segregation was illegal. This Court decision was another important precursor of the civil rights movement, which began with Rosa Parks's attempt to desegregate the bus system in Montgomery, Alabama, the next year.

Rosa Parks Arrested for Trying to Desegregate Montgomery, Alabama, Bus (December 1, 1955)

Rosa Parks courageously refused to sit in the back of a Montgomery bus, challenging the Jim Crow system of segregation that physically separated the races; she sat in the front of the bus in defiance of southern custom at the time.

Rosa Parks riding Montgomery, Alabama bus, Dec. 1, 1955. (Library of Congress)

COINTELPRO Launched (1956–1971)

In the wake of McCarthyism, the FBI launched a counterintelligence program (hence the name COINTELPRO) to seek out and repress domestic radicals; it lasted through the sixties and was used by Richard Nixon to root out white and black radicals. The program involved keeping secret files on the whereabouts and activities of suspected leftists. (These files became available through the Freedom of Information Act of 1966 and the Privacy Act of 1974.)

SCLC Formed (January 10–11, 1957)

The Southern Christian Leadership Conference was a group of largely urban black leaders, including Martin Luther King and Ralph Abernathy, that wanted to be viewed as more mainstream than the National Association for the Advancement of Colored People (NAACP). King spearheaded many civil rights efforts throughout the sixties, until his death in 1968, under the aegis of SCLC, which sometimes allied with SNCC and the Congress of Racial Equality (CORE) to pursue joint desegregation and voter registration efforts, such as in Selma, Alabama, during 1965.

Integration of a Little Rock, Arkansas, High School (September 25, 1957)

Spurred on by *Brown v. Board of Education*, black students attempted to integrate a Little Rock high school called Central High. The National Guard prevented their entrance. Finally, President Dwight Eisenhower sent in one thousand federal troops to assist with the integration, and he federalized the ten-thousand-member Arkansas National Guard, which was standing in the way of integration.

Fulgencio Batista Overthrown in Cuba (January 1959)

Fidel Castro and his Marxist-Leninist revolutionaries, including Che Guevara, overthrew Batista's Cuban dictatorship, in the process extending Soviet influence to the Western Hemisphere and destabilizing cold war–era geopolitics. Members of SDS made trips to Cuba during the sixties to learn about Latin American revolutions and particularly the theories and tactics of Regis Debray, who suggested that revolutions could occur when the rural peasantry was mobilized to spread "exemplary violence" to the urban working classes, a strategy adapted by Weatherman at decade's end.

SDS Formed (January 1960)

This organization, first centered at the University of Michigan, became the biggest antiwar organization of the decade. Initially, it focused on civil rights and patterned itself on SNCC. Like SNCC, it initially favored nonviolent protest and put forward an action plan to reform all of American society around the principle of "participatory democracy," explained in the Port Huron Statement of 1962. Actually, SDS dated back to the late 1950s, when the organization from which it evolved was called the Student League for Industrial Democracy. Al Haber was elected SDS president at the organization's meeting in New York held from June 17 to 19, 1960.

Greensboro, North Carolina, Lunch Counter Sit-in (February 1, 1960)

Four young black men from North Carolina A&T courageously attempted to desegregate a lunch counter in Greensboro, "sitting in" after they were told by a white waitress that they would not be served. Ezell Blair Jr., David Richmond, Joseph McNeil, and Franklin McCain helped bring national visibility to the burgeoning civil rights movement.

Four black students sit in at a Greensboro, North Carolina, lunch counter, Feb. 1, 1960. (Library of Congress)

Sit-ins by Southern University Students in Baton Rouge, Louisiana (March 28, 1960)

On March 28, seven Southern University (SU) students were arrested for sitting in at a Kress lunch counter. They were charged with "disturbing the peace," and their bail was set at $1,500 (the equivalent of $10,000 in 2006 dollars)—an astronomically high bond for a misdemeanor charge. The next day, nine more students were arrested for sitting in at the Greyhound bus terminal. The following day, led by SU student and CORE supporter Major Johns, thirty-five hundred students marched to the state capitol building to protest segregation, the arrests, and the outrageous bail amounts.

Along with Major Johns, the sixteen students who had been arrested were expelled from SU and barred from all public colleges and universities in the state of Louisiana. In response, SU students called for a student strike—a boycott of classes—until the seventeen were reinstated. Said the expelled president of the senior class, Marvin Robinson, who had been arrested in the first Kress sit-in: "What is more important, human dignity or the university? We felt it was human dignity."

NAACP lawyers took the case all the way to the Supreme Court. In 1961, the Supreme Court issued its first decision (*Garner v.*

Southern University sit-ins in Baton Rouge, Louisiana, ca. March 28, 1960. (Bettmann/Corbis)

Louisiana) about desegregation cases of this kind and the students were reinstated to the university. Kenneth Lavon Johnson, then a law student involved in the sit-in and later a circuit court judge, was awarded an honorary degree from the Southern University Law School in 2004 for his role in this landmark effort.

SNCC Formed (April 1960)

In the wake of the Greensboro sit-in, black students across the South staged their own sit-ins. SNCC was formed to organize these efforts, replacing the more top-down organizing models of the NAACP and SCLC with its grassroots approach to organizing. SNCC also had a younger membership.

President John Fitzgerald Kennedy Sworn into Office (January 22, 1961)

The election of John Kennedy to the presidency signaled the beginning of what he called the "New Frontier," a time of optimism, idealism, and activism in America that gave impetus to SDS and the resulting student movement.

President John F. Kennedy's inaugural, Jan. 20, 1961. (AP Photo)

Eight Hundred U.S. "Advisers" in Vietnam
(January 1961)

Kennedy's inauguration saw the beginning of U.S. involvement in Vietnam in the wake of the French defeat. U.S. "advisers" were to give aid and advice to South Vietnamese troops as they engaged the communist North Vietnamese in combat.

The Bay of Pigs Invasion of Cuba (April 1961)

Kennedy supported Cuban ex-patriots living in the United States as they mounted a joint operation to invade Cuba and overthrow Castro. Castro's forces easily rebuffed the invading forces, embarrassing the United States in the process.

Freedom Riders in Birmingham, Alabama
(May 20, 1961)

Freedom Riders, led by CORE's James Farmer, took two separate buses from northern cities to the South in order to test recent legislation (*Boynton v. Virginia* 1960) that outlawed racial segregation in interstate transportation terminals. The white civil rights workers sat in the back of the bus, and the black civil rights workers sat in the front. They used the restrooms earmarked for the other race in the bus terminals. Predictably, the Klan beat the riders, and one of their buses was burned. Attorney General Bobby Kennedy sent his assistant to accompany one of the buses, signaling cooperation between the Kennedys and the civil rights movement.

James Meredith at the University of Mississippi
(October 1, 1961)

Meredith helped end Jim Crow, the segregation of blacks and whites in the South, by entering the heretofore segregated University of Mississippi; federal troops had to protect him against death threats.

SDS Port Huron Convention (June 11–15, 1962)

SDS had been in existence for two years when it convened at a United Auto Workers summer camp on Lake Huron, Michigan, to discuss, revise. and ratify Tom Hayden's manifesto for a "New Left" that stressed participatory democracy in all walks of American life. Hayden's intellectual sources were C. Wright Mills, Albert Camus, and John Dewey.

Cuban Missile Crisis (October 1962)

Cuba, then a strong ally of the Soviet Union, allowed the Soviets to install missiles on its territory that could easily reach U.S. shores. In response, President Kennedy insisted that the missiles be removed, and he deployed a naval blockade around Cuba to prevent Soviet vessels from importing the missiles. In a potentially deadly example of "brinksmanship," the United States called the USSR's bluff; the Soviets turned their vessels around and discontinued their deployment of offensive weapons in Cuba. Americans stockpiled food and supplies in case a nuclear war broke out between the United States and the USSR.

Publication of *The Feminine Mystique* (February 19, 1963)

Betty Friedan (2001 [1963]) launched the "second wave" of the women's movement by publishing her book, which articulated middle-class women's dissatisfaction with their lives in the suburbs. They lived vicariously through their husbands and children and did not develop their own identities, according to Friedan. Millions of American women viewed this as a manifesto urging them to go to college, establish careers, and work politically for women's gains.

Civil Rights Demonstrators in Birmingham, Alabama, Hosed and Set upon by Police Dogs (May 1963)

The emerging civil rights movement in the South, led by Reverend Martin Luther King, met with fierce opposition from the Ku Klux Klan, White Citizens' Councils, and the local police. Birmingham police chief Bull Connor led a particularly vicious police attack on civil rights demonstrators in Birmingham, which caught the attention of the national press and of the Kennedys, who sent federal troops to protect civil rights workers.

President John Kennedy's Call for Disarmament and an End to the Cold War (June 10, 1963)

At a commencement speech at American University in Washington, DC, President Kennedy revealed his evolving foreign policy as he made conciliatory remarks about the Soviet Union and urged an end to the cold war and nuclear disarmament.

NAACP Leader Medgar Evers Murdered in Jackson, Mississippi (June 12, 1963)

The NAACP paralleled SNCC's desegregation efforts. Its leader, Medgar Evers, was murdered as the Klan and other whites violently opposed the spreading efficacy and popularity of the civil rights movement among both blacks and whites.

Medgar Evers. (Library of Congress)

Reverend Martin Luther King Jr.'s "I Have a Dream" Speech in Washington, DC (August 28, 1963)

Martin Luther King addressed an audience of over two hundred thousand in the nation's capital and uttered the famous words "free at last" to express his hopes for the civil rights movement.

FBI Memo Branding Martin Luther King Jr. a "Demagogue" and Warning About "Negro" Involvement in the Communist Party (August 30, 1963)

In an extraordinary FBI memo written just after the "I Have a Dream" speech, the FBI characterized King as "the most dangerous Negro" in the United States and explored ties between the civil rights movement and the Communist Party of the USA.

Four Black Girls Killed in a Church Bombing in Birmingham, Alabama (September 15, 1963)

The Klan's counter-revolution against civil rights continued with the death of four teenage girls in a bombing of a Baptist church in Birmingham. Addie Mae Collins, Carole Robertson, Cynthia Wesley, and Denise McNair ranged in age from eleven to fourteen. (Only recently were the remaining living perpetrators finally brought to justice after years of police and Klan protection.)

President John Kennedy Assassinated in Dallas, Texas (November 22, 1963)

President Kennedy was assassinated in Dallas, Texas. The suspected murderer, Lee Harvey Oswald, was himself murdered a few days later while in police custody. (Conspiracy theories still abound about how Oswald could not have been the lone gunman.) Lyndon Johnson, Kennedy's vice president, assumed the presidency. (Most Americans over the age of fifty probably remember what they were doing when they heard the shocking news that Kennedy was dead.)

More Than Sixteen Thousand U.S. troops in Vietnam (November 1963)

There has been speculation that Kennedy wanted to withdraw the United States from Vietnam; by the time of his assassination, there were over sixteen thousand troops in that country. Johnson quickly escalated the war and increased the number of U.S. troops.

Tom Hayden in Newark, New Jersey, for Economic Research and Action Project (1964–1968)

Hayden, like others in early SDS, was initially more interested in helping the civil rights movement than in ending the Vietnam War, which was barely on the nation's radar screen before about 1964. Hayden lived in Newark, New Jersey, and helped black inner-city residents organize themselves and develop political efficacy through an SDS program called the Economic Research and Action Project.

Freedom Summer (Summer 1964)

Many white civil rights workers from the North traveled to the South to help SNCC and the NAACP register black voters and start "freedom schools," especially in rural areas, to teach black people literacy. Freedom Summer continues today, in a different form, with efforts to teach math to poor, largely minority, kids, a project in which SNCC's Bob Moses plays a major role (see www.algebra .org). Also see Bill Johntz's counterpart program, Project Seed (www .projectseed.org).

Murder of Three Civil Rights Workers (June 21, 1964)

The Klan continued to mobilize against what it, and other southern whites, considered "outside agitators," and in this famous incident murdered two white young men from the North and a black young man from the South who were participating in Freedom Summer. Andrew Goodman was twenty, Michael Schwerner was twenty-four, and James Chaney was twenty-one. This tragic event was the end of innocence for many civil rights workers and sympathizers.

The Civil Rights Act (July 2, 1964)

President Johnson agreed with Kennedy that blacks' civil rights needed federal protection, and thus he signed legislation making it illegal to discriminate against people based on race or gender.

Gulf of Tonkin Incidents (August 4 and 9, 1964)

Johnson used alleged North Vietnamese attacks on U.S. naval vessels in the Gulf of Tonkin as an excuse to increase dramatically the commitment of U.S. troops to the war in Vietnam. The United States took the side of South Vietnam in its conflict with North Vietnam, led by Ho Chi Minh, and with the Viet Cong (National Liberation Front), pro–North Vietnam troops in South Vietnam.

The Mississippi Freedom Democratic Party at the 1964 Democratic National Convention in Atlantic City, New Jersey (August 22, 1964)

The Mississippi Freedom Democratic Party (MFDP) contested the right of the all-white Mississippi delegation to be seated at the 1964 Democratic National Convention, arguing that some of the black MFDP delegates should also be seated. Fannie Lou Hamer, a coleader of the MFDP, made its case in moving testimony to the convention's Credentials Committee. Ultimately, the Credentials Committee decided not to seat the MFDP but to give it token speaking rights, perhaps signaling the "mainstreaming" of the Democratic Party as it moved rightward under Lyndon Johnson, a southern "Dixiecrat."

Fannie Lou Hamer at the Democratic National Convention, Atlantic City, New Jersey, August 1964. (Library of Congress)

Robert Kennedy's Eulogy for His Brother at the Democratic National Convention, Atlantic City, New Jersey (August 27, 1964)

At John Kennedy's funeral, formal eulogies had not been delivered. Instead, selections had been read from his speeches. His brother Bobby made remarks, which were in effect a eulogy, at the 1964 Democratic National Convention. He was interrupted by applause twenty-two times, and he began to cry as he spoke.

SNCC Delegation in Africa and the Turn Toward Black Power (September 13, 1964)

Leaders of SNCC, including Bob Moses, Julian Bond, and Fannie Lou Hamer, traveled to Africa to meet Guinea's socialist leader Sékou Touré. They also met Malcolm X, who supported SNCC's efforts. This began the turn away from SNCC's earlier nonviolent and integrationist strategies and toward a pan-African ("Afrocentric") perspective soon to be called "Black Power." The trip was arranged by the singer Harry Belafonte.

Mario Savio's Speech at Berkeley (December 3, 1964)

The eloquent Mario Savio spearheaded the free speech movement at the University of California at Berkeley, paralleling the efforts of the initially midwestern-based SDS. He said: "There is a time when the operation of the machine becomes so odious, makes you so sick at heart, that you can't take part; . . . and you've got to put your bodies upon the gears and upon the wheels, upon the levers, upon all the apparatus and you've got to make it stop."

Martin Luther King Arrested in Selma, Alabama (February 1, 1965)

King, along with hundreds of other civil rights workers and young students, was arrested after demonstrating at the Selma courthouse at the beginning of a major joint SCLC/SNCC effort to register black voters in Alabama.

Malcolm X Murdered (February 21, 1965)

By the mid-1960s, Malcolm X, along with other black radicals, was beginning to question King's Gandhian strategy of nonviolent protest in the civil rights movement. Malcolm was murdered, probably not by white extremists but rather by fellow members of the Black Muslim Nation of Islam. He was delivering a speech at a meeting of the Organization of Afro-American Unity.

Jimmy Lee Jackson Murdered in Marion, Alabama (February 26, 1965)

A young black man, Jimmy Lee Jackson, was shot and killed by state troopers as he was protecting his mother and grandfather, who were being clubbed during a voter registration demonstration. He died of his wounds in a Selma, Alabama, hospital. His death was scarcely noticed by the white press.

Reverend James J. Reeb Murdered in Selma, Alabama (March 11, 1965)

The Unitarian minister James Reeb heeded the call by Martin Luther King to join him in Selma for major demonstrations designed to draw attention to black voters' rights. Reeb was attacked by white men on the streets of Selma, and he died of head wounds. Reeb's death brought national attention and even sorrowful comments from President Johnson, who characterized him as "that good man" while introducing voting rights legislation shortly thereafter.

Selma-to-Montgomery Voting Rights March (March 21–25, 1965)

King led civil rights workers on a multiday march between these two Alabama cities in spite of police opposition and death threats. This march dramatized the civil rights movement for much of the rest of the country. King's SCLC joined with SNCC to register black voters in Alabama.

Paul Potter's Washington, DC, Speech (April 17, 1965)

SDS president Paul Potter addressed one of the first anti–Vietnam War protests in Washington, DC. He asked people to "name the system," meaning that people should join the New Left effort to analyze the imperialist system of American capitalism in a systemic way and not just propose single-issue Band-Aid solutions. "We must name [the] system. We must name it, describe it, analyze it, understand it and change it. For it is only when that system is changed and brought under control that there can be any hope for stopping the forces that create a war in Vietnam today or a murder in the South tomorrow or all the incalculable, innumerable more subtle atrocities that are worked on people all over—all the time."

The Voting Rights Act (August 6, 1965)

Following the Civil Rights Act, the Voting Rights Act, signed by President Johnson, removed legal obstacles to black voter registration and abolished poll taxes levied against poor and rural black voters in the South. (Even though slavery had ended in 1865, it took another hundred years for segregation in the South to begin coming to an end.)

Race Riots in Watts, in Los Angeles (August 11–17, 1965)

As the civil rights movement spread to the North, American inner cities, with predominantly black populations living in dire poverty, began to explode as police clashed with protesters, who responded to police violence not with Gandhian pacifism but with violent measures; many of the riots led to the burning down of buildings in these inner cities. This week of historic violence began when a police officer pulled over a black motorist who had been driving erratically and an angry crowd gathered.

Affirmative Action in Minority Employment Hiring (September 24, 1965)

President Johnson required government contractors to "take affirmative action" in the hiring of minority employees. He embraced Kennedy's first affirmative action policies, which had urged government contractors and then other public-sector organizations such as universities to behave proactively in ending institutional racism—the tendency of white people to hire and promote white people, creating a vicious circle of poverty among minorities.

Tom Hayden, Staughton Lynd, and Herbert Aptheker in North Vietnam (December 1965)

Tom Hayden, Yale professor Staughton Lynd, and Communist Party of the United States of America member Herbert Aptheker traveled to North Vietnam and talked with North Vietnamese officials and people. They were the first three Americans to do so. The three returned convinced that the North Vietnamese viewed the war as a war of national liberation and would not give up. In the aftermath of their trip, Lynd lost his professorship at Yale.

Eighty Thousand U.S. Troops in Vietnam (January 1966)

U.S. troop strength had increased considerably by the beginning of 1966 to eighty thousand troops. This increase by Johnson, with congressional support, resulted from the probably faked Gulf of Tonkin incidents.

Forrest City, Mississippi, NAACP President Killed by Ku Klux Klan (January 11, 1966)

Vernon Dahmer's house was firebombed by fourteen Klansmen, and he died defending his family. Four Klan members were convicted, but it took until 1998 for Imperial Wizard Samuel Bowers, who had ordered the firebombing, to be brought to justice. Bowers died in prison in 2006.

March of Grape Pickers in California (March 16, 1966)

César Chávez, with Dolores Huerta, organized the National Farm Workers Association in 1962. This later became the United Farm Workers, a powerful union of agricultural workers, many of whom were Latino/as. In 1965, Filipino grape pickers in California went on strike against grape growers, protesting their conditions of employment. Chávez's organization joined the protest, and in March 1966 he led a symbolic march from Delano to Sacramento, the state capital, to bring national attention to the plight of produce pickers.

James Meredith Shot During Voter Registration March (June 5, 1966)

Meredith, the young man who had desegregated the University of Mississippi, led marchers from Memphis, Tennessee, to Jackson, Mississippi, to spark interest in voter registration. He was shot. Three civil rights leaders, Martin Luther King (SCLC), Stokely Carmichael (SNCC), and Floyd McKissick (CORE), continued to lead thousands of marchers after the shooting.

James Meredith shot during march from Memphis, Tennessee, to Jackson, Mississippi, June 5, 1966.
(AP Photo/Jack Thornell)

National Organization for Women Founded (June 30, 1966)

Led by Betty Friedan and Pauli Murray, the National Organization for Women (NOW) was founded as an outgrowth of the Presidential Commission on the Status of Women, which itself grew out of civil rights legislation from 1964. NOW sought to make gender discrimination visible in much the same way that the civil rights movement had made racism visible, on the theory that women needed a kind of NAACP to fight for their legal rights.

Black Panther Party Formed (October 1966)

The formation of the Black Panther Party occurred in the wake of the assassinations of Malcolm X and Medgar Evers, the northern inner-city riots, and the continuing resistance of the Klan and the police to civil rights initiatives. These events persuaded black radicals such as Stokely Carmichael and Eldridge Cleaver that both racial integration and nonviolent tactics were out-of-date. The Panthers urged black separatism as well as armed resistance to Klan

Eugene, Oregon, Black Panther rally, 1969. (Photo courtesy of Ellen Bepp)

and police violence against black people. The image here is of a Black Panther rally in my hometown of Eugene, Oregon.

Floyd McKissick President of CORE (1966–1968)

McKissick joined Martin Luther King of SCLC and Stokely Carmichael of SNCC in the 1965 Selma-to-Montgomery march, and, with King, he was sympathetic to the emerging Black Power movement. McKissick was a family friend who told a packed house at a basketball arena in Eugene, Oregon, that my father was the only white man he ever trusted, making me wonder why.

The Call for Black Power (April 19, 1967)

Stokely Carmichael, a charismatic black leader from the Caribbean, urged black people to love themselves and their "blackness," which became emblems of the Black Power movement. Black Power replaced integration as the goal of this more militant wing of the civil rights movement.

Summer of Love in San Francisco
(Summer 1967)

This name describes the summer 1967 exodus of young people to the Haight-Ashbury district of San Francisco. There they listened to psychedelic bands such as the Grateful Dead and Jefferson Airplane at the Fillmore and Winterland theaters; some of these kids also experimented with supposedly mind-expanding drugs such as LSD, praised by Timothy Leary as a route to insight.

Race Riot in Detroit (July 23–27, 1967)

Detroit, along with other American cities, burned as race riots, lasting several days, devastated the inner city. Armed police and rioters clashed, laying waste to black neighborhoods. This conflagration began when police raided a black bar on Detroit's west side that was supposedly operating illegally. It was not the Summer of Love for everyone.

Tom Hayden in Bratislava, Czechoslovakia,
Saying, "We Are All Viet Cong" (September 1967)

Hayden, predictably, was pilloried by American conservatives for this utterance. But he meant that American minorities and the poor, and indeed all oppressed people globally, had a fundamental solidarity with the Viet Cong, whom Hayden interpreted to be fighting for their liberation from imperialist powers such as France and now the United States.

Viet Cong Release of Three U.S. Prisoners
of War to the Custody of Tom Hayden, in
Cambodia (November 1967)

Hayden negotiated for the release of the first three U.S. soldiers captured by the North Vietnamese in battle.

SDS-Sponsored Grateful Dead Concert in
Eugene, Oregon (January 30, 1968)

SDS sponsored a Grateful Dead concert in Eugene in 1968 to demonstrate the link between the political and cultural aspects of the sixties. The next day, the Tet Offensive shook America's confidence in the war effort.

Tet Offensive (January 31, 1968)

Tet was a dramatic military incursion by North Vietnamese regular troops and the National Liberation Front (Viet Cong) deep into South Vietnam, even extending all the way to Saigon. U.S. military leaders and Johnson had boasted that the United States was winning the Vietnam War. The Tet Offensive convinced many at home that the United States was actually losing the war.

Orangeburg, South Carolina, Massacre (February 8, 1968)

Students at the historically black college South Carolina State University protested the segregation of a local bowling alley. They demonstrated and police opened fire, killing three unarmed young men, Samuel Hammond, Delano Middleton, and Henry Smith. This event received little national press coverage, unlike the killing of four white students at Kent State in Ohio in May 1970.

Two black demonstrators protesting segregation killed in the Orangeburg, South Carolina, massacre, Feb. 8, 1968. (AP Photo)

My Lai Massacre (March 16, 1968)

Lieutenant William Calley ordered his troops to shoot women, old men, and children in the hamlet of My Lai and then burn down the village (using pocket lighters to ignite the fires). At Calley's court-martial, his defense was that it was difficult, in the "guerrilla"-style war in Vietnam, to distinguish between friend and foe.

President Johnson No Longer in the Presidential Race (March 31, 1968)

Burdened by domestic protest and no longer convinced that the United States was "winning" the war in Vietnam, President Johnson announced to the nation that he would not seek a second elected term in office as president. His announcement immediately added momentum to the peace candidacies of Eugene McCarthy and Robert Kennedy, who then decided to enter the race.

Martin Luther King Jr. Assassinated in Memphis, Tennessee (April 4, 1968)

A few days after LBJ's withdrawal from the presidential race, Martin Luther King was shockingly murdered in Memphis, Tennessee, setting off massive black protest across the country. Bobby Kennedy gave a moving speech to a largely black audience in Indianapolis on the evening of King's assassination, explaining his own empathy because he had lost his brother Jack to an assassin's bullets. The president of the University of Oregon wrote a memo (see page 43) to my father, who taught there, twenty days after King's assassination that the university was establishing a committee to investigate and eliminate racism on campus.

Columbia Student Actions (April 23–May 18, 1968)

Led by Columbia University SDS's "action faction," Mark Rudd and other students and even some "outside agitators," such as Tom Hayden, took over the administration building and other key university buildings to protest the building of a gym on university-owned property in Harlem, a largely black, inner-city neighborhood. Leaders of the action faction would become central figures in Weatherman the next year.

Robert Kennedy Assassinated in
Los Angeles, California (June 5, 1968)

On the evening that he won the California Democratic primary against Eugene McCarthy, Bobby Kennedy, after giving his victory speech, was assassinated on the floor of the ballroom of a Los Angeles hotel. His death traumatized the nation, which was still reeling from his brother Jack's assassination and, more recently, Martin Luther King's assassination.

Senator Ted Kennedy's Eulogy for His
Murdered Brother Robert, St. Patrick's Cathedral,
New York City (June 8, 1968)

In a moving eulogy, Ted Kennedy urged people not to lionize his brother Bobby but simply to view him as "a good and decent man who saw wrong." He quoted Bobby's famous lines: "Some men see things as they are and say why. I dream things that never were and say, why not."

J. Edgar Hoover's Program to Disrupt
the New Left (July 5, 1968)

In an explicit 1968 memo from J. Edgar Hoover to other FBI operatives, he outlined a program to declare war on the New Left. Hoover perceptively noted that many members of the New Left "used" marijuana and thus that police authorities should take the opportunity to arrest these radicals on drug charges. But he realized that the local police needed to "be encouraged" by the FBI to take action against these leftist "potheads."

Outgoing University of Oregon President Arthur
Flemming Memo on the Committee on Racism
(July 31, 1968)

With the assassinations of Kennedy and King, 1968 had become a tragic year. Outgoing University of Oregon president Arthur Flemming wanted to extend the Committee on Racism that he forged shortly after King's assassination into a task force that would take a broader look at issues of race on campus. He wanted to appoint my father to this position, as he wrote incoming president Charles Johnson. Tragedy was soon to strike the Oregon campus as Johnson, probably succumbing to the pressure of the job and the times, died in summer 1969.

April 24, 1968

Memorandum to Dr. Robert E. Agger

I am establishing a President's Committee on (Racism) at the University of Oregon. The Committee is to address itself to the issue of racism as set forth in the memorandum of the University Black Students Union presented to me last week.

It is my hope that together we can take steps which will deal effectively with any manifestations of racism that are identified by the Committee and which will also prevent any manifestation of racism in the future, thus enabling the University of Oregon to serve effectively each Black student or other minority group student who becomes a part of our University community.

I am looking forward to the groups' recommendations as to program and policies designed to eliminate any present, or prevent any future, manifestations of racism on our campus.

The full support and resources of my office stand behind the committee in its endeavors. In order to implement the charge to the committee, it should be understood by all University personnel that this committee will have

    a. The responsibility of initiating relations and actions in connection with any segment of the University in their inquiry and development of policy and programs of action where it perceives problems to exist.

    b. Direct access to, and communication with, the total University community, through public statements, memorandums, etc.

    c. The responsibility of transmitting and discussing with me the committee's recommendations.

I anticipate the full cooperation from all areas of the University in the implementation of the work of this committee. Just as there can be no higher priority for this Nation than healing racial bias and cleaning up city slums, there can be no higher priority for the University of Oregon community than eliminating and preventing any racism which may exist on this campus.

Arthur S. Flemming
President

University of Oregon president Arthur S. Fleming sent a memo to Robert Agger in 1968, establishing a campus committee on racism. (University of Oregon Libraries—Special Collections and University Archives)

Democratic National Convention, Chicago, Illinois (August 22–29, 1968)

Democratic delegates and their young sympathizers from the peace movement demonstrated and lobbied to have a peace candidate selected as the Democratic nominee to run against Nixon for president. Chicago police "rioted" and beat up many of these unarmed activists and demonstrators, who chanted, "The whole world is watching [the organized police repression of dissent]." The prowar candidate, Hubert Humphrey, Johnson's vice president, was nominated. He subsequently lost the 1968 presidential election to Nixon.

Boy from My High School Killed in Vietnam (September 18, 1968)

The war came home as eleven boys from my high school were killed in combat in Vietnam. Kreg Viestenz was killed in combat during my junior year after only a month in Vietnam.

Kreg Viestenz, boy from Eugene, Oregon, killed in Vietnam Sept. 18, 1968. (Photo courtesy of the Viestenz family)

More Than Five Hundred Thousand
U.S. Troops in Vietnam (1969)

By the end of Nixon's first year in office, U.S. troop strength had been increased to over half a million, even after the Tet Offensive's demonstration that the United States was losing this "war of attrition." The U.S. military combined carpet bombing of the Ho Chi Minh supply trail from North to South Vietnam with small and often suicidal "search-and-destroy" missions intended simply to kill large numbers of "enemy" soldiers. By decade's end, morale was very low among U.S. troops, many of whom spent their downtime getting stoned and sometimes fragging (injuring) their superior officers.

There were two American bombing campaigns used in the Vietnam War. Operation Rolling Thunder (1965–1968) targeted North Vietnam and primarily deployed F-105D fighter jets. Operation Arc Light (1965–197'3) primarily used B-52s bombers to unload thousands of tons of bombs on both South and North Vietnam. Even after U.S. ground troops had largely left Vietnam in 1972, Nixon still pounded away at "enemy" forces with heavy bombing campaigns to ensure that he did not earn a place in history as the first U.S. president to "lose" a war. He—and we—lost anyway.

Richard Nixon Sworn in as President
(January 20, 1969)

Nixon swept into office on the basis of his campaign pledge to wind down the war in Vietnam and diminish troop strength. Instead, he increased the number of troops and escalated the conflict.

Flacks Attacked at the University
of Chicago (May 5, 1969)

Dick Flacks, one of the early architects and intellectuals of SDS, was brutally beaten and almost died in his faculty office at the University of Chicago. The assailant was never captured, but Flacks recovered and eventually went on to teach sociology at the University of California at Santa Barbara.

People's Park Incident in Berkeley,
California (May 15, 1969)

Protesters in Berkeley were confronted by local police on the University of California campus as the protesters tried to protect a "people's park" created on vacant university land. The police, using shotguns and tear gas, assailed the thousands of protesters. James Rector, a Berkeley student who was not protesting, was killed, and Alan Blanchard, a carpenter, was blinded for life. Governor Ronald Reagan was said to have uttered the infamous line, "If there has to be a bloodbath, then let's get it over with."

Charles Johnson, Acting University of Oregon President, Died in an Automobile Accident (June 17, 1969)

Acting president Johnson was killed when his Volkswagen Beetle crashed into an oncoming log truck on a treacherous curve of Highway 126, along the McKenzie River outside of Eugene. Johnson had weathered a strife-ridden year at the University of Oregon, and there was speculation that he lost control of his car as he succumbed to job-related stress. I was less than two months from moving to Canada.

Weather Took Over SDS (June 18–22, 1969)

At a Chicago SDS conference, the Weatherman faction won control of SDS from the Marxist-Leninist sect, Progressive Labor. Weather believed that bombings would galvanize the urban masses into revolutionary action, a science-fiction scenario, as it turned out.

Stonewall Riots (June 28, 1969)

Gays and lesbians resisted a New York City police raid on an establishment in Greenwich Village catering to people of diverse sexual orientations. This rebellion was the symbolic beginning of the movement for gay and lesbian rights, which extended far beyond the sixties. This event put gay pride on the civil rights agenda. AIDS activism in major cities such as New York and San Francisco, beginning in the early 1980s, can be traced to the spirit of Stonewall.

Woodstock (August 15–17, 1969)

According to many sixties iconographies, this huge rock festival in upstate New York represented the free-flowing, stoned, youth-driven spirit of the decade. Arguably, the concert, which soon became a movie and an album, accelerated the commercialism of popular culture and made little political statement. By late summer 1969, many American kids were turned off by the war, the administration, even the movement. I was two weeks from moving to Canada.

58 Percent of U.S. Population Against the War (October 1969)

Although a majority of people in the United States opposed the war by late 1969, the war was not universally unpopular, as this percentage suggested. Many were still conflicted about what course of action to take in Vietnam.

Chicago Days of Rage (October 8–11, 1969)

Reacting to the disastrous and violence-ridden Democratic National Convention the year before, Weatherman organized an action that would trash Chicago, or "pig city," as they called it. Chicago was also the site of the postconvention trial of the Chicago Eight, and Weatherman seized on the trial as an occasion for its paramilitary "action." A few hundred Weatherpeople showed up, and they were routed by the police. Weatherman's initial effort to "bring the war home" failed.

Millions of Americans Protested War in "Moratorium" Demonstrations (October 15, 1969)

Nationwide opposition to the war mounted, and millions of protesters demonstrated across the country.

Weatherman's Days of Rage, Chicago, Oct. 8–11, 1969. (Photo by David Fenton/Getty Images)

Antiwar "Moratorium" Demonstration in Oshkosh, Wisconsin (October 15, 1969)

Even middle America, here small-town America, witnessed growing antiwar protests.

Huge Protest Against the War, Washington, DC (November 15, 1969)

More than a half million people converged on the capital to demand an end to the war. The White House did not change its course of action in Vietnam.

Occupation of Alcatraz Prison (November 20, 1969–June 11, 1971)

The movement for "red power," called the American Indian Movement, broadened the civil rights movement to include Native Americans. Citing an 1868 Sioux treaty, the "Indians of All Tribes" occupied the vacated Alcatraz prison as an expression of Native American rights to occupy unused federal land.

Murder of Fred Hampton (December 4, 1969)

Fred Hampton, a young Black Panther leader from Chicago, was murdered by Chicago police while asleep in his bed. His murderers were never brought to justice. His murder was part of efforts by the police and the FBI to rid the country of radicals, a campaign begun in 1956 as COINTELPRO.

Altamont Rock Festival in California (December 6, 1969)

Two days after Hampton's murder, another murder took place, this one at a rock festival in Altamont, California. Another young black man, Meredith Hunter, was killed, by members of Hells Angels who were "protecting" the bands onstage (including the Rolling Stones) from the audience. The concert continued, but the decade did not.

Manhattan Townhouse Explosion (March 6, 1970)

The symbolic end of the sixties might be seen as happening on this date in 1970 when some Weathermen blew themselves up while making antipersonnel weapons to be used against soldiers on do-

Fred Hampton, Chicago Black Panther, murdered in his sleep, Dec. 4, 1969. (AP Photo)

mestic military bases. Weatherman, which went underground and became the Weather Underground, rethought its tactics and decided to target buildings, not people. Three Weatherpeople were killed in the explosion: Ted Gold, Terry Robbins, and Diana Oughton.

Four Students Killed by National Guard at Kent State (May 4, 1970)

After Nixon expanded U.S. bombing to Cambodia, the National Guard occupied the Kent State University campus in Ohio. Two days before, a vacant Reserve Officers' Training Corps building had been struck by arson, increasing campus tension. Kent State students began protesting the Guard's occupancy of their otherwise peaceful campus. Tensions came to a head, and during a peaceful demonstration the Guard opened fire and killed four students—Jeffrey Miller, Allison Krause, William Schroeder, and Sandra Scheuer—two of whom had nothing to do with the demonstration.

Weatherman "Declaration of a State of War" Against the United States (May 21, 1970)

The faction that took over SDS at the group's 1969 convention had originally been called the Revolutionary Youth Movement (RYM). RYM acquired the moniker "Weatherman" because its 1969 manifesto borrowed Bob Dylan's lyrics in "Subterranean Homesick Blues." With this declaration of war, RYM went underground and changed its name to Weather Underground. This declaration of war was issued after Fred Hampton's murder and after the Kent State massacres.

National Student Strike (May 1970)

The tragedy at Kent State inflamed the country, and students struck at many colleges and universities across the United States in opposition to the events at Kent State and to the continuing war effort.

Bombing of Army Math Research Center at University of Wisconsin and Death of a Postdoctoral Student (August 24, 1970)

Bombers inspired by Weatherman attempted to blow up the supposedly war-related building Sterling Hall at the University of Wisconsin, inadvertently killing a graduate student named Robert Fassnacht.

Watergate Democratic Headquarters Burgled by Committee to Re-elect the President (June 17, 1972)

As Nixon ran for a second term as president, members of his administration broke into Democratic National Headquarters in Washington in a search for campaign secrets. Police apprehended them during the break-in, and an attempt to cover up this crime was traced to Nixon himself and to his high command, causing a national scandal.

Richard Nixon's Resignation (August 8, 1974)

Under threat of impeachment and conviction for his role in Watergate, Nixon resigned the presidency and was immediately pardoned by Gerald Ford, his successor as president.

The End of the Vietnam War (April 30, 1975)

The nation watched televised images of helicopters evacuating U.S. personnel and citizens from Vietnam as Saigon finally fell to the North Vietnamese, ending the more than twenty-year war and U.S. military involvement in Indochina.

Two People Dead in Brinks Robbery by Weather Underground and the Black Liberation Army (October 20, 1981)

In a weird carry-forward from the sixties, still-militant activists, both white and black, attempted to rob a Brinks truck in Nyack, New York, in order to provide the revolutionary movement with funds. In the process, two police officers, Edward O'Grady and Waverly Brown, and a Brinks guard, Peter Paige, were killed. David Gilbert is doing a life sentence for his participation in the crime, and Kathy Boudin has been released after twenty-two years in prison. While imprisoned, Boudin's son, Chesa, was raised by Weather Underground members Bernardine Dohrn and Bill Ayers.

John Kennedy Jr. Killed in a Plane Crash off Cape Cod (July 16, 1999)

President Kennedy's son was killed while piloting a small plane conveying his wife, Carolyn Bessette, and her sister, Lauren Bessette, to Martha's Vineyard for a wedding. Kennedy, a risk taker, was not certified to fly at night using instruments. Ted Kennedy delivered yet another Kennedy family eulogy, suggesting that the dynastic American family was star-crossed. These remarks were given on July 23, 1999, at the Church of St. Thomas More in New York City, at John Jr.'s funeral.

The chronology just presented could be much longer, hundreds of pages in fact, containing every detail of everyone's experience. That recounting would be as involved and lengthy as a reliving of the decade. And so there are omissions. Readers will construct their own memories of the moment, perhaps deviating from the official sequencing of events. Notable about my timeline is how so much of what we call the sixties involved a "dialectic," pushes and pulls between Left and Right. Movement gains were blocked by state repression, which would incite the movement and bring new rounds of repression. The civil rights movement gained momentum in the

South, and suddenly four young girls were blown up in a Birmingham church by the Klan. The antiwar movement attempted to nominate a peace candidate, and the Chicago police beat it bloody. Fred Hampton, a charismatic Black Panther leader, was murdered in his sleep, and Weatherman seized SDS and moved it in a more militant direction. There was militancy on both sides, with people's positions hardening. People, even of gentle spirit, became "reactionary," responding to events without necessarily taking the long view. That is how I read the Weather episode. The events of the decade were all connected, with every movement gain bringing a setback until the movement was no more, especially after the 1968 assassinations. This was a "negative" dialectic, which resolved itself not in a higher progressive synthesis, but in the nearly forty-year siege of American politics by the Right. Perhaps Obama will get the dialectic moving in a progressive direction.

The end of the movement, and of the sixties, did not erase progressive gains such as civil rights and freethinking. I share the optimism of the Enlightenment and of Karl Marx that history can move forward, albeit in fits and starts. The inertia of the past is powerful; Jim Crow gave way only gradually, with much resistance. The dialectic moves forward by way of contradictions: Gain is matched by setback, which provokes new struggle. I believe in progress, even if I characterize the sixties as a decade of defeat. It was also a decade of great and important victories, without which our world would not have brought forth a black president and a woman secretary of state who challenged his bid for office and nearly pulled it off. It is sometimes difficult to read history accurately as we live it. We often do not recognize small victories as the major achievements that they are. I return to this issue when I address the 1962 Ann Arbor New Year's party at Tom and Casey Hayden's house.

In the next chapter, I consider the legacy of the Port Huron Statement and the New Left generally. I contend that the Port Huron Statement, in its call for participatory democracy, remains one of the most important legacies of the sixties decade. I also consider what it might mean for people today, including young people, to view themselves as "New Left" in their political identities.

❧ Three ❧

Port Huron and the New Left

I was the New and [Flacks] was the Left.
—Tom Hayden

Arguably, the New Left, and indeed the whole decade of the sixties, began with a small conference held by the Students for a Democratic Society (SDS) on Lake Huron, Michigan, in 1962. Tom Hayden, a young student at the University of Michigan and the editor of the student newspaper, brought with him a draft of a document that would be much debated and worked over at the conference. The resulting Port Huron Statement called for a "new Left" in America that embraced "participatory democracy," meaning a full-scale participation of citizens in their communities, polities, and economies that would bring about social justice and help end the cold war. One of Hayden's confidants was Richard Flacks, a red-diaper child (of communist parents) on the East Coast. Flacks, now a retired professor of sociology, was a founding member of SDS, and he helped Hayden think through a "new" Left that derived, but also departed, from Karl Marx. Among their main intellectual influences were the early writings of Marx, the sociological writings of C. Wright Mills, the existential philosophy of Albert Camus, and the pragmatic philosophy of John Dewey. Out of this mélange of influences the American New Left was born.

Initially, SDS took its lead from the Student Non-Violent Coordinating Committee (SNCC), an early civil rights organization that practiced nonviolent protest and also embraced participatory democracy. Bob Moses was its field secretary and later spearheaded SNCC's 1964 Mississippi project. SDS modeled SNCC's grassroots, free-floating organization, which stressed consensus and shunned top-down leadership. This bottom-up model was eventually abandoned as activists turned toward militancy and Leninist models of vanguard organization. This vanguard model vested leadership and authority in a small, tightly knit party such as the Communist Party of the Soviet Union. In the early civil rights and early antiwar movements, people came before "party." SDS and SNCC were pushed toward top-down organization by the mounting forces of right-wing resistance, which challenged the early civil rights and antiwar movements. Interminable meetings designed to build "consensus" were inefficient, and peaceful persuasion gave way to a stress on "action," which included violence.

During the mid-1960s, SDS began to shift gears: It became focused on stopping the war in Vietnam. It was clear from the Port Huron Statement that SDS was not a single-issue protest group; rather, it supported the total transformation of American society. Although SDS did not describe itself explicitly as socialist, so as not to scare off Americans who had little use for Marxism and socialism in the wake of the 1950s McCarthy period, there were clear echoes of democratic socialism in the Port Huron Statement, an issue to which my interviewees turn here.

The sixties opened with John Kennedy's New Frontier, SDS's Port Huron Statement, and the nonviolent civil rights movement, but the decade ended with Richard Nixon's election, an escalating war in Vietnam, the repression of black and white activists on the domestic front, a xenophobic patriotism, and a Left that degenerated into urban violence and revolutionary politics. We can emphasize either the gains achieved during the decade or the setbacks by decade's end. I make room for both perspectives because that provides the most realistic picture. One of my themes is that the sixties proceeded via a dialectic of movement gains that were met by state repression. There were pushes and pulls, not a smooth narrative of uplifting progress. In tracing the legacy of the sixties forward, we need to explain both how the Right has become so dominant in American politics and how women and minorities have flourished, even winning the White House. The gains from the sixties are enduring:

- Civil rights were won for black people and other minorities, as were rights for women.
- Although the antiwar movement did not end the war quickly enough, domestic turmoil forced President Lyndon Johnson out of office by 1968.

- Young people, who are now graying members of the baby-boom generation, learned to challenge authority, think independently, and stand up for social justice.
- The New Left developed the concept of participatory democracy, which remains an important political agenda in a country that lacks an organized socialist tradition.
- The counterculture questioned what we now call "workaholism," persuading people to smell the roses and not allow themselves to be enslaved by the clock, job, or boss.
- Nature was accorded rights, including the right not to be despoiled by the ravages of an industrial civilization.
- Perhaps most important, the "self" became a focus of attention, indeed, the most important agenda of social change. The New Left argued that worthwhile changes must pass through everyday life and affect the quality of life.

This list could be longer, depending on perspective. All of these gains are estimable in themselves. When the sixties unraveled and the Right attacked many of these accomplishments, they remained in play. Sixties people will not give them up without a fight. In spite of the conservative counterrevolution led by Nixon, Ronald Reagan, and George W. Bush, the sixties remain a contested terrain. The kids then are the parents and grandparents now, and we want today's kids to be more like we were. We want them to put their "bodies upon the gears and upon the wheels, upon the levers, upon all the apparatus and . . . make it stop."

SETTING THE STAGE: THE SIXTIES UNRAVEL

You can jail the revolutionaries, but you can't jail the revolution.
—Fred Hampton

The sixties opened with a whimper, not with a bang. Dwight D. Eisenhower's second term of office was coming to an end, and Nixon and Kennedy positioned themselves to run for the presidency as standard-bearers of the two major parties. Kennedy won the 1960 election with a paper-thin majority in the Electoral College, possibly the result of a stuffed ballot box in Illinois where the mayor of Chicago, Richard Daley, utilized his machine to carry the state with its many electoral votes. Kennedy was largely an unknown commodity and was himself an outsider as a Catholic. In his famous Inaugural Address in January 1961, he urged people to "ask not what your country can do for you; ask what you can do for your country."

Many young people were energized by Kennedy's call for public service. However, few were radicals, or even liberals. Only after John Kennedy's assassination did people, especially the young, find it increasingly difficult to remain on the sidelines. They observed the civil rights movement, especially as reporters went south and publicized the increasingly interracial desegregation movement. And in the same year, one year after Kennedy's assassination, Johnson raised the level of U.S. military involvement in Vietnam. In 1965, the nation watched Martin Luther King Jr. lead major demonstrations in Selma, Alabama, on behalf of black voters' rights. Those demonstrations culminated in a televised march from Selma to Montgomery, the state capital, to protest the murder of James Reeb. He had come down from Boston to help King with his integration efforts. (A young black man named Jimmy Lee Jackson had died just before that while defending his mother and grandfather against a brutal beating, but Jackson's death had received much less notice. Reeb was white.) By 1968, the draft, which raised the U.S. troop level in Vietnam to nearly half a million a year later, had become a hot-button issue on college campuses as graduate student draft deferments were ended and then, a year later in December 1969, all student deferments were ended. The military moved to a lottery system that exposed all young males to the risk of deadly combat.

It is fair to say that if Jim Crow segregation had not existed in the American South and if the United States had not become mired in Vietnam (a process probably accelerated by Kennedy's assassination), young people would not have been radicalized as the decade unfolded. These are big ifs. But the social movements of the sixties did not emerge from thin air; they were provoked by events, far away and close to home, but all involving young people in life-or-death decisions about social justice.

Bill Clinton is reputed to have said that how one views the sixties—as the best or the worst of times—determines one's present worldview. He was clearly a sixties person, full of idealistic energy, suspicious of authority, informal, an ally of minorities. He is also infamous for saying that he had smoked marijuana but had never inhaled, an unlikely story designed to make him appear to be all things to all people. Complicating sixties stories is the fact that many of the participants were young and coming of age. Hayden was twenty-three when he drafted the Port Huron Statement. As we came of age, we were undergoing personal growth and crises, adolescence by another name, that were all mixed up with the burning world around us. In reflecting on the decade, I and others are also reflecting on our own youth, which blurs with the momentous events taking place.

This blurring of the personal and analytical marks every sixties book I have read, and with good reason. The sixties are not yet ancient history; people still remember the various marches on Washington, Bull Connor's attack dogs, the Days of Rage. One of the main insights of the sixties is that the "self" is the measure of progressive change, the hallmark of humanism. Thus, people remember the impact of events on themselves, reorganizing their identities around the continuity between who they "were" and who they "are." They are the same person, although different—made different by looking backward. Oral histories "tell" the sixties by working through events and experiences as we achieve the vantage of age and of distance from them.

I prefer an accounting of the decade that stresses discontinuity and an unraveling of progressive energy. Courageous activism and bold theoretical syntheses were juxtaposed to domestic repression and international military aggression that thwarted activism. The cliché that those were the best and the worst of times is how it feels in retrospect. And the best came first, including Kennedy's election, the Freedom Rides, Port Huron, and Freedom Summer, but the worst came last and thus is perhaps more memorable for people who remember a political sixties at all.

And not only did the worst of the sixties come last, from the trial of the Chicago Eight to the Days of Rage to Kent State; the worst endures. Far from being a distant time, the sixties haunt the present. They are haunting because the hard Right, from about 1968 to 1972, beginning with Barry Goldwater and continuing through Nixon, Reagan, and Bush Jr., gathered momentum by turning back the New Left. The sixties opened with Kennedy's managerial liberalism, which was susceptible to influence by the progressive social movements of the time, but ended with the defeat of both liberalism and the social movements. This was not inevitable. It could have turned out differently.

Had Hubert Humphrey been defeated by either Eugene McCarthy or Bobby Kennedy in the 1968 Democratic campaign for the presidential nomination, had Lee Harvey Oswald missed his mark in Dallas, had Robert McNamara, President Johnson's defense secretary, and the military told the truth earlier about the reality of the war, the decade might have unfolded differently and left a more progressive legacy. Had King not been gunned down, the civil rights movement might have endured and blossomed into an interracial poor people's movement. Had Nixon not erected a martial state, with the aid of the FBI, SDS might not have evolved into more revolutionary versions and might instead have preserved the democratic Left's idealism, pragmatism, and base building. Had the Right not prevailed by the end of the decade, the Evangelical Right, as we have come to know it, might have been nipped in the bud. Had economic crisis from the late 1970s through the 1980s not increased class and race warfare, perhaps we would have seen the blossoming, not the defeat, of social initiatives such as affirmative action. Perhaps we would have preempted right-wing evangelism. Perhaps we could have kept some blue states blue, even in the South. The sixties were a decade of what-ifs.

The early twenty-first century, especially the George Bush/Karl Rove regime, has multiple causes, each of which reinforces the others. This world feels locked in, even as we know it is not. Barack Obama may be an opening; it is too early to tell. And hindsight is perfect. It is easy to condemn the Panthers and Weatherman for their extremism, but many of us were desperate then and were willing to try anything to end the war and end racism. The sixties were open to several contrasting outcomes, some of which could have been more progressive than what actually happened, with Nixon's plumbers leading to Bush's Homeland Security force and the scorched-earth policy of Vietnam prefiguring the desert storms in Iraq. Near the end of his second term, Bush was still declaring himself "a war president" as a way of holding on to power that was never rightly his, after the stolen 2000 Florida election. Marines and civilians die every day in Iraq and Afghanistan, some by "friendly fire," but Americans have not mobilized against the war in the numbers or with the intensity of the sixties. The absence of the draft is one explanation. Another is that there is no Left, new, old, or otherwise, in this country. Still another is the dominance of entertainment and even news media, busy selling cultural commodities and diverting attention.

This account risks determinism, which is not what I intend. The sixties taught us above all that people can matter, given courage, imagination, and propitious circumstances. The Port Huron Statement, crafted by intellectually oriented college students, installs the individual as the centerpiece of social change. These changes must transform the ways in which people conduct their intimate lives as well as play their public roles. Port Huron, authored by activist selves, made the self a worthy agenda. And Port Huron, in the climate of Kennedy's energetic idealism and an emerging civil rights movement, added great momentum to the idealism among young people that broke with the conservative Eisenhower years. This idealism, expressed in emerging political movements and in music, was nearly irrepressible. It was not for another roughly six years that the tight coil of radical hopes and dreams began to release, scattering many people's energy into local and nonpolitical projects and concentrating the energy of an angry few, who went underground and set off bombs in symbolic institutions.

The coil of concentrated hopes and dreams began its slow unraveling because the Right mounted a frontal assault in Vietnam and on the New Left. By 1968, America had become an armed camp. Formerly political people grew and ate organic food in communes, learned to play the sitar, and left for Canada or India because their political energy was dissipating.

The year 1969 was especially agonizing. Half a million troops in Vietnam brought the United States no closer to victory. By the end of that year, eight of the eleven boys from my high school who perished in Vietnam had been killed in combat. One survived until 1970 and another to 1974. Weatherman urged people to "bring the war home," and it did, as the death toll and domestic strife mounted. Everything was affected by the burning world. (See Box 3.1.)

There were many other casualties in 1969. Not all of them died. Some were wounded and maimed and still bear the scars. The People's Park incident, a Kent State West, occurring a year before the real Kent State, left James Rector dead. It also left Alan Blanchard, a carpenter who, like Rector, was not participating in the protest in Berkeley, permanently blind. He was a casualty of war, much like the little Vietnamese kids who were napalmed and the U.S. military veterans who lost a limb and navigate their lives using a wheelchair. Blanchard lay wounded on May 15, 1969, in the cosmopolitan college town of Berkeley, California. He could have been in Quang Tri Province lying next to Kreg Viestenz, a young man from my high school who had been killed in September 1968. Berkeley was a battlefield, as was all of America.

By 1970, the bombing of Cambodia drove even middle-of-the-road middle-American college students to angry protest and student strikes. Kent State, a utilitarian state university in the Midwest, was an unlikely place for frustrated students to confront an out-of-control National Guard, only to be murdered in cold blood. The dissent and disappointment—the coil unraveling—were everywhere, from Portland, Oregon, to Portland, Maine. Nixon and J. Edgar Hoover defeated not only the Panthers and SDS but also a whole generation, which by 1970 had turned off politics, the war, college, and adult authority and was searching for escape routes. Kent's mayor asked Ohio governor James Rhodes to deploy the National Guard to keep order in the town and on the campus. Rhodes

────── ∞ **Box 3.1   The Death of a University President** ∞ ──────

In Eugene, two black basketball players on the University of Oregon team were asked to cut their Afro haircuts. The coach wanted them to look respectable. One of the players eventually changed his name from Bobby Moore to Ahmad Rashad; he became a famous professional football player (St. Louis Cardinals, Buffalo Bills, Minnesota Vikings) and is now a television sports commentator. Moore and his teammate Bill Drake protested that white players were allowed to wear their hair long, making a statement about the times. The interim University of Oregon president, Charles Johnson, took the players' side and told the athletic director, Len Casanova, to play the players. Johnson gave the Mormon coach, Frank Arnold, the option to accompany the team on the road trip and accept their hair-styles. Arnold initially refused, and Casanova was poised to replace him. But four days later, Arnold reversed field and allowed the athletes to keep their hair. The campus strife about the war and civil rights imposed great stress on Johnson, and he was a gentle person who did not bargain for this. Wearing the Afros was sym-bolic, an assertion of black pride. There was exquisite sensitivity on all sides then.

One of the most poignant outcomes of the turbulent year 1969 was the fate of President Johnson at Oregon. Johnson, a placid and conciliatory accounting profes-sor, was thrust into the presidency after the liberal Arthur Flemming left the presi-dency for another university. Johnson started well, like the decade, but events thwarted his best intentions. Eugene is now progressive and is sometimes termed "hippieville," but back then Eugene particularly and Oregon generally, a rural state, were quite conservative and the University of Oregon was a liberal oasis. At the same time, Oregonians were pioneers and mavericks, and they elected Wayne Morse to the U.S. Senate. Along with Ernest Gruening of Alaska, Morse was one of only two senators to oppose the Gulf of Tonkin Resolution escalating the Vietnam War. Johnson, a boy from rural Wyoming, genuinely tried to bring people together.

Bobby Moore (then) and Ahmad Rashad (now)—former University of Oregon football player, now a sports commentator. (AP Photo)

During Johnson's year as acting president at Oregon, he was besieged by letters from conservative citizens deploring his stance on the hair issue and on the issue of whether the university should continue to serve grapes in the cafeterias, given the César Chávez–led boycott of grape growers. Johnson was sensitive, and these vituperative letters hurt him. He was also a candidate for the permanent presidency of the university, but the tumult at the time did not serve him well, and he was passed over. That probably troubled him. Eventually, toward the end of the academic year, he contracted Hong Kong flu, lost weight, and was physically and perhaps emotionally weakened. He began to have dissociative "breaks" and was found wandering or driving around after failing to return home on at least two occasions.

At the university commencement on June 15, 1969, Johnson was waiting to deliver his commencement address at Autzen Stadium, the new football stadium on the Oregon campus. Johnson was by then under great strain. A young black man named Ray Eaglin, a member of the Black Panthers, walked onstage and asked Johnson if he could make an impromptu speech. Johnson, who always tried to conciliate and hear both sides, allowed Eaglin to address the gathering. Here are some of Eaglin's words:

"As of this moment we are all under arrest. We are under arrest because we are perpetrators of crimes. We are symbolic of clear and present danger—the danger of ignorance, the danger of racism, the supreme danger of being forced into supporting an illegal war. . . . It is said that the source of all trouble with student anarchists and student radicals is that their sibling days were not up to par, that well-intentioned parental toilet training somehow moved these kids to extremes. We understand par to be a chicken in every pot and two cars in every garage. Par changes from neighborhood to neighborhood. In our neighborhood par means rats in every house, disease in every body, high rent for dilapidated houses, all the avenues of redress closed" (quoted in Metzler 2001: 292).

Two days later, on June 17, 1969—a day that I remember as hot and clear— Johnson drove his VW Beetle up the McKenzie River, along Highway 126, which has many twists and turns. Hundreds of log trucks regularly drove in the opposite direction, bringing thirty or more loaded tons of logs from the dense evergreen forests of mountain Oregon to the lumberyards around Eugene.

Johnson steered head-on into the path of a log truck driven by a young man who was just learning how to drive the big rigs. Inexplicably, according to the young man's telling, Johnson's VW wandered into the opposite lane as Johnson rounded a blind turn. Johnson was killed instantly, suffering crushing blows, broken bones, and internal injuries. At the time, there was speculation that he had committed suicide. Ken Metzler, a journalism professor, wrote a moving book entitled *Confrontation* (2001) that examined the facts of the matter and Johnson's stormy year as president. Metzler implies that it was not suicide but a tragic combination of circumstances that literally and figuratively drove Johnson around the bend. I said earlier that readers unfamiliar with the sixties would do well to start by reading *Diana*, a poignant account of a girl killed by her own hand as she made Weather bombs. Readers will also be repaid by reading Metzler's book, long out of print but found in university libraries and online and recently reissued as a University of Oregon Press book. They will learn that Johnson, too, was a casualty of war. When Eaglin learned of Johnson's death, he wept, and he saw to it that the flag above the student union was lowered to half-mast.

ର

had this to say about the student protesters: "They're worse than the brownshirts and the communist element and also the night-riders and the vigilantes. They're the worst type of people that we harbor in America. I think that we're up against the strongest, well-trained, militant, revolutionary group that has ever assembled in America."

Although all of us at the time thought this was militant right-wing hyperbole, my discussions with Mark Rudd, a former Weatherman leader and member, provide a more nuanced picture, especially where he addresses Weather's role at Kent State. We turn to these discussions in the following chapter.

I recently aired for my students an outstanding hour-long video about Kent State, coproduced by U.S. and Canadian filmmakers. Although the footage was stunning, placing us on the tear-gassed campus in Kent as National Guard riflemen faced down the few thousand protesting and observing college students, even more striking were the interviews with the former college students and National Guardsmen who had participated on that tragic day. Several on both sides were moved to tears as they remembered the catastrophe, when the National Guard opened fire on defenseless students, pumping sixty-seven rounds from their M-1 rifles into the crowd, killing four and wounding more.

The National Guard members interviewed for the film did not varnish their roles in the events. One muttered, crying, "I knew it was wrong, I knew it was wrong," to fire into the crowd of students. His hindsight and maturity allowed him to relive the events without either simplifying them or providing himself an alibi. He remembered that chaos and confusion had reigned, but he did not absolve himself and his fellow soldiers of responsibility. This video, with the interviews and forgotten footage, becomes a piece of the sixties, even forty years later, because it allows self-reflection to invest the events with a meaning that was elusive on May 4, 1970. For those of us who hated the war and even the United States, it was easy to accept a cartoonish image of the events at Kent: innocent students slaughtered by fascist soldiers, probably under orders from superior officers. The reality, we now understand, was more nuanced, even if there is still no justification for what happened. If anything, there was less, given the mendacity of Governor Rhodes, who promised to use "every force possible" in order to enforce law and order at Kent. The Guardsmen were themselves young men not fully convinced that the war was just. They felt imperiled by the student protesters, several of whom lobbed bricks and rocks at the Guard. They chose to open fire, perhaps not responding to orders, because they were caught up in the moment

A Kent State University student lies on the ground after National Guardsmen fired into a crowd of demonstrators on May 4, 1970. (AP Photo)

and could not see things clearly, as many of us were caught up in the sixties as a whole and could not see things clearly. There is less excuse for the Guard's senior officers, who had presumably seen combat before.

The energy seeped out of the sixties with epochal late sixties events such as the Chicago convention (1968), Kennedy/King (1968), Nixon (1969–1974), Cambodia (1970), Kent State/Jackson State (1970), My Lai (1968), and Days of Rage (1969). This was not a natural release of pent-up energy, nor was it a seamless narrative building to a conclusive ending. It was a political and personal tragedy for many millions who had invested themselves in the movement's promise of a new everyday life, new politics, new nature, new bodies, new relationships. The Right defeated the Left and stayed on top and in power. The Right was still there until Obama's election, except that it has become more intolerant and conspiratorial and now claims religious sanction.

From 1962 to 1968/1969, much of a whole generation was radicalized as assassinations turned people into activists disaffected

Chicago police beating up demonstrators, Democratic Convention, August 1968. (Photo by Charles H. Phillips/Time & Life Pictures/Getty Images)

because they could not budge official policy. This radicalization took political, cultural, and personal forms. People marched, burned their draft cards, smoked dope at rock concerts, skipped school, joined the movement, rejected monogamy, grew their hair long, dressed down, and abandoned bourgeois values. First Johnson and then Nixon guaranteed record turnouts at these anti-establishment events by pursuing a hopeless war, even by the Pentagon's narrow strategic standards of winning and losing. Vietnam was a war of attrition where the side with the biggest enemy body count "won." The 1963 JFK assassination began the process of radicalization, followed by the 1964 Gulf of Tonkin incidents, and culminating with Memphis, Los Angeles, and Chicago in 1968. Images of the "police riot," as it was later termed, in the Chicago Loop summarized the late sixties: amassed police beating in the heads of unarmed demonstrators simply protesting the Democratic Party establishment's support of the war.

Other well-known images from afar rival this Chicago tableau for their summary quality: the naked Vietnamese girl burning with napalm running down the rural road and the South Vietnamese officer executing a suspected Viet Cong by shooting him in the head. These images shocked middle-class Americans who could not believe that their beloved country was doing these things.

Naked Vietnamese girl running in the road during Vietnam War. (AP Photo/Nick Ut)

South Vietnamese officer shooting prisoner in the head. (AP Photo/Eddie Adams)

The whole world was watching this decade captured in the camera lens. We did not witness the concentration camps until after World War II, and they shocked us. We understood the trench war conducted with machine guns and mustard gas during World War I only from survivors' accounts. The sixties, however, were televised and photographed, beginning on November 22, 1963. This began the process of radicalization for many of us, even if we could not have come close to putting this into words until much later. We sensed that the New Frontier was over, and we could not yet know that the subsequent Great Society of Lyndon Johnson would be based on the Gulf of Tonkin hoax.

My sixties did not become clearer as a coherent "narrative" until I visited Dallas for the first time in summer 1993, when I was forty-one. My wife was at a family reunion in the panhandle of Texas, and I flew down to join her and our young daughter. Dallas was terra incognita to me, although I had visited south Texas, enjoying the balmy winter. My first agenda was to visit the Book Depository, triple underpass, and grassy knoll, the tableau of Kennedy's assassination. I had not realized from television that the motorcade was traveling downhill as it passed the book depository. We actually drove the route and went partway to Parkland Hospital, near where we now receive our medical care. We moved to Texas the next year and have lived near Dallas ever since. Could I have been drawn to the crime scene? Dallas for me will always be one of the landmarks of the sixties, enveloping not only JFK, Jackie Kennedy, John Connolly, Lee Harvey Oswald, Jack Ruby, and the Oak Cliff Theater, but also my life as a kid who watched his father cry on that dismal day and could not understand what was happening to his world.

I could not believe how difficult were the shots that Oswald squeezed off in rapid succession with his World War II bolt-action rifle. They were through a tree and downhill. Three shots in approximately eight seconds, two of them finding their mark? I still do not believe it, although not accepting the Warren Commission's finding that there was a lone or unaided gunman does not restore my faith in America. If anything, it deepens my mistrust. I now understand that my journey to Dallas and the assassination site, a journey I have repeated now that I live nearby, was a search for my identity, which was bound up with the demystification of America that began on that fateful day when I was in fifth grade.

The devil is in the details. We know that Oswald purchased his Mannlicher-Carcano rifle through the mail. He ordered it on March 12, 1963, eight months before the assassination. He paid $21.45 for the Italian World War II vintage firearm. It was sent to an alias, A. Hidell, at a post office box in Dallas—P.O. Box 2915, Dallas, TX. The firm that sold the rifle was Klein's in Chicago.

For many sixties people, identity is inseparable from the startling events of the time. We remember where we were when the shots sounded on Dealey Plaza, and then we watched events unfold on television. We realized that this was a monumental event and that we would be forever different. This sense of living a history in the making made the sixties so exciting and in some ways so different from times today, when history seems closed to earth-shattering events. Today, for the most part, history is experienced as tragedy, the outcome of someone else's bad intentions; think of 9/11. Traveling to Dallas was part of my self-exploration. I needed to settle my score with those events, especially since I left America before the decade was out.

For me, November 22, 1963, occurred before Port Huron (1962), which only came into my view as the Vietnam War escalated after Tonkin in 1964. By mid-decade, in 1965, I had begun to observe my parents' intense involvement in the civil rights and antiwar movements. I remember 1964 as an epiphany for me: That is when I became political. The 1964 presidential election was the occasion for this. Even by 1964, the rightward shift of the Democratic Party was occurring, as I remember watching the August convention with my father, who explained to me how the mainstream party had blocked the Mississippi Freedom Democratic Party, led by the eloquent Fannie Lou Hamer, who wanted to desegregate the all-white Mississippi delegation.

By the time I entered high school, draft protest had become draft resistance and there was a growing militancy on the New Left. I turned sixteen one day before Bobby Kennedy was gunned down, and a couple of months after King was assassinated. Later in that summer of 1968, the police riot in Chicago took place, followed by the show trial of the Chicago Eight and the unraveling of Port Huron into Weatherman. Time compressed and events piled one upon another as the decade crashed and burned on the fate of the Vietnam War. Even high school students were drawn into this vortex as we considered the draft and began to protest.

The powerful "values" section of the Port Huron Statement expresses the Zeitgeist of the New Left and indeed of the progressive movements of the sixties: Social change should change the person and her or his social relations in family, workplace, environment. (See Box 3.2.) "Progress" should not be an abstraction but rather a choice made by moral people who oppose injustice and dedicate themselves to eliminating it. The SDS campers persuaded Hayden to move up this section so that it begins the document; it summarizes the basic moral philosophy and political theory of early SDS and its agenda of participatory democracy.

—— ❧ **Box 3.2   Excerpt from the Port Huron Statement** ❧ ——

We regard men as infinitely precious and possessed of unfulfilled capacities for reason, freedom, and love. In affirming these principles we are aware of countering perhaps the dominant conceptions of man in the twentieth century: that he is a thing to be manipulated, and that he is inherently incapable of directing his own affairs. We oppose the depersonalization that reduces human beings to the status of things—if anything, the brutalities of the twentieth century teach that means and ends are intimately related, that vague appeals to "posterity" cannot justify the mutilations of the present. We oppose, too, the doctrine of human incompetence because it rests essentially on the modern fact that men have been "competently" manipulated into incompetence—we see little reason why men cannot meet with increasing skill the complexities and responsibilities of their situation, if society is organized not for minority, but for majority, participation in decision-making.

Men have unrealized potential for self-cultivation, self-direction, self-understanding, and creativity. It is this potential that we regard as crucial and to which we appeal, not to the human potentiality for violence, unreason, and submission to authority. The goal of man and society should be human independence: a concern not with image or popularity but with finding a meaning in life that is personally authentic: a quality of mind not compulsively driven by a sense of powerlessness, nor one which unthinkingly adopts status values, nor one which represses all threats to its habits, but one which has full, spontaneous access to present and past experiences, one which easily unites the fragmented parts of personal history, one which openly faces problems which are troubling and unresolved: one with an intuitive awareness of possibilities, an active sense of curiosity, an ability and willingness to learn.

This kind of independence does not mean egoistic individualism—the object is not to have one's way so much as it is to have a way that is one's own. Nor do we deify man—we merely have faith in his potential.

Human relationships should involve fraternity and honesty. Human interdependence is contemporary fact; human brotherhood must be willed, however, as a condition of future survival and as the most appropriate form of social relations. Personal links between man and man are needed, especially to go beyond the partial and fragmentary bonds of function that bind men only as worker to worker, employer to employee, teacher to student, American to Russian.

Loneliness, estrangement, isolation describe the vast distance between man and man today. These dominant tendencies cannot be overcome by better personnel management, nor by improved gadgets, but only when a love of man overcomes the idolatrous worship of things by man.

As the individualism we affirm is not egoism, the selflessness we affirm is not self-elimination. On the contrary, we believe in generosity of a kind that imprints one's unique individual qualities in the relation to other men, and to all human activity. Further, to dislike isolation is not to favor the abolition of privacy; the latter differs from isolation in that it occurs or is abolished according to individual will. Finally, we would replace power and personal uniqueness rooted in possession, privilege, or circumstance by power and uniqueness rooted in love, reflectiveness, reason, and creativity.

As a social system we seek the establishment of a democracy of individual participation, governed by two central aims: that the individual share in those social decisions determining the quality and direction of his life; that society be organized to encourage independence in men and provide the media for their common participation.

In a participatory democracy, the political life would be based in several root principles:

- that decision-making of basic social consequence be carried on by public groupings;
- that politics be seen positively, as the art of collectively creating an acceptable pattern of social relations;
- that politics has the function of bringing people out of isolation and into community, thus being a necessary, though not sufficient, means of finding meaning in personal life;
- that the political order should serve to clarify problems in a way instrumental to their solution; it should provide outlets for the expression of personal grievance and aspiration; opposing views should be organized so as to illuminate choices and facilit[ate] the attainment of goals; channels should be commonly available to relate men to knowledge and to power so that private problems—from bad recreation facilities to personal alienation—are formulated as general issues.

The economic sphere would have as its basis the principles:

- that work should involve incentives worthier than money or survival. It should be educative, not stultifying; creative, not mechanical; self-directed, not manipulated; encouraging independence, a respect for others, a sense of dignity and a willingness to accept social responsibility, since it is this experience that has crucial influence on habits, perceptions and individual ethics;
- that the economic experience is so personally decisive that the individual must share in its full determination;

- that the economy itself is of such social importance that its major resources and means of production should be open to democratic participation and subject to democratic social regulation.

Like the political and economic ones, major social institutions—cultural, education, rehabilitative, and others—should be generally organized with the well-being and dignity of man as the essential measure of success.

In social change or interchange, we find violence to be abhorrent because it requires generally the transformation of the target, be it a human being or a community of people, into a depersonalized object of hate. It is imperative that the means of violence be abolished and the institutions—local, national, international—that encourage nonviolence as a condition of conflict be developed.

These are our central values, in skeletal form. It remains vital to understand their denial or attainment in the context of the modern world.

───────────────────── ∾ ─────────────────────

The 1962 Port Huron Statement belonged to the best part of the sixties, as did Rosa Parks's courage in 1955 when she defied segregation and sat at the front of the bus. Indeed, a good argument can be made that Jackie Robinson began the sixties back in 1947 when he broke the color line and joined the Brooklyn Dodgers. By the end of 1969, early SDS had been surpassed by Weather, which was the dialectical negation of Nixon's counter-revolution against the movement. It was as if Nixon's truculence about Vietnam gave birth to the Weather vanguard, which shared his pathology. From baseball to carpet bombing. Port Huron was formulated by youngsters committed to socialist humanism, even though they might not have understood those sources fully. Weather sprang from V. I. Lenin, Mao Tse-tung, and Regis Debray. These differing orientations are bookends of the sixties. In the following section, I explore the origins of Port Huron and the legacy of the New Left in discussions with the movement's leadership.

RICHARD FLACKS

What It Means to Be New Left

"[To be New Left] means a sense of democracy as a living, breathing standard for every institutional situation, every personal situation. It's not that we always live up to it. I mean, I tell my class to speak so much that I'm drowning out your voices. But that's a critique. You have every right to criticize that because I profess to be a democratic teacher. I'm not that skilled at doing it. If there's an essence, this is the essence: a belief in the potentials of democracy in every kind of relationship and social situation, and trying to put that into effect would be what I would take as the fundamental."

Did the Sixties End?

"Everything went aground . . . and that . . . is what Todd's story is in the book *The Sixties.* It's not the story I experienced, because there was a tremendous amount of grassroots movement in the late sixties that SDS had little to directly do with. When I came out to Santa Barbara in '69, tremendous energy, tremendous! Energy that I had not seen even at the University of Chicago, by students who were newly radicalized and that was one phase that had many ambiguities to it, but the real point that I think is missed is how much serious activism came after '69, at a local level, creating what gets to be called new social movements, or by the environmental movement, feminism, and the like, based in communities, and many of the people who of course were active in the sixties New Left and antiwar movement. That's the turn they took, so the fate of SDS as an organization is one thing, but the fate of a wider movement, and even what might be called the New Left, or the way I would put it now, the project of democratization, of participatory democracy, that's a different story."

The 1962 Port Huron Convention

"If you take the early new SDS and the Port Huron period, the emphasis on trying to articulate a new ideological perspective as a collective enterprise, and being . . . very involved in that kind of work as well as activism, a lot of the possibility of collective intellectual or ideological development began to really die, you could say it started, you could see that in 1964. We had a convention at SDS which was supposed to adopt a third manifesto. . . . We had the first two documents and the third, but that convention couldn't arrive at a consensual perspective. I don't even remember what the debates were at all, but of several different documents prepared, none of them could speak for the consensus, so no new document arose. Well, if you think that those were rather interesting and important achievements, which I do, partly because I helped write them, it is a disappointment not to be able to continue. On the other hand, what I concluded even then, I think, but certainly later, was that no single perspective is going to encompass the complexity of social reality that we were living, so the idea that you could simply, each year, update the Port Huron Statement as a collective effort was illusory. The other thing, of course, that you're alluding to in your question, is that SDS grew beyond the boundaries of the face-to-face organizing that had enabled it to grow in the first couple of years. Most people joined SDS in the first few years because they had met organizers or leaders of the organization. . . . There's nothing like personal contact to build trust even if you don't necessarily completely agree. We were able to sustain a kind of trusting communal organization for a couple of years because people knew each other, and even if we disagreed, we trusted people beneath the disagreements. Once you get a real growth spurt where people are coming in, not because of personal contact, but because they identified with the organization as a symbol or because they saw it written up in *Life* magazine and were attracted to it, a kind of growth takes off, which it did by the '65 demonstrations against the war that SDS led. There's an amazing amount of media coverage around that and after that in a format which is completely obsolete, which was the mass magazine, the *Life* magazine depictions, those were really important. It wasn't so much TV as those, but I really felt, "Okay, now people are joining" . . . and I think I've written about this. Now people . . . and Todd wrote about it in his book *The Whole World Is Watching*, people are joining because of how SDS is represented rather than how we represented it. And that's tremendously energizing for an organization, that we have this tremendous growth spurt, the ability to have intellectual consensus, or to even imagine that its primary goal would be intellectual. . . . What Marcuse seems to imagine was possible was just not possible. The other thing that I always like to point out to people is how young this group was . . . a group of twenty-year-olds."

Hayden's Role in the Port Huron Statement

"People came there with the idea something was in the wind, and we were maybe able to articulate it as an organization, and on paper. And some great deal of credit goes to Tom Hayden because he was like a magpie, picking up all of these threads and putting, having the skill. . . .

"He was a tremendous synthesizer, and an eloquent writer, and he understood something that was lurking in the history of the American Left, which is that the language of an American Left has to be attuned to American speech and American understanding.

"I can talk at length about where it came from in his own personal history. It's not a big mystery. It's been talked about before, but . . . what would I change about the Port Huron Statement? In some ways, maybe to my great discredit, I've been living off it ever since. Everything I've taught intellectually has its roots there. When the fortieth anniversary of it was [a few] years ago, I used it in a class. They had to read it, and I was struck by how many students thought it still spoke to them."

Intellectual Origins of Port Huron

"The main lines of it still really resonate, but what 'America in the New Era,' which I was one of the primary authors of the following year, tried to do, as I recall it now, without looking it up, is take the next step, which was to be more concrete about energies, for a New Left, for a New Left coalition or New Liberal Left coalition. We were deliberately trying to bypass debates over third party or work within the Democratic Party, or electoral versus direct action. We embraced everything, like all of those things were valid, in one way or another, and we would try to carve out something that was more of a synthesis, and I don't know if it was successful really, in its own terms, but I still think that a lot of what we were thinking at that time was on target for the time, and still is what I identify with as the right way to be a Left person in America.

"Oh, I think people understood sources. There's another thread which I think is very important which comes down from American pragmatism, John Dewey in particular, and people understood that the term 'participatory democracy' had a link to socialism but was not simply reducible to any standard use of the word 'socialism' by people who were socialists, and that it had the beauty of being a euphemism for radical change that sounded more American, was more American in that socialism had no resonance, is not a positive term in the U.S., unlike the rest of the world.

"It not only helped end the war, I think [the New Left] set the stage for a lot of developments. The whole women's movement comes out of, to a great extent, the New Left. Is that a defeat of the New Left? Is that a defeat of the New Left, or is it a further evolution? You know, it's partly interpretive."

TODD GITLIN

Is Todd Still New Left?

"I don't know that I [still view myself as New Left]. It's not a designation that refers to a living politics. It's a designation that refers to a moment. I don't know that anybody is New Left anymore."

Tom Hayden's Organization and Intellectual Skills

"Tom was one of the very few New Left leaders, really only a handful—who had mastery, the skill and the passion for instrumentalism . . . to manage a political career, and interestingly enough, of the people I knew well, his only rival was somebody who walked off the edge of a political cliff and became a guru follower, Rennie Davis. Rennie was the only other person at the high levels who had that sort of instinct for how to get and use political power.

"I argue in *Letters to a Young Activist* that there were very few people, precious few in the New Left, who were of the character type to be a successful politician. We were more—again, a giant generalization—free-form, anarchic, ambivalent about power, self-generating, self-controlling individuals, and uneasy with organizational discipline. We talked a lot about building a new politics, but mainly that turned out to be not doing politics. In a way, the pure expression of that mentality today is Ralph Nader, who, if he had set out to do for the Left what the Christian Coalition did for the Right, and before that, the Goldwater movement, would have created a force in the Democratic Party that would actually have weight. As it is, the only practical thing he could accomplish was to elect George Bush.

"Given the fact that Tom was confined to local politics, he went as far as he could go. He was a considerable player in California politics for a long time until he was term-limited out, but he couldn't win national office. He could tell you in detail how he was foxed out of various congressional possibilities by people with more money or better connections."

Causes of Sixties Social Movements

"Jim Crow is not by itself causal. . . . What has to happen first is the civil rights movement, and the civil rights movement was not the product of Jim Crow alone. It required the perception on the part of a critical mass of activists that they could actually bring it down.

"There had to be also a critical mass of people who imagined themselves to be intellectuals affiliated with the movement, or who might, à la Mills, themselves constitute a group that had a bigger goal than to achieve civil rights. The uproar against the draft came later—since college students were exempt through 1966—and the proof of it is that the movement grew even as college students were protected. . . . The war obviously was pivotal in spurring the movement and in the exponential growth of the movement, but the movement precedes the drafting of students, and this is crucial; a lot of people miss this. There's a little riff on this in my book *The Sixties*. I think it's important that the movement was recruiting people at a time when students still had exemptions up until '66."

Impact of the Draft on the Student Movement

"Through part of '66, at least part of '66, Mike Locker and I wrote a quiz that we were using as an organizing tool at universities to alert students to what was waiting for them if they actually suc-ceeded in going to Vietnam, and that was in '66. It was a counter to the Selective Service System's test. . . . Their idea was that you could exempt yourself by passing their test, so we countered it sometime in '66. I can't tell you exactly when those students started to be drafted, but it was sometime in '66.

"The big escalation was in April '65; that was when Marines landed and the bombing became steadier, and then the numbers of troops started growing. At some point in that year, the year '65, '66, they recognized that they were going to run out of guys. But there were SDS people who were actually eligible for student ex-emption, who threw it over because they decided to do something militant against the draft, so they were willing to jeopardize their safety. And then it's also important to recognize that the SDS at least was acutely aware that if students didn't get drafted, that somebody else was going to get drafted, and we were at pains to be something other than a self-interested or class protection project."

The Origins of the Right in California Politics

"I recommend here, in my discussion, I forget which letter it is, in *Letters to a Young Activist,* about this asymmetry between Left and Right. I refer to a couple of books that I think are really important on this, and one of them is a book about the right wing of Orange County, California, by Lisa McGirr, called *Suburban Warriors*, and she tracks, from the fifties on, this network of Birchers and Chris-tian anticommunists and other such types, and how they were fa-natical and staunch, stalwart, unflappable. There was a crucial moment for them—after 1962, these people had gotten big enough in Southern California that they thought it was time for them to nominate a gubernatorial candidate—and they ran a guy named Joe Shell against the more moderate Nixon in the primaries, and they got defeated. Nixon won the nomination, and then the right-wingers were very angry and disturbed because they had been working for years to take over the Republican Party and now they had been defeated, and some actually thought at that point of going off and organizing a third party, and they approached their major tycoon, who was Walter Knott of Knott's Berry Farm, and they put this proposition to him, and he told them they were crazy because the system was rigged for two parties. He told them to go back to work in the Republican Party and do their proper work, which was, in effect, *becoming* the Republican Party, and, of course, in '64 they did that. These people were the shank of the power of the California delegation at the Goldwater convention, and nominated Goldwater, and that seemed like a gigantic feat at the time, but from it came Reagan. Reagan became prominent as a national figure, as a deputy of Goldwater's, and from Reagan's prominence in that campaign came the notion of pushing him forward as governor of California in '66 and so on. The rest is history.

"But it told you something about who actually lived in California. Not so many, in fact, were hippies, radicals, or militant blacks. I made the point in passing in my *Sixties* book. I went back and looked at issues of the *Berkeley Barb* to the year 1966 when Reagan was running for governor, and there was just one brief mention of the campaign. I mean, Berkeley was living in another world. And, of course, Reagan knew that well and capitalized on it by running against Berkeley, and won by a million votes. My point about 1962 is that the right-wing Republicans were realists, at that moment, which could have been pivotal. If they'd gone off to become Ralph Nader, they would have gone off the edge of a cliff, but they stayed, and they got themselves a Republican Party with a lot of work—it took years. You remember, Reagan ran for president twice before he won. He lost the nomination in 1968 and 1976 but kept up the inner-party struggle until his time arrived."

TOM HAYDEN

The Relationship Between the Kennedys and the New Left

"In Kennedy's 1962 period when the Port Huron Statement was written, there was every reason to believe Kennedy was vulnerable to pressure on civil rights. We described him as a form of managerial liberalism, not oppression, but managerial liberalism meaning if we intensified the heat on the streets enough, he will make some concessions in order to keep managing society. Vietnam had started, but it was quite insecure.

"There's some evidence of that, but much of this is a test of where you are, not an evidentiary assessment, but what we know is that he was riling up the military-industrial complex and the conservative Republicans because he was proposing an end to the nuclear arms race, an end to the cold war, and a turn towards peace, and he was shot shortly after making that speech.

"Those of us who were in the movement at the time were deeply suspicious at the time, finding ourselves as radicals who wanted to change the system and not just desegregate a lunch counter. I think deep down there was a sense that it was possible for our agenda on the Left to converge with Kennedy's agenda . . . if we pushed.

"[Bobby] Kennedy was a continuation of the first Kennedy regime that had been stopped by assassination, so it was probably on that level, but I also thought that he'd be fine on Vietnam and that he had a much greater ability to organize the urban poor and mobilize them.

"There was another thing that was very different about their experience than ours. The movement itself, it seems just filled with instances of revolutionary possibilities. Whether you were an effective organizer or you just stood by, there was always a demonstration coming down the street. There was always a riot. There was always a development. It was as if history had been kicked into motion, and it did seem that history was out of control, that all the managerial liberalism of Kennedy was gone and the fight was on. They were, I think, very stimulated and reactive to that sense of possibilities, which didn't really exist in '61, '62, or '63 except in pockets of the South, maybe."

Marx's Influence on the New Left

"It's almost impossible to discuss Marx because people have such confused impressions of the subject matter, and because he lived a long life and wrote many hundreds of thousands of words and participated in many events, so it's for you to sort it out.

"Oh I had read [Marx], but they were lifted, if you will, from Catholic theology, from Erich Fromm, from C. Wright Mills above all. At this point, you had a hybrid organization. There were some people, like Flacks, who were red-diaper babies and descendants of the Marxist tradition, and there were others, like myself, that felt it wasn't clear whether it was for substantive reasons or otherwise, but it had become so laden with baggage that, you know, we needed something else. So I was the New and [Flacks] was the Left maybe, but I was very reluctant to see this project as just the revival of the Left. I was swayed that way because more experienced people told me that's how it had to be.

"It wasn't a conscious effort in the early sixties. It certainly was not conscious of me. . . . It was absolutely not conscious with SNCC."

SNCC's Impact on SDS

"If there had been no SNCC, there would have been no SDS. . . . We were motivated by the experience with SNCC. Now, Gitlin came out of Harvard academics . . . its peace program. . . . He tried to develop a countertheory to deterrence, and that was his part of Port Huron. Flacks came out of the communist party and the popular front. He wanted to leave all that behind. He would be the most likely, but I just don't remember him talking about the recovery of the early humanism of Marx.

"Well, this is the sharp break. There's nothing really in Marxism that would help you understand SNCC, and so your analysis of the evolution of these ideas and theories and practices and so on could well be accurate, but I'm just telling you that almost nobody I knew was trying to recover the 1844 manuscripts."

C. Wrights Mills and the New Left

"I thought of him as a Texas wild man who slept with women on the tops of desks and rode a motorcycle, and he was a kind of a repressed Irish guy, hadn't dealt with his roots, and I placed him as much in the anarchist tradition as the Marxist tradition. But be that as it may, what he called for was something we could all live with, which was something that was radically new. He called it a New Left, but it was also radically new from the history of the Left."

MARK RUDD

Is Mark Still a New Leftist?

"I don't talk about myself as a Leftist, because we're not a factor. We are not a political entity. I'm a union activist, I'm an environmental activist, a peace activist, but I wouldn't say that there is a Left.

"Of course, [I still consider myself a New Leftist]. I was a New Leftist. I'm really still a New Leftist, but it would seem to me a Left would involve the postulation and the attempt to create the party, a political party of the Left. That to me is the minimum requirement.

"And there is no such thing and there's no possibility, and there's no fantasy even of a communist party, which I think was pretty much all it ever was—a fantasy.

"But there were plenty of people who spent a lot of their lives attempting to build a communist party of some sort, and there are still entities that exist. But there's nobody who thinks about a party, which really was what a Left means. Now there are a lot of social movements. Women, gays, environmental movements, various aspects of a Latino movement: They all exist, but nobody thinks of a party.

"Well, I think theory probably precedes organization. We have neither."

Impact of Port Huron Statement

"I came in contact with SDS people in '65 and actually joined SDS in '66. At that time I did read the Port Huron Statement. . . . That was a full . . . three or four years after it was written, but at that time I read it, I was really galvanized by the idea of opposing the cold war. I don't know if they had corporate liberalism, but that the cold war could be opposed and that anticommunism could be opposed, and that these were great wastes of the resources of this country, anticommunism and the cold war. I was galvanized by that and the idea of participatory democracy. Why not? That was kind of an anarchist notion; I liked that."

Marxism and the New Left

"We pretended to be Marxists. I would say that [we were Marxists] . . . with a lot of anarchist tendencies. We hit many different Marxist notes. We liked Lenin, and we liked Mao. Some of the people even liked Stalin, that hard core.

"When I was a freshman, sophomore, junior, we were reading the Frankfurt School, and especially early Marx. . . . Early Marx, very important; Gramsci, I've read that."

Impact of the New Left Today

"My estimate is that there are somewhere around 5 to 10 million people in the country who are directly touched in some manner or participated in some manner in the New Left endeavor of the era of '65 to '75.

"There were 3 million students who went on strike in May of 1970. That's 3 million right there. There were 3.8 million GIs who went to Vietnam. Of that 3.8, my guess is approximately half were antiwar. They had some connection, maybe just reading, some context within the antiwar movement. I also believe that the antiwar movement itself was in the millions of activists.

"There were demonstrations in the hundreds of thousands, and there was one that was forgotten, May Day 1971. . . . The DC police arrested ten to twenty thousand people. They didn't arrest them, they held them in a stadium, or several stadiums, so I think to say that there's 5 to 10 million people who at one point or another were touched directly by the antiwar movement or the New Left is correct.

"And there's another interesting bunch of people who are thirty-five to forty-five who are cusp people, and they were young, but they were fascinated. . . . [Like] . . . Sam Green and Bill Segal, who made *The Weather Underground* movie, they're thirty-seven and forty-one. Those cusp people are very important people; they really are."

ROXANNE DUNBAR-ORTIZ

Is Roxanne Still New Left?

"In the early 1970s, I totally rejected the New Left identity, or perhaps even earlier as I helped pioneer the women's liberation movement in 1967–68. I think it was a way of shirking responsibility for the many mistakes and apparent failure of our capacity to move to a more effective level in bringing down the U.S. empire and changing the social and economic order. In the 1990s as I wrote a memoir of the 1960s, which was published in 2002 as *Outlaw Woman: A Memoir of the War Years, 1960–1975*, I was able to gain a distance in placing myself in history. I have a doctorate in history, and I'm trained to do that in writing history, but it's not so easy to be professional and objective about one's own life. I had to concede that not only I, but the women's liberation movement, and even the American Indian Movement with which I became involved in the early 1970s, were a part of the New Left, which had been born out of the post–World War II mass civil rights movement. As to whether I am still New Left, whether I like it or not, I am, we are.

It's like asking whether I'm still a part of my family. How can I not be? I still consider myself a full-time revolutionary, at least wannabe, and I carry the values that nourished me and that I contributed to the New Left. I like being a part of history, that history, and being able to place myself there."

Marxism and the Port Huron Statement

"I agree that the Port Huron Statement was in effect a Marxist document, not because any of its authors were consciously Marxists, and probably none were Marxist specialists or had even read Marx. But as with Freudianism, Marxism was 'in the air' by the early 1960s. In the U.S., for young people coming of age, we heard a great deal about Marxism and communism, all of it negative, but nevertheless it entered our consciousness. I read what were actually cold war tracts like Milovan Djilas's *The New Class* in the late 1950s, and although he was a Yugoslavian living in exile, condemning the Soviet-dominated bloc of countries, he was prosocialist. The book was a best seller; otherwise, I doubt I would have even known about it in Oklahoma in 1958. I took a cold war course on "The Theory and Practice of Marxism," taught by a crazed anticommunist, but we read *The Communist Manifesto*, which I found made perfect sense. I'm certain that I was having these kinds of experiences in Oklahoma, and being from an impoverished rural family, that the urban youth my age were likewise being exposed to Marxism in this way. Then, of course, there was C. Wright Mills, who didn't come my way at the time, which so influenced the Port Huron creators. Marcuse was soon to follow. I think it's ahistorical to maintain that Marxism was out of the picture; it was fundamental."

Origins of the Women's Movement

"I think there were a number of forces that converged to produce the women's liberation movement that burst into the public eye in 1967–68. There was already a reformist women's rights movement in the early 1960s that came more out of the Old Left, the communist party, and its affiliates. That's where Betty Friedan came from, and her book *Feminine Mystique* became a best seller . . . leading to the formation of the National Organization for Women. JFK responded by establishing a women's equity desk in the White House; then, of course, women's rights were included in the 1964 Civil Rights Act. All of this was closely connected with the consciousness of rights created by the civil rights movement, and by the Universal Declaration of Human Rights by the United Nations, very much the work of the Communist International.

"Young women were not involved in significant numbers in the women's reform movement of the early 1960s. However, most of the young, white women who started the radical women's liberation movement came right out of SNCC, where they learned invaluable organizational skills and political consciousness. SDS also made its transition to an antiwar movement from the same source of experience and knowledge. Radical young women were shocked, I think (I certainly was), at the negative responses of most, not all, radical men. At the same time, the gay and lesbian movement was bursting out, and radical lesbians became key leaders in the women's liberation movement. I would say that the earlier reformist movement, being far more savvy in mainstream politics and ensconced in the Democratic Party, overtook and co-opted the radical women and began calling themselves feminists. Certainly, this became the highly publicized face of the women's movement— a special-interest group of white, middle-class women competing for jobs and wealth with blacks and other oppressed groups. So the women's liberation movement was a flare, like SDS, that was consumed and consumed itself, although thousands of young women and men were radicalized as they joined in while it was on fire. The radical women created and joined various radical groups. Young women of color who hadn't paid attention to the women's liberation flare, or it was gone before they could get a handle on it, certainly were not attracted to NOW and the abortion and equal rights amendment movements that were reduced to lawyers' work and ritualistic protests, but they began forming very radical groups and producing dynamic literature."

Port Huron's Concept of Participatory Democracy

"Participatory democracy came about to address the alienation young people felt about their self-determination as human beings, where everything seemed to be controlled from the outside. This was also the main pillar that the civil rights movement and the later women's liberation movement were built on. That every human being counts and should have a voice. I think the urge activated young people and created tremendous kinetic energy. But, certainly, it had its limitations, which young people discovered, especially as the civil rights workers from Mississippi discovered at the Democratic Party Convention of 1964, when the Mississippi Democratic Freedom Party was not recognized as representing the people of Mississippi, allowing the racist white oligarchy to remain in control of the Mississippi Democratic Party. Most New Leftists came to see capitalism and imperialism as evils to eliminate, with various ideas about new societies, mostly on some variation of a socialist model. Of course, the U.S. was founded as a capitalist/ imperialist state and will not volunteer to change itself any more than it must in order to survive intact."

CASEY HAYDEN

Is Casey Still New Left?

"I came to SDS through the Liberal Study Group [LSG] at the USNSA [United States National Student Association] Congress in 1960. I gave a rousing speech to this primarily white organization of student political leaders in support of the sit-ins, in which I was a participant. I was scooped up by Al Haber (who in a brilliant move had created the LSG as an organizing tool for SDS) and the emerging SDS leadership. I was a religious, small-town University of Texas student who had come to student politics through the National Student YWCA [Young Women's Christian Association] and an offbeat, intellectual Christian existentialist commune where I was living in Austin. Here I'd already been exposed to the idea of a student movement and to critiques of race and sexual roles and the cold war. The New Left felt like home. Deep in the southern movement on SNCC staff, I was dedicated to democratic organizing and Gandhian nonviolence. From those perspectives, and failing as we all do, I've tried to wear the original face of the New Left. That face had many aspects, but to me the lasting sensibility invests one's own values and experience above all else, and seeks other people of like mind to love and trust. With them one can take great risks to live with radical and intelligent integrity for the sake of all beings."

DAVID GILBERT

Is David Still New Left?

"Yes! To me 'New Left' was a refreshing and necessary way to say that we did not see the bureaucratic and repressive regimes of the USSR and East Europe as positive models. I was inspired by the civil rights movement and by the national liberation struggles in the Third World, not by the USSR and East Europe or the parties

David Gilbert with his son Chesa. (Photo courtesy of Chesa Gilbert)

that followed them. New Left also connected with the vibrancy of the cultural rebellion, with rock 'n' roll at the center of it. I still consider myself New Left in the sense of opposing that statist model of 'socialism,' and in emphasizing national liberation, racism, and sexism as well as class, but in too many ways our generation now represents an Old Left in the mechanical recitation of Marxist-Leninist formulas and very commandist organizational structures."

Democratic Socialism

"I very much think of myself in this way. I can't say that I read or followed the theorists you mention, but in my own thinking it was essential to be both democratic and socialist; in fact, you couldn't have one without the other: (a) big money undermines democracy; (b) socialism means running the economy by/for the oppressed, which can be achieved only through democratic forms."

JOSÉ ANGEL GUTIÉRREZ

José Angel Was Never "New Left"

"New Left identification. I never identified with the term. I was neither Old Left much less New Left in 1961 when I began my activism at age sixteen as a Chicano kid. As far as I can recall, the elementary teachers pinned 'I Like Ike' political buttons on our shirts just prior to going home from school in 1952 and again in 1956. The secondary teachers at Crystal City High School openly preached an anticommunist ideology, beginning with the *Sputnik* alarm in 1957. If I had identification with any political movement, it was the Political Association of Spanish-Speaking Organizations (PASO), headed then by Bexar County commissioner Alberto A. Peña Jr. of San Antonio, Texas, during the early 1960s.

José Angel Gutiérrez. (Photo courtesy of Stefanie Hogan)

"The English-language media from San Antonio and the local newspaper or radio never published items about the [Port] Huron Statement, SDS, Old or New Left. Television was not affordable by the Chicano masses yet, and reception was bad. Cable had not begun. All Chicanos simply saw in the world of that era was us and them; and them were the bigoted, racist Anglos we called 'gringos.' I am sure that Anglo youth then were as ignorant about our historic presence in these Americas as they are now. Education in the U.S. is about making Anglos out of all of us; no need to study anyone else.

"I have evolved since the 1960s and become appreciative of the social struggles of other minorities and of New Left advocates and progressives in general. I remain a Chicano nationalist."

CARL OGLESBY

On What It Means to Be New Left

"I think that [New Left] is an important term and that it continues to be important because there's a political niche between liberal and Marxist that I think New Left fills, and I think it's legitimately called New Left because it doesn't harken back to any of the basic ideologies of Marxism and liberalism. It's an attempt to take democracy seriously and to build it back into the grass roots.

"What got me into SDS was the simple fact that they weren't calling themselves one thing or the other. It's not to say there weren't socialists in SDS and probably some communists, too, but the organization itself, at least so far as I could tell, didn't take a position on the economic form that society had to be based on. It was, so far as I could tell, exclusively concentrated on the manner in which decisions were made."

In the next chapter, I address the topic of Weatherman, a phenomenon of the late sixties. The activists address my contention that Weather sprang from great movement frustration about persuading Johnson and then Nixon to stop the war. They also address my concern that the Right today wants sixties radicals to repent for their misdeeds as a way of condemning the progressive projects of the sixties. This agenda is made possible in part by the political climate in the United States since 9/11.

The Right attempted to demonize Barack Obama in the 2008 election campaign by linking him to Bill Ayers, a Weather founder.

This fact alone keeps the sixties—and Weatherman—alive. And Ayers's publisher seized a commercial opportunity by reissuing *Fugitive Days* (Ayers 2001) after the election, when Ayers could no longer hurt Obama by their supposed affiliation. The Right has made Ayers more famous than he ever used to be. Such are the media politics of demonology.

ဢ Four ❧

Bringing the War Home:
Weatherman and Radical Dissent

Memory is a motherfucker.
　　　　　　—Bill Ayers

On September 11, 2001, a fateful day, the *New York Times* ran an interview with Bill Ayers, the author of his controversial memoir. During the protracted surreal chapter of the Weather Underground from the late 1960s and 1970s, the Weather fugitives hid from the law in plain sight, using aliases and addresses to elude the FBI. His "lifetime partner," Bernardine Dohrn, the charismatic Weatherleader, was pictured alongside Bill, just a regular professional couple making dinner in the kitchen. Both are professors. The interview was described as "fawning." But the interview and Ayers's book were largely ignored because much more dramatic events were unfolding in New York City, at the Pentagon, and in the air over rural Pennsylvania. These events—now called 9/11, playing on the emergency that they posed for America and the world—were termed "terrorism." Predictably, the Weather Underground Organization (WUO) was also labeled terrorist in retrospect, using the newfound term for middle-class revolutionaries who unpredictably blow up buildings and people, including themselves. After 9/11, a film mentioned earlier was made about the Weather Underground that romanticized some of the drama of the late sixties and offered interesting insights into the protagonists in the group, such as Mark Rudd. In this chapter, I consider the legacy of Weatherman and also, peripherally, the issues of violence and terrorism.

Weatherman issued a "declaration of a state of war" against the United States following the Black Panther Fred Hampton's 1969 murder and Kent State in 1970. It is at this point that Weatherman went underground, fighting the Debrayist battle against U.S. "imperialism." Regis Debray (1967), a theorist of Third World revolution, argued that a revolutionary leadership group could incite rural violence, which would then spread to cities as a revolutionary ("red") army formed to overthrow capitalist imperialism—not, obviously, a theory suited to the United States. Weatherman was the informal name given to the Revolutionary Youth Movement (RYM), which took over the Students for a Democratic Society (SDS) at the 1969 annual SDS convention. Weatherman, while aboveground during the late 1960s, turned SDS into a top-down vanguard party, replacing the grassroots orientation of the earlier Port Huron SDS. Weatherman became the Weather Underground with a manifesto, issued by Bernardine Dohrn in May 1970, extending the sixties into the next new decade and declaring a state of war in "Amerika." According to Dohrn's manifesto, "All over the world, people fighting Amerikan imperialism look to Amerika's youth to use our strategic position behind enemy lines to join forces in the destruction of the empire." She ended by saying: "Within the next fourteen days we will attack a symbol or institution of Amerikan injustice. This is the way we celebrate the example of Eldridge Cleaver and H. Rap Brown and all black revolutionaries who first inspired us by their fight behind enemy lines for the liberation of their people ("Never Again Will They Fight Alone" 1970).

After this communiqué was released, the WUO began a series of strategic bombings of symbolically important American buildings as part of its campaign to galvanize urban American workers and youth. They, in turn, would join a "red army" and overthrow the state.

SETTING THE STAGE: BAD WEATHER

All of us up here [on stage] are stone communist revolutionaries.
—Jeff Jones

By 1968 and 1969, movement kids utterly stymied by Lyndon Johnson, Hubert Humphrey, Richard Nixon, and J. Edgar Hoover had dropped acid and dropped out. A few already affiliated with the post–Port Huron version of SDS decided not to retreat from politics. They became Weathermen, and their goal was to bring about a Marxist-Leninist revolution in the United States and throughout the world. Just as the sixties evoke rock, drugs, and free love, somewhat misleadingly given the surrounding political turmoil, so they bear the imprint of the Weather Underground's campaign of bombing at decade's end. Weatherman was, at most, a few hundred souls, not much of a movement, even for hardened cadres seeking to foment revolutionary discontent. Nevertheless, Weatherman represented an important moment because, perhaps more than anything else, it signaled the transition from the sixties' Dionysian to Euripidean phases, from ecstasy and eros to tragedy, even self-destruction.

Jeremy Varon (2004) has written an excellent study of the Weather Underground, comparing it to the German Baader-Meinhof group and probing its intellectual and political underpinnings. Bill Ayers's memoir remains an important retrospection on the late sixties and early seventies, told by a child of privilege, a self-confessed all-American boy who became an SDS activist and helped move that organization in the direction of desperate and sometimes violent extraparliamentary politics.

Bill Ayers, Bernardine Dohrn, Jeff Jones, Terry Robbins, Kathy Boudin, Diana Oughton, Ted Gold, and David Gilbert were sixties

Bernardine Dohrn, former leader of the Weather Underground, and her companion Bill Ayers are escorted by federal authorities after surrendering in Chicago, Illinois, Dec. 3, 1989. (AP Photo)

people, and they even belonged to the same organization started by Al Haber and spearheaded by Tom Hayden. Yet these SDSers were younger than the founders and experienced the early and mid-sixties differently than the elders of Hayden's age group. For the most part, Dohrn and the other Weather leaders missed the existential transformations of the 1962–1965 Port Huron period; they gravitated to the antiwar movement and took over the New Left toward decade's end after early SDS, in its prior hopeful phase, had atrophied. Early SDS evolved into a revolutionary movement partly because the antiwar movement had not stopped the war and partly because the antiwar movement became a focused, essentially single-issue campaign only tenuously connected to Port Huron's critical social theory, which called for thoroughgoing radical change in America.

Early SDS both failed and succeeded. It failed to persuade the movement to adopt a radical critique of American society and international imperialism both because that critique was derived from an unfamiliar European leftism and because the swelling antiwar movement between about 1965 and 1968 put aside the overarching critique of the military-industrial complex and instead focused simply on stopping the war. Early SDS succeeded because it politicized hundreds of thousands of prepolitical college students and adults and brought them into the antiwar and civil rights movements at a time when the Democratic administration of President Lyndon Johnson not only supported the war but also was escalating it. SDS offered an alternative to the major political parties that made sense to young Americans worried about being drafted and increasingly convinced that U.S. military aggression in distant Southeast Asia was immoral and insane.

The Columbia University uprising in spring 1968 figured centrally in the transition between the Port Huron phase of SDS and later, more militant configurations of SDS. The so-called action faction at Columbia, as Rudd indicates, evolved into Weatherman within a year. But Hayden was also at Columbia, although as an outside agitator. In a memorable image, a conservatively attired Hayden is helping Frances Fox Piven, a young Columbia faculty member, into an occupied building. After the sixties and the movement were over, Hayden continued his political work and Piven became a radical academic of considerable repute. Indeed, she was recently elected president of the mainstream American Sociological Association, thereby demonstrating that radicals not only now occupy a building and a campus but also have embarked successfully on what German New Leftist Rudi Dutschke called the "long march through the institutions" (Dutschke et al. 1980). Dutschke initially survived a right-wing assassination attempt in Germany in 1968, but he died from his injuries in 1979.

By 1967 or 1968, the Port Huron leadership had either left SDS or been eclipsed by new and less patient blood. Within a year, the whole movement was plunged into despair by assassinations, the Chicago convention, the hunt for reds. At the fractious 1969 SDS convention, Weatherman outmaneuvered the Progressive Labor faction for leadership as the younger New Left leadership gave up on peaceful mass protest—which clearly did not work—and embarked on a strategy that included military actions. Reading the speeches and manifestos of this new hard Left makes one cringe because these young people did not fully understand the theoretical formulations—"revolution," "smash the state"—they were mouthing as they turned against Port Huron's generous idealism and instead decided to bring "Amerika" to its knees. In particular, this new SDS Weather leadership sought to expose America to violence so that citizens would be radicalized and mobilize against the martial state, which was conducting the pointless Vietnam War and repressing and murdering dissidents at home.

The Weatherpeople, cadres totally committed to revolutionary ideology, rejected an existentialism that regards the self as infinitely valuable, as Port Huron expressed it. The revolutionary Debrayism of Weatherman drummed out individuality through political education, a means of consciousness-raising since the Soviets and Chinese began their experiments with command socialism.

In a sense, then, one might regard the Weatherman/Weather Underground phenomenon as postsixties, having abandoned the central tenet that the individual is valuable and not fodder for the revolution. One might view Weather as a product, albeit a dialectical one, of Nixon and FBI repression and the military hegemony of the Pentagon: Had the war ended by 1968 or 1969 in response to mass protest, Weatherman probably would not have come into existence as a militant expression of total frustration. Young radicals were frustrated, especially at the time of the Chicago Democratic Convention, that they could not budge the government (or "state"); indeed, the state was cracking down harshly on all dissent. Weatherman's subordination of the self to the radical cause was provoked by the state's disciplining of dissent, extending an earlier fifties McCarthyism via mechanisms of police terror and federal intelligence gathering such as COINTELPRO.

Most stories of the sixties include the Weather phenomenon. This is an intriguing moment in twentieth-century American history as upper-middle-class children gave themselves over totally to the "revolution."

In general, young people have less stake in a society (no family, fewer debts, etc.), are more open to new ideas (they have not been brainwashed for so long or so well), and are therefore more able and willing to move in a revolutionary direction. Specifically in America, young people have grown up experiencing the crises in imperialism. They have grown up along with a developing black liberation movement, the liberation of Cuba, the fights for independence in Africa, and the war in Vietnam. Older people grew up during the fight against Fascism, during the cold war, the smashing of the trade unions, McCarthy, and a period during which real wages consistently rose—since 1965 disposable real income has decreased slightly, particularly in urban areas where inflation and increased taxation have bitten heavily into wages. ("You Don't Need a Weatherman to Know Which Way the Wind Blows" 1969)

There were communal living, group sex, Maoist gut checks, criticism/self-criticism, robotic military drills. All of this was un-American, or was it? Was this not just the other side of a soured liberalism and individualism? Although Weatherman deserves notice because it represents the spiraling downward of SDS and reflects the fatigue of the movement by the late 1960s, Weather should not overwhelm Port Huron in our memory of sixties politics. These phases, one early and one late in the decade, are each other's counterpoint, perhaps each other's negation. There is connection, too: Hayden, on trial for his role as an outside agitator at the Democratic Convention in 1968, addressed the Weatherpeople just before their October 1969 "action" in Chicago. Using a bullhorn, he addressed a small crowd of activists gathered at night in Lincoln Park before they sprinted through affluent neighborhoods and smashed cars, buildings, property, eventually succumbing to the police, who outmanned them. Hayden did not chastise the young cadres but wished them well; he dispelled the rumor that he and the other Chicago defendants disapproved of bringing the war home.

The Weather leadership had a lot to learn. But these young people were outraged at the refusal of the administration to change course in Vietnam even after millions of peace-loving Americans had joined in protest of the war. They were passionate, if misguided. They were zealous and committed, even if they did not understand fully the Left revolutionary traditions from which they were drawing. V. I. Lenin was serious and sober by contrast; he had mastered G. W. F. Hegel and Karl Marx before he stormed the Winter Palace in St. Petersburg in 1917. Weathermen were adventurist; they were on an adventure that contained distinct Oedipal overtones of killing their parents. And their strategy of using selective violence, such as bombings, to radicalize high school students and the working class had little appeal to post–World War II Americans. It was telling that the Weather leadership (Weatherbureau,

Two Chicago policemen arrest a member of the Weatherman faction of the SDS during a disturbance on Oct. 11, 1969, following a march from Chicago's Haymarket Square to the Loop. En route, marchers broke windows in the downtown area and clashed with police, who arrested 103 people. (AP Photo/ Fred Jewell)

predictably) planned for thousands of revolutionary youth to join them in Chicago during autumn 1969, rampaging through "pig city" and destroying property on the Gold Coast. Only hundreds showed up. The Weatherpeople knew that they faced prison, injury, and perhaps death. They persevered both because the macho male leaders had something to prove and because they were angry that Nixon had been elected and the war was escalating.

On March 6, 1970, the New Left was shaken to its foundations as a townhouse they occupied in Manhattan exploded, killing three of the Weather inhabitants. They were making antipersonnel bombs to be used against military personnel on American bases. The death of their Weather comrades caused the leadership, especially Dohrn, to rethink their strategy of "exemplary violence." They decided to limit such violence to the destruction of unoccupied buildings, a "softer and gentler" Weather doctrine laid out in a Weather publication called *Prairie Fire: The Politics of Revolutionary Anti-imperialism* (Power 1974).

By 1970, the Weather leaders had regrouped and decided to modify their plans for violence. Now only buildings would be targeted, and they were careful to forewarn the custodians of these buildings so that occupants could be evacuated. There were no subsequent human casualties; the Weather Underground exercised care to target unoccupied buildings with national symbolic import, such as Congress. This was protest in its ultimate form. They risked everything—lifetime imprisonment and death—in order to make the points that the war was wrong and that the government was impervious. More than wrong—the war was a symptom of arrogant American imperialism. The "system," American capitalism, had to be changed, and these changes could not be piecemeal. They had to go to the heart of a system of private profit in a market economy.

Although theoretically unsophisticated, Weather was Marxist. It had a total theory of what was wrong with American capitalism, and its solution was an international communist revolution. Revolutionary images and practices from China and Latin America were largely irrelevant to post–World War II America, where the most pressing problem was ennui. WUO did not have a well-conceived strategy, given the absence of revolutionary agents in the United States, especially after the student movement petered out and regrouped at Woodstock in late summer 1969. Weather's argument that selective bombings would mobilize the working class and high school students was naïve at best. But Dohrn, Ayers, and their comrades, mostly in their twenties, were committed and passionate. And at the time, who had a better idea?

In our interviews, Hayden remarks that one should understand the Weather phenomenon as an expression of frustration with traditional peace politics and protest. It is easy to dismiss Weather as having been irrational—suicidal, even. But Hayden is saying that there was real rage against the American war machine, rage that Hayden had begun to feel as he made a 1965 fact-finding trip to Vietnam and in 1967 played a key role in negotiating the release of the first three American military personnel captured by the North Vietnamese. In spite of the media spectacle of "Hanoi Jane" (Jane Fonda, eventually Hayden's wife), Hayden worked behind the scenes for the release of U.S. soldiers and for better relations with the North Vietnamese.

Hayden had already indicated during the sixties that "democracy is in the streets," meaning that participatory democracy must play out in the everyday venues of community, school, and family and that the movement needed to take back the public sphere— the streets, at least metaphorically. Weather actions were a way of reclaiming or at least redefining the public sphere, even if the odds against succeeding were very long. The key word in all this is "rage," the emotional reaction of many movement people during and after 1968 as it became clear that the White House and the U.S. military were not listening. If anything, they were escalating the war, even after the Tet Offensive in early 1968. Tet should have signaled to the Pentagon and White House that the war was being lost and was probably not "winnable" in conventional terms.

The war was unwinnable not simply because it was a "guerrilla" war fought opportunistically without a defined battlefield but also because it was a popular war, with much of Vietnam's civilian population mobilized against the American intruders. Hayden, in his 1988 memoir, wrote that he wished that he had not been so uncritical of the North Vietnamese, with their Marxist-Leninist orthodoxy and authoritarianism. There was a sense that "the enemy" was necessarily "our friend," and morally and politically righteous. "Amerika" was evil and its "enemy" was saintly. There was, and is, too much dichotomous thinking. But Ho Chi Minh, his Leninist orthodoxy aside, was a popular leader who promised to rid his country of another imperial intruder, just as the Vietnamese had rid Indochina of the French in 1954. Even after the United States had killed a million soldiers and civilians, the will of the Vietnamese people was iron; they were going to fight to the death to send the Americans home, and they succeeded in 1975.

The U.S. government and military did not understand any of this because the prevailing cold war mentality—evil Soviet and Chinese empires versus good United States and its allies—prevented them from viewing the world with nuance and complexity. Hayden and other movement leaders who traveled to North Vietnam during the war were impressed by the steely resolve of the Vietnamese even as their cities and hamlets were being pounded from the air. It was easy for Hayden to believe that North Vietnam was a utopia in which gentle folk, with almost Zen patience, steeled themselves through sheer force of will. Although this was partly correct, North Vietnam was not a utopia; it was a hierarchical society organized around the perception—no, precept—of revolutionary necessity. It was a one-party system in which the communist party was unchallenged.

This model of socialism was anathema to the Port Huron New Left, and yet it was idealized by New Left leaders during the war as the alternative to U.S. aggression. Eventually, by the late 1960s, many American soldiers had turned against the war and were biding their time until their tour of duty was over. They got stoned, avoided missions, and sometimes even fragged (injured) their officers. Vietnam-era GIs protested at the entrance to the Ft. Dix stockade in New Jersey. The slogan over the gate, "Obedience to the Law Is Freedom," was reminiscent of the Auschwitz concentration camp slogan, "Work Will Set You Free."

There are many evils afoot, and it is entirely possible for all sides to be wrong. This is a postmodern lesson, emphasizing the importance of perspective. Absolute truth is obstructed by perspective, which is necessarily distorting. The sixties bred dogma, preventing the Left from viewing itself critically. Weatherman sprung from this hubris. Young people during the late sixties fugitive days were full of themselves but untested by either experience or knowledge of history. This is a very American failing. Richard Nixon and General William Westmoreland were also afflicted with hubris, but for them, and for us, the stakes were much higher as they vigorously escalated the war.

Today, those who reconstruct the sixties as a simplistic morality play, especially in this post-9/11 climate, paint Weatherman as "our" terrorists. But the real terror then was wrought by Klan nightriders and B-52 bombers, not by those who made small-potato bombs to disrupt business as usual in vacated federal buildings. Days of Rage had a minuscule body count; a single day of fighting in Khe Sanh expended many more lives. I have never been comfortable with the term "terror" as a theoretical category. Terror is the unpredictable upsurge of violence in everyday life. By that definition, infant mortality is terror, as are gang shootings, as is prison violence. We ignore the millions imprisoned in the United States today (but see Kann 2005) for whom the American dream has become a nightmare. We have decided to throw away the key, warehousing a sizable portion of humanity, predominantly poor and nonwhite, in miserable institutions guaranteed only to create subcultures of future criminality. Life in prison is defined by terror, fear of imminent but unpredictable violence, little different from living in Jerusalem or Baghdad.

Terror defined the sixties for American blacks in the South. Vernon Dahmer was murdered by fourteen Ku Klux Klan (KKK) members on January 10, 1965, in the small town of Forrest County, Mississippi, where he was NAACP chapter president. The Klan nightriders torched the Dahmer family home; his wife and eight children escaped unharmed, but Dahmer was burned and died in the hospital. It was not until 1998 that the mastermind of this terror, an Imperial Wizard of the KKK named Samuel Bowers, was finally brought to justice. Southern blacks experienced the same nighttime terror as Jews did during the early stages of Adolf Hitler's Germany; they did not know if they would make it through the night.

Instead, since 9/11, terror has had an Arab face or, in the case of neoconservative reconstructions of the sixties, the face of Weather. Lost in all this is the reason SDS unraveled into Weather—the administration's intransigence. A more meaningful parallel is between the lies we were told about how "we" were winning the Vietnam War and the lies we have been told about how Iraq harbored weapons of mass destruction. Once the national media, both mainstream and alternative, began to document that we were not winning in Vietnam after all, the credulous public began to doubt the self-serving official accounts of the White House and Pentagon. The domino theory then (if Vietnam falls, "we lose" all of Asia) was as ridiculous as the George Bush/Karl Rove axiom that we must bring American influence (read: a military presence) to various rogue dictatorships, especially in the Middle East, lest terrorism prevail.

What we are learning, after more than half a decade in Iraq, is that terrorism, again that dubious theoretical construction, is impossible to contain; the targets and tactics simply shift. Islamic fundamentalist zealots, who hate America as much as they hate Israel and women, are willing to sacrifice themselves, much as the Vietnamese were willing to fight guerrilla skirmishes for more than two decades to rid their countries of uninvited intruders and as Weatherman risked liberty to make a point. These dynamics are dialectical: Thrust begets parry, for which we reserve the term "terrorism." Had Johnson, Nixon, and Westmoreland heeded the protests, they would not have produced Weatherman as a response. These youthful cadres were reading and breathing Debray at the time when America was coming apart, deconstructing into terror—a perfect word to describe the midnight murder of Fred Hampton in Chicago, the Klan murder of Dahmer in 1961, and the napalmed children in Vietnam, for which we still have not made adequate moral reparations. We have not, I suspect, because we are a country often in denial about the implications of our actions for others.

How else can we understand the hatred of much of the civilized world for the United States today? Interestingly, this is the same hatred of America shared by Weatherman, which was anti-American and internationalist in ways that early SDS was not. Weatherman shared with the rest of the world today a rejection of American manifest destiny, which is why it adopted the rhetoric of revolution to characterize its political aims. Who could blame WUO, given the seemingly never-ending Vietnam War and the arrogance and truculence of the White House, FBI, Pentagon, and police? I cannot blame Weatherman because my family fled the United States in the same month as the Chicago SDS convention at which Weather took over leadership of the organization. I spelled America with a "k" because I realized, even as a teenager, that fascism was afoot and that the movement was going down in defeat.

In the next section, I explore with my interview subjects the topic of Weatherman, its origins, and its parallel to modern terrorism. Weather made itself hard to love, given its rhetorical excesses and sophomoric social theory. But its critique of American imperialism and adventurism rings true today, although we replace the term "imperialism" with "globalization." I am particularly interested in whether the former activists view the Right's call for repentance by movement radicals as a genuine act of reconciliation or merely as a vehicle for demonizing dissidents, then as now. Although Weatherman did not succeed in its revolutionary goals, did it fail? Did the selective bombing of symbolic infrastructure hasten the end of the war? Did Weather bring the war home?

RICHARD FLACKS

Suspicions About Weatherman

"I was upset with Weather from the outset, though I didn't use the term 'Debrayist.' I despised Debray in any case. It's not about Port Huron idealism in my mind but about whether one has democracy as both means and end. Weather is a species of elite youth history-making; many of these folk in the early sixties were morally disciplined by nonviolence, which is the only way to morally practice 'vanguard'-style political initiative. All of the key factions in SDS were 'revolutionary' breaks with Port Huron and the New Left, and I thought all of them were pathological right from the get-go.

"They weren't just lashing back at the war and the administration. They wanted to become revolutionaries, challenged by the Vietnamese and Cuba on one hand and black revolutionary nationalism [on the other]. These exacerbated their already strong guilt over their privileged class and racial position, and so, as I wrote thirty-five year ago, they came to want to overcome that guilt by making themselves pure, self-destroying instruments of revolution. But their ability to actually implement this in any kind of practical terms was severely blocked by their tight in-group cohesion, a cohesion that blocked free expression internally and limited their connection with reality. They took all these turns in the midst of mass opposition to the war on campuses that was unparalleled—they turned their backs on that. They were unable to consider antiwar resistance as a serious strategy (as distinct from a 'revolution fantasy'), nor, as Hayden did, were they at all able to contemplate parliamentary strategies.

"As I say above, that is what they thought. Or more precisely what they said is that the black ghettoes would be erupting in revolution and they as whites would die in an effort to support that uprising. They also seemed to believe that if they could become thugs, to quote one of my Weather students at the time, they'd win a following among white working-class kids. Revolutionary fantasy as a product of sectarian group cohesion is not unique to Weather Underground but was observable in some Trot[skyist] groups in [the] late thirties, and in the communist party formations right after the Bolshevik Revolution in the United States."

TODD GITLIN

Sectarianism Within SDS

"I wrote in 1969, in an essay for a radical Methodist magazine called *Motive*, that all the factions were guilty of bad faith, because the New Left had an unprecedented social identity as an expression of students, intellectuals, etc.—what some people called educated labor. I wasn't really inside these categories, mind you, but I did find them useful. I thought that there was a failure of nerve to accept the novelty of our historical situation. I still harbored the hope that there was a utopian possibility, and that the student movement should stand for that and not run away from itself. I was under the sway of the idea of postscarcity consciousness at that

Todd Gitlin. (Photo courtesy of David Shankbone)

point, for a couple of years. I thought that the beginning of sensible theory was with the ways in which we were not the working class or a Third World country. Insofar as I had a theoretical project, it was that. It seemed to me that all the factions scrambling for power in SDS were desperately refusing to face the new situation and instead were straining to burrow into the old. That's how I would have put it in '69. Over time, I came to think the problem was worse than that. I came to think that Marxism altogether was a mistake. I hadn't been *exactly* a Marxist, but I'd been reasonably comfortable with that vocabulary. Certainly by the time I wrote *The Sixties*, in the mid-eighties, I'd concluded that the effusion of Marxist language was itself in need of fresh thinking."

The Eclipse of the Port Huron Generation

"But you asked, when did I think that it was doomed? Certainly by '68. Let me see if I can reconstruct my state of mind in '67. . . . I was sufficiently impressed by the existential imperative of our situation vis-à-vis the war that SDS's floundering in '67 didn't really strike me as doom; it struck me as honorable. I would say '68 is when it's clear to me that it's going down. The rising power of [progressive labor], which I saw face-to-face in San Francisco—I was involved in the strike there as a sort of outside agitator but also as a journalist in late '68—it was clear that they were off-the-wall, and the rise of the action factions also struck me as dangerous. I liked Columbia. I liked the Columbia uprising, but I didn't like the attempt to implant that model everywhere regardless of condition. By late '68, with the election of Nixon, it was clear that the New Left was both marginal and deluded. What wasn't clear was what, if anything, could be done about that."

Opposition to Weatherman

"I was aghast. I did certainly oppose them, but not as vigorously as I should have. A number of us who were of the earlier, so-called old guard generation did think we ought to do something direct about it. The person I remember talking with most about that was Nick Egleson, who had been the president of SDS in '66–'67. He was the last president before SDS, in a fit of formalistic leveling, abolished the office. Anyway, Nick and I talked about writing a countermanifesto, a sort of new Port Huron. Earlier, in 1967, there had been an effort to create a poststudent organization, the so-called drawing boards conference, which I wrote about in *The Sixties*. That was a disaster. Also in '67, there were radicals in the professions conference in Ann Arbor, which produced some initiatives, but was, all in all, scattered. There were attempts to create a movement for a democratic society (MDS), but that was scattered, too. Either in the fall of '68 or the spring of '69, Nick and I talked about writing another sort of statement, a values and analysis *pronunciamento* that wouldn't be either primitive Marxism or revolutionist fantasy, but we didn't do it. We couldn't even get up a good draft. I would say that all of us who were appalled by the direction of SDS stood and stared at these mounting factions with a sense of horror and futility, and mostly we got depressed. Carl Oglesby and I were in San Francisco feeling this way. Nick and others were in the Boston area feeling this way."

The Use of Revolutionary Discourse

"I think I flirted with it in . . . a sort of nominal way, as if to say, 'This is the language my tribe is speaking now, and there's no real alternative.' I began the essay on the identity of the student movement, the one that was eventually published in *Motive*, to try to clarify my thinking, but it began with a kind of a hedge. I think I used the first person plural . . . you know, 'We say . . . that there is, or will be, or must be a revolution,' or something like that. I was in a sense insinuating myself into that category, but did I do it without reservation? . . . No. [The Weathermen] were living in dreamland."

TOM HAYDEN

The Generational Origins of Weatherman

"[Weatherman came] out of a genuine experience in the movement in the States. First of all, they took a Bob Dylan quote; second, they rooted themselves in their perception of youth culture; third, there was a generational separation between the early sixties and the late sixties. The experience was quite different. I believe people are molded to a very great extent by the experience they go through when they're about twenty years old.

"It's quite simple. Mark and Billy Ayers, for example, and many others were second-generation SDS. I was the founding generation of SDS.

"So we would have seen a world in which there was some temptation to believe in the promise of the New Frontier. On the other hand, a big suspicion that that was an illusory temptation, but that's a lot different than having Johnson in office when you come of age. . . .

"By [late 1967 and 1968] Mark and Billy and Bernardine, I think, saw the early SDS as having been liberal rather than radical.

"They would be able to cite Gitlin . . . a few others. I think I was in the middle. I was probably a question mark because I could relate to both sides. Nobody knew where I was coming from.

"Well, I think that we had different viewpoints. I think that the second generation [of SDS] that produced Weathermen did not have the direct experience of possibilities that the first generation did."

Roots of Weatherman in Third World Revolutions

"I took one of those trips to Cuba. I thought that Debray had a lot to say, and I still do. I was very sympathetic to the Vietnamese revolutionaries [and the] Cubans. I was not governed completely by ideology; I was governed by experience, to try to make sense of it, and my experiences were contradictory. One thing I learned was that there's more than one possibility in the situation, and you have to think in several scenarios. One scenario would be gradual reforms catalyzed by radical action, and then on the other hand there could be a breakdown of the social order and repression, and then several strikes, and then in the middle would [be] instability, including a lot of selective repressions. What I think probably happened [is that] the system simultaneously opened its doors to reformers through the McCarthy campaigns and closed the door to radicals by the COINTELPRO programs.

"I think that they perceived that the possibilities were virtually closed before they knew that there was a COINTELPRO program. I think it was their sense, because of the escalation of the Vietnam War, because of the rebellions in several hundred cities in the ghettos, because of the assassinations of the Kennedys and King and Malcolm X and Fred Hampton, it was their sense that the system was closed.

"There were some people at the time who had dismissed them ideologically because they were against violence, or they didn't think anything would come of it. What I would say about the Weathermen is that the reason they have a lasting appeal is that there was something genuine about their reading of the situation. They weren't so wrong about what was going on, and to one extent it was caused by Vietnam, the assassinations, the repression, the urban rebellions, its generational rivalries, the early SDS, and the later. . . . Who knows? It's a mixture of all of those."

Conservatives Demonizing Sixties Radicals

"There's nothing new in American history about the establishment going after certain people as symbols. It happened in the era of the Rosenbergs; it happened to Sacco and Vanzetti. If you go into the slave rebellion, you read the history of Nat Turner. If you go further back, Tom Paine. There's always some of this scapegoating which seems to be premised on the view that you can attack a person for their alleged excesses, and unite the middle, the moderate middle, and isolate the radicals. Some people think this goes on because it's good politics for the Republicans, demanding apologies, and then people refusing to give apologies, and then the Republicans and conservatives saying, "Well see, they don't repent. . . . They haven't grown up, you know. They're . . ." etc. I don't think it's that. I think it's an attempt by the conservatives to continually divert public attention away from the issues that the conservatives are really concerned about. The conservatives are the political expression of the market. The market is insatiable. The market is restless because it's had these impositions from the populist era to the New Deal to the sixties. The markets can't tolerate imposition. They can't tolerate the interventions of the regulatory structures because they block the true nature of the market. And so what the Republicans and conservatives have to do . . . they're compelled to do, it's inevitable, is fight against all previous generations of reforms.

"The problem is, those are popular. You know, they do it indirectly. They want to get rid of Social Security. They want to get rid of the progressive income tax and so on. They want to get rid of environmental policies, but they realize from their polls that these have become popular, that what was radical at one point becomes acceptable later, and so they're left with demonizing radicals per se, and then carefully trying to undermine radical achievements in an indirect way, by vouchers for private schools."

MARK RUDD

The Recent Weatherman Movie

"No, the movie's not accurate. It's just a great movie. The movie's inaccurate in certain key places, but that doesn't matter because it's accurate about the context that we were living in. That's its mostly useful part.

"For one thing it did not really tell the story of the Weather Underground . . . the history of what was actually going on within the Weather Underground, in terms of twists and turns of life. The biggest inaccuracy, however, is that the movie is . . . remember, this is just me talking. Other people might agree with it. In fact, I did get in an argument with an old comrade of mine about this very point. The movie creates the impression that we demonstrated and petitioned and did legal protests for years and years, it didn't work, and out of frustration, it couldn't survive. The movie shows us as having turned to violence out of frustration. We also had a theory of revolution, the 'foco' theory."

Origins of Weatherman in Revolutionary Theory and Practice

"Here's what I believe happened. Here's my experience: Starting in '67, I became aware of revolutionary movements throughout the world that were defining U.S. imperialism, so I was exposed to an anti-imperialist understanding of the world, a global view. I was also exposed to revolutionary struggles that existed.

"I was eighteen in 1965 and at Columbia I met people, SDS people, who taught me anti-imperialism. In about '67 you have a global war against U.S. imperialism. In '67 I got exposed to a book called *Revolution in the Revolution?* by Regis Debray. Debray is into neocon now, but at the time [his] book put forward a theory of the struggle, of guerrilla struggle in Latin America, called the 'foco' theory, so it's based on discussion that he had with Fidel and Che in 1966. By '67, the book came out and Che went to Bolivia. The book basically analyzes the Cuban revolution and other revolutions around the [world], and says that guerrillas that were building a revolutionary army led the struggle, and that when you start guerrilla warfare the people join in . . . it's called the 'foco,' and it opposes the Trotskyists who had another theory called 'armed self-defense,' and it also opposes the communists, whose basic theme was to talk rather than to do.

"At Columbia, I took courses in the Russian Revolution, and all of us read Lenin and Trotsky and tried to understand the revolution, and also China was incredibly important to us. We had study groups on a book that came out I think in '67, '68, mid-'68, called *Fanshen*, by William Hinton; he died [recently].

"Well, anarchists are vanguardists, too, but the question was, 'What do you do with the vanguard party?' It's not like these guys were anarchists. They weren't, but their notion was that the vanguard party builds a revolutionary guerrilla army, and so that's what communists have been doing for generations in Latin America, including Cubans. According to their line, the communist parties were urban intellectuals who would easily organize among the workers, but the basic thing they would do would be talk about revolutions rather than to start [them]. So Che Guevara, he had this line, 'The duty of every revolutionary is to make the revolution.' Well, that sounds like a tautology, but it really is saying, 'Don't talk about it; do it!' And that was the foco theory, and so, in 1967, I recall that it may have been Bob Pardun (who doesn't remember this incident) who handed me a copy of this theory, or the book, and he says, 'This is our future,' in 1967. In '68 I went to Cuba, in January or February, and I was exposed to the idea of guerrilla warfare. Che was already a cult figure because he had been murdered in October of '67, and I was there in January and February . . . the first student trip for four years . . . in Cuba. We went to Cuba, and we were the predecessor. We were kind of like the beginning of the contact between Cuba and SDS that eventually led to that famous [Venceremos] brigade [in 1969].

"We came back from Cuba all fired up with this, and then the events at Columbia seemed to bear it out; we were a small group, one hundred active members of SDS. We had done a lot of educational work, but we took the initiative. We were aggressive. We seized buildings, and the whole place erupted and joined us; and so, aha, foco theory is working. From that point on, many of us began to think that we should be Debrayists. We should be *foquistas*. We should begin guerrilla warfare, so we kept upping the ante. Now, meanwhile, what was actually happening—and what we did—was we differentiated ourselves from the antiwar movement as a whole; we were revolutionary and we were also anti-imperialist. The antiwar movement was liberal and not specifically anti-imperial.

"And we also didn't see that the antiwar movement was winning. So we actually attacked the antiwar movement at numerous times. It was not, for myself, a question of frustration. I suppose in some manner you could say it was frustration, but you could also say it was wishful thinking . . . that this country was revolutionary and that if we began a struggle, the masses, including the youth masses, would join us. That's not in the movie.

"I had this argument with a friend, and his view was that for himself it was frustration, and that for a lot of people maybe at lower levels in the organization, in the Underground, it might have been frustration also, rather than theory.

"[Carl] Davidson [national secretary of SDS] was great, but he became a lifelong Marxist in this little California grouping called the Revolutionary League, RL, and then it became something else, and they had a newspaper for many, many years. You can probably Google Davidson and find out what party he's still connected with. He's a Marxist dogmatist.

"That's not in the movie . . . that whole link to the Third World struggle and the fantasy of Debray and of an exemplary guerrilla warfare that would build an army. That whole thing was left out. We made a choice. We made a wrong choice. It wasn't out of frustration. Well, maybe it was out of frustration; you see, I can't say that for everybody."

Mistakes Made by Weatherman

"First of all, Debrayism was wrong everywhere. It was probably not even right about Cuba. It probably was the wrong analysis of what actually happened in Cuba, in the revolution of Cuba; the many years of organizing by communists and other labor organizers and the work in the cities was very, very important, and so it was not just the guerrilla army in the countryside. So I'm pretty sure that if you look at subsequent analysis put out by the Cuban Communist Party, they repudiated the view of their revolution that Debray wrote in 1966. I think that would be an interesting kind of thing for somebody to do, to compare their own history. So I don't even think Debrayism was right in Cuba, and around the world thousands of people lost their lives, including Che Guevara, around this stupid theory. The theory is basically that if you start armed struggle, people will join you, and that's not how it works. This isn't how it works. It isn't even how it works in a very revolutionary situation, a situation where there's terrible suffering and repression, like Bolivia.

"All of that sounds [like a] wonderful, idealist, anarchistic, utopian fantasy, and probably all of us thought in those terms. But just participatory democracy, that was a slogan of SDS from 1962. Let the people decide. I mean, what a wonderful democratic fantasy, but it got to the point in Weathermen that what was going to replace this thing was very little discussed. What we were really thinking of was bringing it down, and we had the fantasy of revolution that could destroy the system, and we figured [that] as we destroyed it, we'd be creating the structures that would replace it. And, of course, it was ridiculous. I mean, the biggest ridiculousness of all, from my point of view, is the fantasy of armed struggle. You asked about hindsight, and all of this theory stuff is interesting, but the real failure is the failure to realize the inherent dangers of armed struggle, mainly that you would get creamed, and also it would just not build a mass movement. We thought because we were Debrayists, we thought armed struggle would build a mass movement. What a stupid idea. And mass movements are possible in this country, but not revolutionary [ones]. There could definitely be a mass movement to end the war in Vietnam, and we should've organized for that mass movement. Our slogan should have been to unite as many people as possible to end the war in Vietnam, and also as we did, to develop an understanding of the nature of imperialism, but that doesn't involve bombings; in fact bombings work to the advantage of the government."

The Fantasy of Armed Struggle

"And that's the biggest error. It's not anything theoretical or ideological; it's just the fantasy of armed struggle, where that came from. There's a lot of places that came from. I've identified myself as macho, and Gitlin always talks about too much identification with the Third World, but that's problematic, because Gitlin doesn't really identify at all with the Third World. I believe Gitlin supported this [Iraq] War."

Repentant, but Still Committed to an Analysis of U.S. Global Imperialism

"We knew what the nature of the United States was in the world, and that our problem was we didn't know how to deal with it; it was too big. We didn't know what to do, but nothing's changed. Our analysis was right. We're the same imperial bully. So, yeah. And I think, as far as repentance goes, the only thing I'm repenting for is the Weather Underground. I'm not repenting for believing that the United States is a global empire and doing terrible things; I'm not repenting for that. But you're right. The attack on the New Left is some way of reclaiming the lost patriotism. It's a culture war."

What Really Happened at Kent State

"Dohrn [was] from Chicago, although we knew Dohrn in New York when she was at National Lawyer's Guild. Columbia was a key. There's a direct line from Columbia to Kent State to the Weathermen. This is an interesting story, which I'll probably tell if I ever write my book [Rudd 2009] of the direct line from Columbia to Weathermen to Kent State, [about the] events of May of 1970. We figured in those events as predecessors, preceding organizers at Kent State. We had a huge SDS chapter at Kent State that was virtually all Weathermen.

"By then they had smashed the chapter; a lot of people were in jail, or we had taken a lot of people underground with us, so the chapter did not exist by name, but the politics remained on the campus, and so we were predecessors, and also the politics of confrontation.

"When I first went out touring the country in the fall of 1969, one of my stops was Kent State. There was a very active chapter there. The regional organizer was Terry Robbins, based in Cleveland, but he seemed intimately involved with the chapter. That was when I first met Terry.

"The chapter was an action faction chapter, meaning much emphasis on confrontation, less on talk and 'base-building.' The theory was that base-building would happen through action. So if you look at the history of Kent SDS, you see confrontation after confrontation, around Oakland Police recruiting, ROTC [Reserve Officers' Training Corps] on campus, several other issues. It was a very militant chapter. Many of its main organizers went into Weatherman in the summer of 1969: Howie Emmer, Candy and Rick Erickson, Colin Neiburger, many others. I run into these people occasionally. At the SDS convention in June 1969, the Kent chapter was one of the most important supporters of the split with PL [Progressive Labor].

"If you look at the 1976 Senate Internal Security Committee Report on Weatherman, many of the people listed came from Kent.

"Kent was so combative that many of their people did time in Portage County Jail.

"By May 1970 SDS at Kent was gone, but the legacy of militancy lived on. I went back there in 1989 for an SDS reunion. Two guys came up to me and confessed that they had started the fires and riots which caused the National Guard to be called in. They had never told anyone because they always felt guilty for beginning the chain of events that led to four deaths.

"I think there may be more, but that's the beginning of the story. I'd need to do more research, flesh out the names and events.

"But Kent was a thoroughly Weather chapter. It's not a coincidence that the shooting happened there: There had been years of provocations."

The Undoing of Port Huron SDS

"In the course of things, my little faction seized control of the SDS national office and several of the regional offices. We then made the tragic decision—in 1969, at the height of the war—to kill off SDS because it wasn't revolutionary enough for us. I am not proud of this history.

"I often read references in historical literature and commentary to SDS 'self-destructing.' This seems to refer to a constellation of generalized forces, including Maoist sectarian infiltration, the development of various brands of Marxist dogmatism among the 'regulars,' the drive toward hypermilitancy, violent confrontation, and ultimately 'armed struggle,' all within a bitter context of government repression. In some renditions of the death of SDS story there is the consoling air of historical inevitability—no matter what we in the national leadership would have done, SDS was destined (by the God of history, I suppose) to implode.

"But I don't agree. I remember a certain meeting with no more than ten people present—out of a national membership of twelve thousand and perhaps ten times that many chapter members—at which we in the Weatherman clique running the [national office] decided to scuttle SDS. I remember driving a VW van with Teddy

Gold from the NY regional office in the basement of 131 Prince St. to the Sanitation Department pier at the end of W. 14th St., just a few blocks from here, and dumping the addressograph mailing stencils and other records from the regional office onto a barge. These were insane decisions, which I and my comrades made unilaterally, to the exclusion of other, much better, choices. We could have, for example, fought to keep SDS in existence so as to unite as many people as possible against the war (which is what the Vietnamese had asked us to do) while at the same time educating around imperialism. I often wonder, had we done so, where we would have been a few months later, in May 1970, when the biggest student protests in American history jumped off. Or today, when imperialist war rages yet again, would we have had to reinvent the anti-imperialist movement almost from scratch? Alas, with all the best intentions of promoting revolutionary solidarity with the people of the world, the Weatherman faction, by killing off SDS, did the work of the FBI for them. Assuming we weren't in the pay of the FBI, we should have been."

Rethinking Revolutionary Violence

"The subsequent Weather Underground did not, of course, lead to the growth of a revolutionary movement in this country. It led to isolation and defeat. The guerrilla foco did not help build either a revolutionary army or a mass movement. One thing I'm absolutely certain of, having learned the hard way, is that political violence in any form can never be understood in this society.

"No amount of rhetoric around revolutionary heroism and solidarity with the Third World can mask the Weather strategy as anything other than sure revolutionary suicide. Revolutionary suicide may serve some psychological or existential function, but politically it produces nothing. So the greatest lesson I draw from my disastrous history is the Left must absolutely stay away from violence or any talk of violence. The government is violent; we oppose [its] violence."

ROXANNE DUNBAR-ORTIZ

On Radical Repentance and the Right

"Oh, yes, the Right hates the sixties and sixties radicals with a fury that is very telling. They work so hard to destroy that which was changed forever by the civil rights movement/New Left. And they've had some success at chipping away, particularly in with-drawing or greatly reducing government funding for the arts, poverty reduction, and highly successful programs like Head Start and WIC ([Women, Infants, and Children,] the pregnant women and mothers' nutritional program), and privatizing, deregulating, union-busting, etc. They want to stamp out every vestige of the 1960s and make us cry uncle. I've never for a moment felt like re-penting for my actions or apologizing for the New Left. I do think it's essential and useful to analyze the mistakes, bad judgment, and often wretched behavior, but no apologies, certainly not to the Right, although many are owed to comrades, sisters, and brothers in the struggle I mistreated or hurt."

Weatherman and Women's Liberation

"I was critical of Weather at the time, not that they went under-ground, but their embracing of the idea that their mass base was the turned-on, dropped-out youth, their mission to bring more young people, especially working-class youth, into the fold, a sort of *Lord of the Flies* vision of revolution. I and many other radical women were working very hard to bring the emerging women's lib-eration movement into a powerful anti-imperialist, antiwar force, at the same time insisting on a very radical feminist perspective. The Weather women hurt that effort and infuriated me by charac-terizing and trashing the women's liberation movement as a bunch of 'sad-eyed sisters,' rather than embracing those of us who were struggling politically within the hugely diverse women's movement. They changed in the mid-1970s to claiming feminism as if they had invented it, but the moment had passed."

CASEY HAYDEN

Ambivalence About Revolutionary Violence

"As we put it at the time, was nonviolence a way of life or a tactic? Mostly a tactic, but it varied from person to person and was a com-bination of many, many factors. Besides those you cite, I'd add a belief that time was on our side; a lack of knowledge about weapons, which would have meant a lot of effort to get 'em and learn to use 'em; fear of upping the ante from clubs to guns; and on and on."

DAVID GILBERT

Weatherman: Utopian, Not Frustrated About Failing to End the War

"While there was anger and frustration about the war, Weather emerged much more out of a sense of hope, and especially a deep sense of identification with the black movement and with national liberation movements around the world. The sweeping successes of the latter—never in world history had there been anything like that number of successful revolutions in a couple of decades— gave us great hope that the most oppressed, the wretched of the earth, were totally reshaping the world in a more humane way. Also, we deeply identified with the black struggle and could not sit passively while so many were being gunned down or imprisoned. Because the new level of militancy was so new and scary to us, we went through a horrid period (ca. July 1969 to April 1970) of psyching ourselves up by glorifying violence. In that period many in Weather argued a Debrayist view that exemplary violence would create a red army.

But the heart of the theory over the years was the politics of solidarity. We knew there was no magic formula for instantly organizing the majority of the white working class on an antiracist basis. We saw youth as the most promising sector, and many of them responded well to well-done (with no casualties) attacks on symbols of power. At the same time, we were trying to extend the repressive apparatus so that it could not focus all its resources on people of color. I do not believe that North Vietnamese cautioned Weather against militancy—I've seen too many examples of white Leftists opposed to such militancy scrambling to hide behind a revered revolutionary authority. Those I knew who met with the Vietnamese say they never told the U.S. movement what to do. Certainly, they valued a broad antiwar movement, which was basic and essential, but they also appreciated intelligent, humane militancy."

Ego and Revolutionary Violence

"Broadly I'd define 'the sixties' as a long decade from the *Brown* decision [desegregating public schools] in 1954 until the end of the Vietnam War in 1975. You're right that Nyack came very late, although in the broader world about seven different national liberation struggles took power in 1979. I'm not the best one to try to sum up or assess the strategy of the unit of the Black Liberation Army which led that action. In terms of my own thinking in 1981,

I guess I fell back into foco theory, that a small group's heroic actions could reignite a broader movement. But I certainly knew better than that in terms of political theory. So I think that foco was a rationalization, and my poor judgment was based in ego (as so many of all our mistakes are) in that, after the collapse of the WUO, I was superanxious to redeem myself as a 'revolutionary at the highest level of solidarity with third world struggles.'"

The Right Demonizing the Sixties

"You're right about the Right's demonizing the 1960s in order to take away the gains. I still absolutely embrace the basic principles of standing with the oppressed and striving for fundamental social change. In fact, we didn't do well enough in being antiracist, pro–Third World, for women, gays, the working class, and the environment. At the same time, I regret not doing better and the many mistakes we made (including the Brinks case, which led to the loss of lives and setbacks to the struggle)."

CARL OGLESBY

On Weatherman's Revolutionary Orientation

"I thought that it was a lot of talk and too much talk about revolutions. They had not made the case for revolution. They didn't know how a revolution, even if it were necessary, was going to be manned and equipped. They had not bothered to think about any of the practical questions. It is almost beside the point that they hadn't stated a philosophical case for revolution. I thought that you could make a very strong argument that our democracy had been corrupted, but the answer to the corruption of democracy was to uncorrupt it, and I thought we [of early SDS] had in our hands the means to do that."

JOSÉ ANGEL GUTIÉRREZ

On Demonizing

As a Chicano nationalist, I have always been demonized simply for stating a historical fact that we as peoples of mixed bloods, native and European, mestizos, have long existed in these lands, our homeland. The borders and the flags have crossed us; we did not cross them. There was an Anahuac/America before there was a New Spain, New Santander, New Mexico, Tejas, United States, Texas, Southwest, or any border. We have been made foreigners in our own lands.

"I still believe that foremost in our struggle is to confront the reactionaries and racists in our midst and expose them for what they are. We must never forfeit any political agenda, social issue, cultural trait, geographic space, or human right to those in opposition to us. Life is a struggle, and a meaningful life is commitment to struggle."

In the following chapter, I explore the parallel between patriotism during the sixties ("America, love it or leave it") and patriotism during the present era of Homeland Security ("These colors don't run"). There are interesting disagreements in our discussions about whether patriotism can be endorsed and adapted by the Left or whether it needs to be abandoned in favor of internationalism. Certainly, the issue of love of country was important during the Vietnam War and is again today, after the events known as 9/11.

∞ Five ∞

Love of Country

I'll never fly an American flag.
—Mark Rudd

In this chapter, I pursue themes of patriotism, nationalism, and love of country. Early in the decade, activists and reformers such as Tom Hayden viewed themselves as homespun midwesterners who never doubted that they were American, and proudly so. By the late sixties, radicals such as members of Weather and the Black Panthers were developing theories of the complicity of the United States in international imperialism. Some of us did not even want to live in the United States any longer.

Nation is on the agenda because we live in a "global village," as Marshall McLuhan (1989) terms it. It is also on the agenda because President George W. Bush's foreign policy drew derision from much of the world community. Barack Obama's presidency promises to restore American credibility in the international community, even if issues of uneven development bedevil American attempts to export democracy. The New Left, as early as Port Huron, recognized that global economic inequality was the source of geopolitical instability. As such, the New Left was "international-ist" in its orientation to domestic and global problems.

Although the New Left stressed global interconnections, it also focused on small and local issues of bodies, families, schools, and communities. The individual was the benchmark of social change. Perhaps it is possible to love those closest to us just as one loves all people, humans as well as humanity. These are not settled issues, as we explore here.

SETTING THE STAGE:
VIETNAM/NIXON AND IRAQ/BUSH

> *Iraq is George Bush's Vietnam.*
> —Ted Kennedy

I emphasize not only the parallels between Nixon/Bush and Vietnam/Iraq but also their connections, the Right's triumph by the end of the sixties making way for Ronald Reagan and George W. Bush's unilateralist foreign policies. Indeed, the Gulf of Tonkin incident in 1964 and September 11 in 2001 are examples of paranoia as a presidential posture. This is a question of the role of the United States in the world and of the very idea of "nation." The Right wants to conceal the early sixties, both Students for a Democratic Society (SDS) and civil rights, because it has a stake in portraying dissenters as anti-American. The iconography of the American flag is an important part of the American consciousness. Even Leftists have to embrace this nation (and perhaps nation in general) as a defensive maneuver. It should be enough to say that peace is patriotic.

In the sixties we were mired in a bloody war in Vietnam, a distant country. Neither President Lyndon Johnson nor President Richard Nixon would listen to protesters, who numbered in the millions. The Right was well organized and used the FBI and police to muzzle radicals. The gap between rich and poor was largely a matter of a person's race. Patriotism took ugly forms.

Now we are mired in a bloody war in Iraq, a distant country. Former president Bush would not listen to protesters. The Right is well organized and uses Homeland Security, the police, and the FBI to muzzle dissenters. The gap between rich and poor is largely a matter of a person's race. Patriotism takes ugly forms.

John Kennedy's administration held the possibility of a more open America, even if his original agenda did not necessarily include Americans of color, women, and students. Kennedy eventually aided the civil rights movement, and there were important links between Tom Hayden, the author of SDS's Port Huron Statement, and Bobby Kennedy, who eventually became a peace candidate.

The sixties are often portrayed as a time of activism and progressive causes. It is less often noticed that the organized Right destroyed the civil rights movement, repressed and even killed black leaders and radicals, and ignored the antiwar movement (even though LBJ took himself out of the running for a second term as president in March 1968). The Left was not totally blameless in this, as we discussed in the preceding chapter on Weatherman.

However, the radical turn of SDS and the Black Power movement in the late sixties largely responded to the increasingly repressive and well-organized Right that controlled the White House, Congress, and agencies of social control such as the police and FBI. However idiosyncratic the "Debrayism" of Weather seems in retrospect—young radicals fomenting a violent revolution by bombing buildings and thus stirring the masses to join in a revolutionary cause—at the time many peace-loving liberals were becoming furious because Nixon would not listen. As a result, young people began to hate America, not just Nixon's policies. This was unprecedented in American history.

Today, Regis Debray (2007) has interesting things to say about nationalism and the idea of America. Debray was a foreign policy adviser to President François Mitterrand in France, and he now writes on political and social philosophy. He adds his voice to discussions of globalization, which flow from discussions held in the sixties about American imperialism.

Not only are there parallels between the sixties and the present; there also are connections. Nixon's counter-revolution against the New Left prepared the way for right-wing dominance of American politics ever since he and the FBI orchestrated a campaign of repression against the white and black Left in the late sixties and early seventies. The Weather Underground and the Black Panthers became symbols of Leftist "extremism," but in large measure because they were pursued so relentlessly by the police and FBI. In this sense, my sixties contain the continual alternation between Left and Right, pushing and pushing back, with "revolution" bringing counter-revolution and internationalism prompting nationalism, which quickly metastasized into a hatred of "others." The SDS kids and civil rights workers were not revolutionaries; that rhetoric was not used much before decade's end with Weather and the Panthers (who mouthed the words but could not really have believed that this was St. Petersburg or Cuba). SDS wanted participatory democracy, and the civil rights movement, via Gandhian means of protest, sought voter registration, an end to poll taxes, and the abolition of racial segregation.

The alliance, although hesitant and fragile, between the Kennedy brothers, Jack and Bobby, and Hayden was an important framing of the sixties. He pushed them further to the Left, especially Bobby, while giving hard advice. Hayden played both sides of the street, working outside and inside of channels, allowing him to have impact in the ghetto of Newark and the back rooms of the White House. This is partly why he was so devastated when Bobby was assassinated, arguably ending the sixties for Hayden, in 1968.

And 1968 only got worse, with the Chicago Democratic National Convention.

Perhaps the most notable parallel between the sixties and the present is the spirit of manifest destiny behind U.S. foreign policies in the Johnson/Nixon administrations and in the second Bush administration. Notable here is that LBJ was a Democrat. In fact, on domestic issues he was a New Deal liberal, supporting civil rights and launching a war on poverty. Although the decade ended with Nixon's administration, which added momentum to the rightward shift taking place in the country—momentum that has brought us to the present day, at least until Obama's election—the manifest destiny that led us to engage in two distant and unjustified acts of military adventurism was supported by both major political parties. Democrats endorsed the Vietnam War, just as most Democrats went along with the Iraq war, although perhaps in both cases out of expediency. On issues of foreign policy, Democrats then, such as Hubert Humphrey, weirdly belonged to the Right—the forces of reaction.

In that sense, attitude toward nation may be one of the strongest connections between the two eras. America's crushing defeat in Vietnam has been repressed in the national memory since the end of that war, so that Bush Jr.'s belligerence in the Middle East went largely unprotested. The domino theory was matched in absurdity by Bush's claim that Iraq was behind 9/11 and that Saddam Hussein possessed so-called weapons of mass destruction, as if nearly half a million U.S. troops were not also a weapon of mass destruction.

Underneath nation, we find a distinctively American penchant for conquest. Nixon and Bush Jr. had imperial intentions, reflected in their approach to nation-building through forced regime change. But the issue is not just a matter of these two parallel presidents. American society is conflicted in ways that European countries and Canada are not. During the sixties this violence was institutionalized because the police and the National Guard were often out of control; just think of Chicago and Kent State. But violence bred its negation, which shared many of its elements, in the military movements of the Left. One of the most tragic images of the sixties was of inner cities burned down by black ghetto dwellers. And most of us remember Columbine in 1999, where two disaffected high school kids, acting out video game vengeance, murdered their classmates and then killed themselves. These are all self-inflicted wounds.

America's imperial tendencies have congealed into a militarism that can be traced all the way back to slavery and our shameful

Detroit race riot, July 23, 1967. (Photo by Rolls Press/Popperfoto/Getty Images)

treatment of Native Americans. The mythos of the Wild West flavors foreign policy. Since about 1900, it seems that the United States has been embroiled in a war every thirty to fifty years or so—the Great War, World War II, Korea, Vietnam, the two Iraqs. Sometimes, as in the case of Korea, the long cycle shortens. About fifty years before the Great War (now called World War I), the Civil War saw the death of at least 620,000 American soldiers, from both sides. These cycles can be linked to our ambitions for global empire. Why a war every few decades? Perhaps that is the time it takes for national consciousness to repress the disastrous consequences of the previous war. Seen in this historical context, Weatherman's urban guerrilla strategy and the military Black Panther Party are of a piece with our national legacy of violent conquest.

The sixties and the present also are connected by what Guy Debord (1983) calls "the spectacle." In 1964 Johnson exploited supposed attacks on U.S. naval vessels by the North Vietnamese to leverage escalation of the war from Congress. Al Qaeda hijackings of U.S. commercial airplanes and the implosion of the World Trade Center towers were leveraged into the new federal Department of

Homeland Security in 2002 and into a Middle East war that has already claimed more U.S. lives than the tragedy of 9/11. The government and media spun events into military adventures, even though 9/11 was covered live on global television, whereas the Gulf of Tonkin was but a rumor. I never saw a photo of Tonkin until I did research for this book. Both were spectacles in the sense that they were inflated to acquire mythic significance, a necessary preface to the launching of war against distant enemies.

The sixties presented other spectacles as well—the first Kennedy assassination and its funereal aftermath, which in the span of a long weekend created a media culture in which the reporting of news became news and also entertainment; the images from the South of Bull Connor's attack dogs and fire hoses directed at civil rights demonstrators; the Chicago Democratic National Convention, at which the police were the criminals; and the daily reportage from Vietnam of the grinding and inhuman nature of search-and-destroy missions that brought the carnage home.

The reporting of these events, like 9/11 today, became value-laden narratives supporting one policy course or another. News

Gulf of Tonkin, Vietnam incident, 1964. (Naval Historical Center Photo Archives)

Burning World Trade Center, New York City, Sept. 11, 2001. (AP Photo/Amy Sancetta)

during the sixties was revealed to be riddled with perspective; even images were partisan—think of the pile of bodies at My Lai or the Viet Cong officer executed summarily on videotape. Today, we have images from Abu Ghraib, a U.S. prison in Iraq in which Iraqi prisoners of war were tortured, ridiculed, and otherwise mistreated.

The American humiliation of political prisoners did not begin in Iraq. There are parallel images of Viet Cong prisoners of war, blindfolded and crying before their interrogation by U.S. forces. We did not view most of these images until long after the war was over.

Politics became visual during the sixties and remains so today. Although this adds depth and a human perspective on events, it also simplifies issues and overtakes analysis. The dominant media before November 1963 were largely print. After Kennedy's assassination in Dallas, the electronic and visual media, perhaps unwittingly, replaced analysis with image as people obtained their news from television (and now the Internet) instead of from pulp sources. This has had a significant impact on public opinion, which is more readily manipulable in a post-textual age.

The major difference between those times and today is that there is no contemporary mass movement against the Iraq war, let alone in support of the sweeping changes advanced in the Port Huron Statement. As I note throughout the book, the absence of the draft is one factor. This is not to say that young people lack social concern. After all, a careful demography of the New Left reveals that "kids" like Hayden were actually children of the fifties, when discontent was already brewing.

However, there were stirrings of revolt as lame duck Bush escalated the war in spite of majority will against it—a "surge," in the Orwellian language of military strategy. Protests mounted, often led by sixties veterans. On January 27, 2007, thousands attended a rally in Washington, DC, to protest the war.

Will these protests spread? Will a larger critique of American society emerge? Obama's election and the conduct of his presidency hold answers to these questions.

As I explore with the activists, the question of patriotism is really a question of America's role in the world. The United States is not just any nation. Today, it is the only remaining superpower, even as China becomes a major economic player. The United States is the only country that pursues "regime change" and "nation-building." Love of country is an abstraction; at stake is love of this country, a country built on slavery and immigrant labor. There are real differences of opinion about how one should view the idea of America, especially after the travesty and tragedy of Vietnam.

RICHARD FLACKS

Dewey and a Distinctively American Radicalism

"I'm no expert on Dewey, but the more I've learned about his project [of pragmatism] in the thirties, [there is a] quite astonishing parallel, astonishing because you don't identify Dewey with the Marxist tradition, but on the other hand he was a very conscious Leftist. He articulated the need for an American Left, distinct from European. He was looking for organizational forms as well as ideological, philosophical foundations for that. He really was looking for a New Left, and he certainly was not ignorant of European Marxism, probably not ignorant of the whole 'critical theory,' so if you ask Habermas [a neo-Marxist who viewed a socialist good society as a site of communicative democracy] about Dewey, he'd say, 'Yeah, there's a great deal of parallel with the incorporation of Dewey into Habermas.' So how much did people of Port Huron [understand their foundation in early Marx]? . . . I think, maybe, just talking off the top of my head, that most of the people there understood the foundation or effort that went into the ideological foundation of the

Richard Flacks. (Photo courtesy of Richard Flacks)

statement had something to do with a critique of not only the communist party, but the socialist party as well as the American Socialist Party, and other established groups. But whether people knew about [early Marx] . . . I can't remember when I knew about Marx. I know I was teaching a course in Marx when I got started at the University of Chicago, and we were focused on the young Marx. . . . But how much did I know? Hayden knew a lot of what he knew from Arnold Kaufman, who was a Deweyite philosophy professor at the University of Michigan, but I know that was another foundation. It's almost a cliché now, about Camus, but Bob Moses [of SNCC] had read Camus. In fact, if you were to ask me what I remember about [Hayden's] philosophical understandings when I first met him, it was Camus combined somehow with Mills. I don't remember when his book *The Marxists* came out, was it before . . . ? [Mills's book came out in 1962, the same year as the Port Huron Statement. In *The Marxists* Mills describes himself as a 'plain Marxist,' a characterization that fairly describes much of the sentiment of the Port Huron document.]"

The American Left and Patriotism

"I wrote a piece with Peter Dreier that was in *The Nation* several years ago, on the Left and patriotism, the main point of which was just to call attention to the degree to which the main symbolic expressions of patriotism in the United States were created in the Left. When you talk about the Pledge of Allegiance in terms of its fascinating history, the inscription on the Statue of Liberty, the song 'America, the Beautiful' . . . who wrote that, why did she write it . . . 'This Land Is Your Land,' the whole popular front, Woody Guthrie kind of patriotism, which is still very vibrant to people like Springsteen. . . .

"It is important for people on the Left to examine its own patriotic tradition rather than be ignorant of it, and to see what it was that people in the past, and even now, are trying to do with the question of patriotism coming from the Left. It seems to me that one could make the case that the behavior of Bush in this war is profoundly unpatriotic. He has refused to honor our troops by going to honor the dead. I like the fact that the Veterans for Peace in Santa Barbara have a weekly Arlington West site where they put up crosses for everyone who's died in Iraq with their names, and some photographs are appearing there now, and they have ceremonies around this. They're the only grassroots group that I know of that's honoring the dead in Iraq. I like the fact that John Kerry's quoted Langston Hughes's poem 'Let America Be America Again.' If you read the whole poem, it's a very radical critique. . . .

"He was reported to be learning how to sing 'This Land Is Your Land' and play it on the guitar. Woody Guthrie and others, Josh White, people wrote songs during World War I supporting the war effort, and there's really a kind of interaction between what Roosevelt was saying from the presidential pulpit and what these people were articulating in filmscripts, in songs, in radio plays, all kinds of stuff that left-wing popular culture creators were doing at that time to support the war effort. So it struck me that Kerry is looking back to those very same sources. There's an opportunity to talk about what America means from our side and really inject that into the discourse. I know that's what Springsteen is up to, and he's not the only one. There's quite a lot of effort in pop music to try to do this.

"Michael Moore, he is the greatest example. Michael Moore is trying to express patriotism, and I don't think it's been successful by the right wing to paint him [as a] 'domestic enemy.' There's no way that's the case. I don't even think it's an argument anymore that needs to be made, and it's not about putting a flag on your balcony. I was in New York right after 9/11, and we were driving around the East before that, and there was a lot of flag display, but when we got to New York, yeah, there was flag display, but there were also a tremendous number of public sites where people had put other kinds of flowers, and candles, and poetry. And a lot of it was about healing and peace, not about revenge in any way. I fly a global flag on my house. I have ever since 9/11. I have a bunch of flags that I use on my house. I like doing that, but the global flag is the one we put up after 9/11 and we still fly it. It's a picture of the planet. . . .

"I don't think Gitlin empathizes, or he might, but he covers up his empathy with the kind of strictures that he is constantly making about the Left. It would be terrible for the world if the whole discourse of the U.S. narrowed down to a [discourse about] what's the best way of defending the United States rather than having voices that speak beyond national sovereignty and speak to building global peacekeeping forces to replace national military power. All of that has to be restored as legitimate. That's not anti-American, and I have no objection to people framing everything they say in terms of what's good for America or the American people, especially given this government. This government has made it easier for the Left."

TODD GITLIN

Anti-American Americans

"I don't know that I ever named a number [of anti-American Americans]. I rather doubt I did. The numbers don't matter, really. But the legions who gobble down Chomsky's books are surely not an insignificant number. As for the '60s, at one level, I never doubted that I was American either. But there were levels and levels. We were bitterly self-contradictory, and it wouldn't have been the first time human beings tied themselves in knots that way. Nothing dishonorable about the push-pull tensions we felt. I'll stand by my characterization of the anti-American mood of those days.

"As for Mark Rudd's point [about nations built on violence], show me the major nation that wasn't built on violence and I'll show you a nonstop orgasm. History is a slaughterhouse. But it is not *only* a slaughterhouse. It sounds as though you, or Mark, are imputing to me a nostalgia for some bygone America. Really, I'm not so simple-minded!"

Patriotism and Internationalism

"I consider myself both a patriot *and* an internationalist. At times this gives me some trouble, because in a given situation there are tensions. Sometimes, the two coincide—as in Afghanistan, for example, where the call of justice after 9/11 was also the call of humanitarian intervention against the Taliban (unfortunately left in the lurch by the unserious Bush, whose default was not nearly so predictable as was his all-around botch in Iraq). At this moment, I consider it both patriotic and internationalist to urge a decent withdrawal from Iraq. Sometimes there's a tension. It can't be patriotic to support the movement of manufacturing jobs outside the country, but it might be internationalist. One wants to finesse the difference by saying we want retraining, a social floor, etc., and that's all very well and good, but when push comes to shove, and the Ohio ex-steelworkers want to know what you're going to do for them, easy rhetorical formulas don't really get you off the hook.

"At the risk of repeating what I say in the book, to concede that the xenophobes are the true patriots is bad judgment—for who is to force a wiser policy and a more habitable world if not the Americans? And if you don't fight in their behalf, in whose, then? Surely bands of intellectuals can't accomplish a grand change on their own. But patriotism is more than expedient—it's ethical. If you do not proclaim a politics in the name of the people you aim to persuade, then what does your politics amount to beyond a gesture?

"Democratic patriotism is the truest kind, in my view. The patriotism of shared commitment is what we have to offer against the right-wing maniacs."

TOM HAYDEN

Is Gitlin Waving the Flag?

"I'll take another look at Todd's book. I thought Naomi Klein took him to task [in *The Nation*]. I found that, maybe you can clarify for me, but my sense was that Todd was . . . how to put it? . . . I think he was overreacting to a bogeyman. There aren't that many anti-American Americans to worry about.

"And . . . also, sort of internalizing . . . what the Bush administration is trying to cultivate is kind of a blind reflex of flag waving and can be rationalized in any number of ways, but the effect of it is to legitimize the flag waving by Todd, with no appreciable gain for women, minorities, or immigrants, not to mention victims of U.S. imperialism, so it's kind of dangerous territory there. Flacks, on the other hand, follows the popular front tradition, which tries to Americanize radicalism."

Plain Patriotism

"And it's a tradition that starts with a lot of immigrants, like Sacco and Vanzetti, who were demonized as immigrants, in part, and had a struggle for acceptance, whether they were Irish or Jewish or Italian or anarchists or communists. They were seen as foreign, foreign inspired, and they were plunged into having to seek acceptance. I come from a different tradition than New York, obviously, and would be more Mills and Texas and the Midwest, and places where I never thought patriotism was a question. I didn't think of myself as anticountry. I thought of myself as being against the violation of the American ideals that I grew up on, so I think that would be classified as a kind of plain patriotism. On the other hand, I think the deficiency in that that I saw as I grew in experience is that the main challenge is not for the Left to prove that it's patriotic; it's to peel back what lies under layers of patriotism and discover the genocide, which is like the blood at the birth of the country itself.

"And how to come out of that with any kind of coherent view, how to come out of it at all, is very difficult, but the only way that I've found is to emphasize that the struggle for democratic reform cannot be separated from the issues of colonialism and slavery and the Crusades, which are deeply, deeply rooted in the American character, and that's why you have so many social movements that are half populist and half racist."

Identity Politics

"I believe in identity politics. I've believed in identity politics since the Port Huron Statement. It wasn't called that at the time, but it started with the recovery of black identity among a new generation of students. It came with Michael Harrington's rediscovery of poverty in *The Other America*. It came with the first feminist literature, which was all about recovering an identity. It came with Chicano nationalism. It came with the gay/lesbian movement. The whole history of the sixties can be seen as a project of recovery.

"And then you have to figure out what are the linkages here, and the linkages include class and other traditional categories, but with respect to Irish identity, I think one's racial or ethnic identity is part of multiple identities. It's not your only identity, but the question of ethnic identity is supremely important in a society where a majority of people are classified as 'white.' That's a census category and that's a terminology you grow up with, and I think it's essential to reject that, not out of guilt or an unreal desire to be black or brown, but you have to recover the radical traditions that were carried by some of your own family and some of your own ancestors: what they achieved, how they fell short, how they were, perhaps, forced to internalize Americanism to get by. You have to pick up that thread and then reclassify yourself in the racial debates in the world. I don't understand what footing a so-called white person would have in the debates about global justice and multiculturalism and diversity. I mean, is anybody seriously seeking a category for whiteness? I don't think there'd be a second to the motion. But I think if you said, 'We want certain qualities of Irishness to be preserved and not smothered under some kind of empty Europeanism or whiteness,' I think you'd get a lot of people saying, 'Yes, absolutely!' And you would then be able to align yourself with anticolonial traditions that have been more successful."

Hayden's Internal Irishness

"I would say that you've got to get to the roots of American history and the roots of your own family. That story is essential, and if you don't do it, you'll be stranded as white or you will be forced to buy into a completely false version of the Irish story, the melting pot, and so on. And if you unlock the story, you will be better grounded as a person, but you'll also be able to understand the current generation of immigrants from Central America who are going through very much the same experience as the Irish. You'll be able to understand why people pick up the gun when they're under colonial government. You'll be able to understand why some people fall into the gang life when they live in the underclass, and you'll find a place in the mosaic of politics and culture. I read some people, probably in *The Village Voice*, arguing that there's nothing special about Irish, that they're white racists like everybody else. That's completely false, and it's important to recover the Irish struggles against racism, but even if it were true and we were to go with the idea of the Irish being universally racist and chauvinistic, we could learn from that experience, how it came to be, because the Irish clearly were not racist in behavior or philosophy before they became immigrants to America. And what happened in the years between the 1840s and the 1860s could give us a clue as to how racial politics are formed. But if you don't know anything about yourself, you're kind of blind and deaf in the most important political discussions going on in the world.

"It's highly personal—knowing your story and grounding yourself is the first point. It's not political. But the second point is the political implication; you have an opportunity to relate to other people that you've considered alien or 'other' by overcoming the alienation of yourself, you alienated from your own story. When you can overcome that, you have a lot in common with the kind of stuff that is written, has been written for a long time, by Albert Camus and Fanon, and many others. You start to understand neurosis and self-hate and inferiority and victimization. You start to understand a lot of experiences as historically caused, and not the sort of things that can be sorted solely in the therapist's office, but they're also universal in character. The language and color and experiences may be somewhat different, but you're able to be part of a dialogue that's going on in the world.

"My Irishness was always there, but it was like C. Wright Mills's Irishness; it would come up in an occasional fit of pique, but I never incorporated it into my analysis. What affected me were the trips to Northern Ireland, and the gradual feeling that I had something to learn there and it was something that I could do about the ending of British rule that had been inflicted on my own ancestors, that the reason I was in America was because of British expulsions from Ireland. And it drew me in, and more in the '90s during the time when the peace process brought a thaw in the 'troubles' and opened a lot of closets in Ireland and in Irish America that had been closed. So it's a phase, and I'm trying to introduce it to my own children earlier so that they grow up with it as part of their being.

"It doesn't mean you have to be an obsessive or an Anglophobe; it just becomes part of your understanding of who you are and why you're here and what your heritage really is, and how similar it is in some ways with other oppressed peoples, and also how you came to have privileges that they don't have by buying your way into or accepting a role in the system which required leaving your own rebellious past behind. There's no accident that most of the people that died in 9/11 were Irish; the biggest percentage of the dead on that day were Irish Americans.

"No, I don't think it's close. You're talking about the firefighters and the police. There's even some of the stockbrokers, the ones that have finally made it out of the ethnic ghetto into the stock market. Whole legions of Irish people died in the building."

Hayden on Canada (to Which I Emigrated in 1969)

"Just generally the quality of life overall [in Canada], including the health-care [system], but the tolerance. My leaning on multiculturalism would be to favor Quebec nationalism despite the potential for a kind of religious and national chauvinism there. I think that the French Canadians are entitled to separate if it's a will of a strong majority, and I find that the English-speaking Canadians react with horror to that point of view, so I'm careful about expressing it. I've questioned [whether I am] projecting something out of my situation onto them, but I've been up there, I've studied the history of the French, the history of the Irish in Quebec. I was up there looking around graveyards last year.

"The Quebecois had a revolutionary movement that was part of the sixties. I was part of it then. I recognize legitimate aspiration when I see it and feel, as times have matured, I find much of the argument against them is simply keeping Canada together. If you weigh it, I just think that the national argument wins and the divorce settlement is what's left. Do I think it's going to happen? I don't know. That last referendum may have been the high point because it's changing demographics. On the other hand, I believe that the Quebec nationalists are going to sweep all the elections this time in Quebec."

MARK RUDD

Internationalism, Not Patriotism

"I'm an internationalist, and patriotism for the imperial country of the world, the sole superpower of the world, is an imperial patriotism. I think it's a bizarre concept to think of an American nation

Mark Rudd. (Photo courtesy of Thomas Good/Next Left Notes)

when you think of all the contemporary immigrants in this country who are making up this nation, all the conquered peoples that live in the Southwest where a lot of the conquered people still exist, where in the East they've all been killed off. Well, not all, because there are a few survivors in casinos, but where the blacks in the East are a conquered people, and all of the immigrants are conquered people, so American nation and patriotism, what's the identification? It's identification with conquest—I'm sorry, that's what it is. I heard Garrison Keillor last weekend; he was talking about torture. Do you ever listen to *Prairie Home Companion*? Garrison Keillor was talking about torture, and he was saying he doesn't want to live in a country where enlisted men are ordered to torture prisoners, and then when it gets known, when it gets found out, the brass escapes responsibility and blames it on the enlisted men. That's what he was saying, and the audience went crazy.

"And then he said, our country, our sweet country has been taken away from us by people who are torturers; basically, he said that they've smudged our wonderful sweet country. So I'm sittin' thinking about this, and I realized that Minnesota is a settler state. Minnesota is a place where the Indians were smashed, conquered, murdered, defeated; where's our sweet country? I mean, had the Germans won World War II, could we talk about sweet Poland, sweet Czechoslovakia? What's so sweet about America, about the history of America? If Todd Gitlin hasn't read Howard Zinn, then he ought to read Howard Zinn. So I'm sorry; I got no room for that. I'm sorry.

"I'll never fly an American flag. I had a 'No War in Iraq' sign, and it got vandalized. The 'No' was painted out, and somebody painted on there, 'Kill 'Em All.' But no, I'll never fly an American flag ever, and I'm sorry."

ROXANNE DUNBAR-ORTIZ

Problems with Patriotism

"If Dick Flacks thinks Woody [Guthrie] was a patriot, he needs to listen more closely to what Woody wrote. Even Hughes. I think they're just old and trying to find relevancy, which is understandable as the past twenty-five years have been very rough for Leftists, not for the weak of heart or commitment. Certainly, those who have embraced the flag have fared better and are probably personally happier than those of us who haven't. After all, there's absolutely no punishment for it; on the contrary. But if they wish to play a part in making change, they're dead wrong to embrace patriotism, love of 'country,' and the flag. It might be all right if you are a citizen of New Zealand, Canada, or Australia, although wrongheaded, because those states can do minor harm and not on a large scale.

Most of these New Left patriots also talk about 'saving' the 'original' democratic principles of the United States. But that's a problem, because its founders created the U.S. as a 'republic for empire,' as Jefferson put it. The first century, although with hundreds of interventions overseas and in foreign countries (for instance, annexing half of Mexico in 1848), saw the largest territorial expansion of any empire in history, dwarfing the direct ownership of colonies by Western European colonial powers, and that was the armed seizure and colonization of indigenous peoples' lands, building the capitalist wealth necessary to become the most militarily and economically powerful state in human history, indeed more powerful than all the rest of them combined. U.S. independence was not anticolonial, but analogous to the independence of the union of South Africa or Rhodesia. The first responsibility of the Left is to acknowledge those origins and figure out how to deconstruct the empire that is the United States. The Weather Underground is the only fraction of the New Left that came to realize that burden, which also contributed to their passion and mistakes. They didn't have faith in people that they could be liberated by the truth, which I consider possible because it is necessary."

Internationalism, Nationalism, Identity Politics

"Internationalism can be just as much an escape from acknowledging the historical character and danger of the U.S. state as patriotism and the flag, although solidarity with those oppressed and exploited by the U.S. military and corporations is a moral necessity. Yet without revealing the roots and irredeemable aspects of the U.S. to our revolutionary surrogates elsewhere, we are no more than Peace Corps volunteers in our effectiveness. I think it has been a great failure of the U.S. Left to not use the mechanisms of the United Nations as Malcolm initiated in the early 1960s. Wisely, the American Indian Movement started doing so in 1974, forming the International Indian Treaty Council. They recruited me to work on that, and I have ever since, but I probably would not have without that. I have tried to persuade many other groups to get involved on a consistent basis (not just attend a world conference), with no success.

"The best organizing from the civil rights movement to the present has been local and regional. There's just no national in the

U.S. People don't believe in it, because it's not real. It's a state, and if a group goes national or has a nationalist (U.S.) identity, then they are subsumed by the state, absorbed, or 'neutralized.' Therefore, I see identity politics as a better alternative (if one needs an identity) than patriotism or U.S. national identity. Probably the most effective international solidarity in fact has come from 'identity' groups, such as the pan-Indianism of the Western Hemisphere and further, pan-indigenism (which also includes the Pacific, Arctic, and even groups in Asia and northern and southern Africa). Then there is pan-Africanism, which has long been a source of revolutionary movement in the U.S., Latino solidarity, gay and lesbian, labor solidarity. The alliances forged among such groups can be quite effective. I think it's fine for Tom Hayden to claim his Irish heritage, but I don't think he would argue that being an Irish American is the same as being a person of color in the U.S. I'm part Indian (raised white), but I've become quite interested in my father's family roots, Scots-Irish. I see the Scots-Irish settlers as the 'foot soldiers of empire' in the United States. Frankly, I think any identity other than 'American' is preferable. It won't make a revolution, but it can be transformative, which Americanism cannot."

CASEY HAYDEN

Love of Country as Rootedness

"America is always aggressively patriotic, and of course more so in times of war or threat, the real threat now being the fact that the petroleum is running out, which, as Leonard Cohen says, 'everybody knows.' I must say that I do love this country, not so much as a political/social/economic system [but] as natural world, as dirt, as regional ecosystem, as watershed, because I'm deeply rooted here. I think a sense of local place, of rootedness, is very important, a key political element for visioning a sustainable future."

CARL OGLESBY

How to Salute the American Flag

"Authoritarianism and one of its chief forms, militarism, contradict the Declaration of Independence and the Constitution. American patriotism obligates a critical stance toward state power. Note that

Carl Oglesby. (Photo courtesy of Jennifer Fels)

militarism is pushed hardest by the heirs of the Confederacy—e.g., Texas. . . . Speaking truth to power is the only way to salute the American flag. Anything else is idolatry."

DAVID GILBERT

Humanism, Not Patriotism

"The fundamental reference point for me is humankind. In a country that intervenes in and exploits other nations, there is a tremendous danger of patriotism being the cover for arrogance and aggression. There are aspects of this country I love, its ideals, diversity, many of its people—but first and foremost that has to be separated from rationales for imperial dominance. Solidarity with oppressed nations has to be a centerpiece for us. I do not think that identity politics for oppressed groups necessarily contradicts universalism. The only way to build principled unity is to challenge oppression, so independence and power for oppressed groups are necessary steps on the long march to a universal humanity based on equality and respect."

KENNETH JOHNSON

In Defense of Love of Country

"The concept of nation and patriotism has always meant a lot to me. A very, very lot to me, because I was raised in southern Mississippi and my county borders would keep me in line, and way down in Mississippi. We grew up very religious, Baptist, and my parents, my mother and my father, taught me that. My mother was a schoolteacher in 1921 and my father was a farmer, and he also had a public job, and they taught us patriotism and religion. Patriotism towards your country, God second, always. That's the way it was. And I went off after I graduated, I was expelled from Southern [for civil rights protests], and I graduated from Howard, went into the army. The first year I was prosecutor in the JAG [Judge Advocate General's] Corps prosecuting in Fort Belvoir, Virginia, and that's where I saw the 'I Have a Dream' speech on August 28, 1963, and I was on the command staff. At JAG I was a legal officer on the command staff, and I was in the helicopter field taking pictures flying around the Washington Monument, and so then one year there and one year in Korea and the rest in Okinawa and Thailand and some other countries that I can't tell you about; it's still top secret. And Vietnam through there, I got shot at twice. And when I came back to Mississippi after four years in the army, and I didn't come home that whole stint I was overseas. After the disastrous eight Bush years, . . . the U.S. has been discredited overseas. [Obama wants to restore] America to what it used to be and what it could be.

"I came home in '66, and the first thing that happened to me was, I went uptown and I got called a nigger by a white woman because I walked through the front door [of a restaurant]. But still, they are unpatriotic; the right wing, as far as I'm concerned, are unpatriotic, and I am [patriotic]. I've kept the faith. I was angry then and I'm still angry.

"As I sit here and look at what's happening in the war in Iraq and the fool in the White House and his vice president who's not a fool, pretty smart, but evil, it makes me not reconsider my patriotism, but makes me more determined to see that the country turns around."

In the following chapter, we consider Gitlin's contention that the Right won the political sixties, while the Left won the cultural sixties. Even to frame the issue this way acknowledges that the Right gained more advantage during that decade, a point that provides one of my main theses about connections between yesteryear and today. The sixties ended badly for the New Left, which Nixon vanquished using organized state repression. Can we return to the positive, progressive energy of the early sixties, when SDS issued the Port Huron Statement and the nonviolent civil rights movement helped improve America for black people?

🔊 Six ଔ

Who Won the Sixties?

The Right won Washington, and the Left won the English Department.
—Todd Gitlin

In this chapter I explore the outcome of sixties tumult, especially for progressive politics. Todd Gitlin's framing of the issue—"The Right won Washington, and the Left won the English Department"—is a place to begin. The sixties started out so well, and ended so badly, largely because the Right controlled not only the means of production but also the means of social control, such as the police and the FBI. The sixties also ended badly because smoking dope contributes to lassitude, as Karl Marx well understood when he said that bourgeois ideology is the opiate of the masses. During the sixties, the opiate was "weed" and stronger hallucinogens. Young people who gave up on politics got high. (Some were never even political in the first place.)

But another reason that the sixties ended badly was that the New Left (think of the Port Huron Statement) was never "Left" enough, could not be, because Americans were not willing to swallow even a watered-down version of cold war–era social democracy, let alone stronger doses relying explicitly on early Marx. Keep in mind that the Port Huron Statement was written less than ten years after the McCarthy period. That it went as far to the Left as it did was a minor miracle. The Right's defeat of the movement during the sixties led to the Right's dominance of American politics since Ronald Reagan's presidency (he had been elected governor of California while the sixties were still unfolding).

The question of who "won" the sixties is a matter of the sixties legacy, an underlying theme of this book. Those for whom the sixties were the best of times, even if they acknowledge the blood spilled and the hopes dashed, tend to emphasize progressive outcomes such as civil rights legislation and the women's movement. Those who lament the sixties as libertine seek to turn back the clock to earlier decades, when comfortable consensus about values concealed deeper fissures.

SETTING THE STAGE: PROTEST MARCHES, POT, AND MUSIC

> *The sad thing about the Sixties was the weak-mindedness of the so-called radicals and the way that they managed to get coopted. I think one of the things that helped that happen was LSD. It's the only chemical known to mankind that will convert a hippie to a yuppie.*
> —Frank Zappa

Against many retrospectives, I emphasize politics over cultures and countercultures in my account of the decade, even though I acknowledge their intersection. The Age of Aquarius was largely a rhetorical device used to sell albums and incense and perhaps to deflect young people from the political tasks at hand. The other sixties were found in Washington and Watts, Selma and Saigon. A major legacy of the sixties is the dominance of the Right and of global unilateralism, which, as I have noted, joined mainstream Democrats and Republicans in common cause until the very end of the decade. By then opportunistic Democrats realized that the war was folly, and they jumped on the antiwar bandwagon, perhaps five years too late to prevent Lyndon Johnson and then Richard Nixon from claiming the support of a "silent majority" of patriots.

But were psychedelia and music somehow less "real" than politics, as I just implied? I still recall the smell of incense at local dance halls in Eugene such as the Wesley Foundation, just as I remember the music of Hammond Typewriter and Searchin' Soul Blues Band. We all remember concerts by Jefferson Airplane and the Grateful Dead. Many hours spent listening to albums—Simon and Garfunkel; Bob Dylan; Crosby, Stills, and Nash—were "real"; they transformed us into sentient selves, open to experience. The Doors' "Riders on the Storm" could have been the track playing during our first kiss or first joint. There was a cultural politics of music, hair, dope, that set us apart from the fifties and from our elders.

My sixties were intensely political, but they were also cultural. In high school I listened to bands for whom an ecstatic politics emerged from a rock culture inseparable from the political culture of the times. Politics and culture were distinct and even antithetical for many of my less political but nonetheless pot-smoking friends. For others of us, to whom the label "radical" might have been applied, there was a continuum along which we could locate both cultural and political resistance. San Francisco and local Eugene bands sang against the war and for an ecstatic politics of Marcusean new sensibilities to supplement the traditionally boring politics of our parents.

To be sure, rock music expressed and promoted rebellion. Indeed, white rock devolved from black blues, which was protest music, too. And the counterculture was not against "culture" but deeply suspicious of workaholism and the Protestant ethic, much as the beats had been during the fifties and slackers are today. Hippies were often making interesting choices for existential lifestyles and against bureaucratic jobs and suburban conformity. Herbert Marcuse (1969), in *An Essay on Liberation*, identifies the sixties temperament as the "new sensibility," one that refused to postpone liberation to a distant future time and insisted that radical change must not bypass people's everyday lives. This was very much the sentiment of the Port Huron Statement.

The sharp edge of protest contained in San Francisco and British rock endured beyond the sixties. The angst-driven "new music" of the present resonates with anxieties of the self and fails to galvanize a generation as we were galvanized by Bob Dylan and the Airplane. This whole matter of cultural and aesthetic politics has been treated by cultural theorists (see Frith 1978; Grossberg 1997) searching for nondiscursive forms of protest and theoretical insight. Many of the millions who attended concerts during the sixties, especially those younger boomers for whom Woodstock was more emblematic than the bus boycotts or the John Kennedy and Martin Luther King assassinations, did not notice the political lyrics or theorize music as a critical vehicle. They were too stoned to theorize at all, and having grown up in pragmatic America, they were impatient with analysis, one of the foibles of the sixties as a whole and an enduring quality of American anti-intellectualism (see Hofstadter 1963).

One might say this: The sixties were stretched between political and cultural preoccupations, but at times—for the briefest of moments—cultural politics bridged the gap. Protest music, transcendent rock, political theater, and communal concert events prefigured a New Left community of like-minded "new sensibilities" such as the Port Huron campers, who shared a taste for direct democracy and opposed utilitarianism. The counterculture was against only high culture, dictated from above by mavens of mandarinism, including corporate cultural producers. This era was the briefest of moments—perhaps 1966 to 1968—before cynicism set in, with Woodstock degenerating into Altamont and paralleling, on the cultural side, the spiraling downward of Port Huron into the Weather Underground. At Altamont in California on December 6, 1969, the Hells Angels stabbed to death a young concertgoer while they were protecting the bands onstage, at that moment the Rolling Stones. Peace and love were not supposed to be homicidal. But even this brief moment suggests that we need to rethink traditional boundaries between politics and culture, taking our lead from the gentle and political souls of the sixties who well understood that socialism (or whatever we call the good society) must be lived and experienced; it must be embodied, sung, played, danced, eaten, and exercised.

There was a blending of politics and culture as political thinkers and activists shared the stage with musicians and cultural figures. Timing is everything: A speaker and performance event was held at the Fillmore East ballroom in New York City exactly one year and a day before Altamont and after the murder of Fred Hampton, the young Chicago Black Panther. Roxanne Dunbar-Ortiz attended, and she describes a fractious moment at which H. Rap Brown stalked out, accompanied by his bodyguards. She reports that only Marcuse kept his cool. Already the New Left was unraveling.

The New Left and the counterculture understood that the self is an embodied subject, thereby rejecting the mind-body dualism that has prevailed since the eighteenth-century Enlightenment. The challenge for the New Left was to preserve the rationalist goals of "enlightenment"—what Jürgen Habermas (1987) calls the "project of modernity"—while escaping the straitjacket of dualism, which denigrates the body, nature, and play in favor of a technologically driven industrialism involving the domination of nature. Earth Day, April 22, 1970, manifested these ecological sentiments, a carry-forward from the previous decade. Another way to summarize the legacy of the sixties, especially its short-lived cultural politics, is to say that sixties people rejected "productivism" and the domination of nature as worthy societal and personal goals, a sentiment already found in the Port Huron Statement and its various theoretical influences.

During the sixties, culture followed politics, escape and inebriation buffering political defeat. The surreal politics of body counts led people to take hallucinogens, which afforded access to out-of-body experience. Political vision, extinguished with JFK's assassination, became a nightmare for much of the decade. Gitlin is certainly correct that the Left was outmaneuvered by the Right as it escalated the ungodly war in Vietnam even in the face of a protest movement that by 1968 had swelled into the millions (see Wells 1994). One of the dominant political experiences of the sixties, which was also a personal experience penetrating to the inner core of people's existence, was the utter futility of protest and resistance. This futility bore both the stoned disengagement of the counterculture and the quixotic engagement of Weather's revolutionary agenda.

All the while, the Dionysian side of the sixties was unfolding. It was difficult not to be moved by the cultural politics of the time, which was embedded in the erotic, psychedelic, and nonlinear aspects of rock music and light shows, especially of the San Francisco bands. The hippie new sensibility learned to differently experience the world, including space and time, by listening and dancing to this sixties rock, providing a utopian imagery of transcendent experience and decent interpersonal relationships at a time when politics was going bad. Our sense of political alienation after Dallas, not to mention Memphis, Los Angeles, Chicago, and Kent, was somehow redeemed by listening to this pulsating, imaginative music. Although we certainly used this music for "escape," much as we smoked pot and used other mind-altering drugs, there was more to it than that: Jefferson Airplane's album *Crown of Creation* embodied our hopes and dreams of rapprochement with nature, intimate community, sharing, and democracy. Port Huron's vision was reinforced at rock concerts where people shared and shared alike and experienced their bodies and the world in transforming ways.

Political tragedy changed the ways in which we related to music through cultural politics. Ecstasy and community were replaced by transcendence and escape as Woodstock Nation formed in 1969. This "nation" was located off the map; it was a state of mind and a means of escape from that official map. Rock energized young people and eventually became a significant political medium. As the hopes and dreams of the Kennedys and Port Huron were extinguished by the martial state, music, like drugs, became escapist and lost its political edge. Middle-class white kids, especially those born after about 1953, replaced (or supplemented) beer with grass and Elvis with the Stones without having experienced the liberating effects of early Students for a Democratic Society (SDS) or the early San Francisco bands, which supported New Left politics and viewed themselves as cultural-political agents.

It is possible to romanticize the sixties as an Aquarian age dominated by freethinking, free love, music, and drugs. But many of

us experienced the sixties as a sustained moment of disenchantment as we came to understand that sweet reason, multiplied by
a million or more, was having little impact on policy, let alone on
social structure. Johnson and then Nixon gained strength from
their cavalier dismissal of the protest movement; protest validated
them and gave them an excuse to lower the boom as they tried to
repress the New Left, particularly with the FBI run by the perni-
cious J. Edgar Hoover. So many of us were obsessed with the Vietnam War because we watched it on the nightly news; we recoiled
from the banality of evil encoded in the body counts measuring
how the war was going. Perhaps music and other inebriants were
our ways of dealing with being ignored and even vilified as activist
citizens.

Sometimes, politics and culture were contradictorily juxtaposed,
occupying the same moments in time but involving very different
constituencies. American cities such as Detroit had race riots,
which destroyed the black inner city, in the long hot summer of
1967, while middle-class hippies gravitated to San Francisco for
the so-called Summer of Love. Meanwhile, the war in Vietnam
raged. The juxtapositions and overlaps were the crazy things.

By the time of the 1968 assassinations and then the Democratic
National Convention in Chicago, millions of young people had
begun to wear their hair long, dress in nonconformist ways, smoke
marijuana as their party drug of choice, experiment sexually, and
also march against the war and in support of civil rights. As their
antiwar politics was choked off during the late Johnson and early
Nixon years, they gave up on politics and drowned their sorrows in
music and drugs, their alienation becoming a wellspring not of political praxis but of escape. The anguish of Janis Joplin and Jimi
Hendrix reflected the disaffected mood of the moment, and the
Grateful Dead rode the wave of existential release that followed political disappointment. The later double entendre "Deadhead" captures the apolitical turn in rock and youth culture. Although SDS
sponsored concerts, SDS itself had wandered far from its Port
Huron roots and was now preparing for radical "actions" in order
to "bring the war home."

Even the apparently apolitical rockers were not immune to
COINTELPRO and other efforts at organized surveillance. Before
she achieved national prominence, Janis Joplin lived in Austin,
where the University of Texas campus police were busily docu-
menting political and cultural subversives. Here is an image from
handwritten notes taken by an informant who identified Joplin's
fondness for amphetamine drugs; these notes were found in the
files of the campus police many years later.

University of Texas campus police chief Allen Hamilton document listing Janis Joplin as a subversive to be kept under surveillance. The document was first revealed to the public in an article by Thorne Dreyer titled "The Spies of Texas," which appeared in the November 17, 2006, issue of the Texas Observer.)

Janis Joplin's Influence During the Summer of Love

In a candid remembrance, Mark Naison (2002) shares his personal and political awakening with his students. Here, he recalls hearing Joplin's music for the first time. Profiles in courage, presented throughout this book, involve the courage to establish relationships, an embryonic politics of the personal. We were all in Mark's shoes during that time, and we all needed a little help from our friends.

It is the summer of 1967. The Vietnam War is raging, but it's also the "Summer of Love" when the nation is becoming aware of an emerging counterculture involving hundreds of thousands of young people who are calling themselves "hippies." Race relations are tense. Riots are breaking out in Newark and Detroit. The Black Power movement is spreading like wildfire on college campuses, putting people in interracial relationships in a difficult position from the Black side as well as from Whites. It's exciting, it's scary and it's confusing. It's war and revolution, sex and drugs, and the most incredible music blasting from the airwaves, because in that summer, FM radio comes into its own with a new progressive format that allows for the playing of whole albums and songs lasting more than 3 minutes. Anyway, back to the home front, Ruthie and I are both working at Project Double Discovery, the Columbia University Upward Bound program, Ruthie as a counselor, me as a division leader. We are both living in the Columbia residence halls, but periodically have time off to see each other at our off campus apartment. It's a Saturday night and I have off and Ruthie is busy. I decide to go to the West End bar (the bar near Columbia where Jack Kerouac and Allen Ginsberg once hung out!) for a drink and run into my friend Michel, a former Columbia soccer player from France who I lived with for a year. We start drinking and are soon joined by a very attractive woman named JR who I used to work with in the Columbia chapter of CORE [Congress of Racial Equality], and who, to be fully honest, I had the hots for along with every guy, and probably some of the women, in the group. Well after a few drinks, JR starts talking about this amazing new singer she's heard named Janis Joplin, and invites me and Michel to come to her apartment to hear her. Michel says he can't go, so I find myself walking down the street with this very hot, very hip, and very interesting woman, hoping none of my friends or Ruthie's friends will see us. This is not one of my better moments. During the five block walk to her apartment, one part of me says I am doing something very wrong and another part says "go with the flow." Everything is very innocent—there's no touching or holding of hands. When we get to JR's apartment, we sit down on the couch in her living room and start to chill. JR pulls out a water pipe and shows me this album with the most bizarre, picaresque graphics on the cover (drawn by a cartoonist named R. Crumb). The album title is "Cheap Thrills" and the name of the group is "Big Brother and the Holding Company." What a strange name for a group, I think. Then JR puts the record on and a voice comes on of a kind I have never heard before. The singer wails, cries, screams and begs, never letting up for a second even with the drums and guitars crashing behind her. It is pure unadulterated passion and pain and longing and it touches me in places where I usually don't want to go—a place where my own insecurities and desires and need for love reside. I thought of moments of loneliness and isolation, of times when I felt ugly and unlovable, and I felt grateful for the love of the beautiful person who I had been with for the last year and a half but WHO WAS NOT THE PERSON I WAS SITTING NEXT TO ON THE COUCH! What comes next is a little embarrassing but very much in the spirit of Janis Joplin, whose hunger for new experience took her to some strange places. As the music, and the contents of the water pipe, took hold of me, I slowly put my arm around JR's shoulder, curious to see how she would respond. If she snuggled close to me and pulled me to her, I am sure I would have kissed her and let nature take its course. But when she didn't respond at all, I felt a kind of relief. I just sat there with my arm on her shoulder till the album was over, then said good bye and walked home, feeling a mixture of gratitude, regret, disappointment, and a certain amount of pride that a former "Supernerd" like me could even KNOW two women like Ruthie and JR, much less be loved by one of them. And this is where Janis's music really spoke to me. See, if you grow up thinking you are ugly, or unlovable, as Janis did, and to some degree I did, to find that people actually are attracted to you can be a powerful thing. Janis bared her soul to get love from her audiences and I understood and identified with her need. When you think you are unlovable, you need a lot of reassurance, and while Janis apparently never got enough reassurance to keep her alive, the emotions she expressed in her music enriched the lives of her listeners by reminding them that they were not alone in their pain and isolation. I know I felt that way. I walked back from JR's apartment feeling more alive and ready for the challenges of life than I had before. I now had a friend that I could turn to in my darkest moments just by turning on the record player. Janis Joplin created beauty out of darkness and expressed it in her music. What a wonderful gift that was, to me and countless others. Thank you Janis.

One can distinguish sharply between apolitical college kids who replaced (or supplemented) beer with grass and harder-core activists like Tom Hayden who worked with a plan, and organized, to bring the war to an end and win civil and economic rights. There is validity to this distinction; many of my high school classmates tried marijuana and liked it, but were miles away from burning their draft cards. However, as the decade wore on and they entered college, they became politically aware and almost as quickly experienced disillusionment as the White House appeared impervious to the massive protests. It is equally possible to read sixties rock music as merely escapist when in fact it contained political cadences and social commentaries, suggesting alternative modes of experience and existence that appealed to young people disgusted with the politics of the day. Even Timothy Leary offered a political theory of sorts as he extolled the virtues of LSD, which was not to be a party drug but a philosophical methodology—a way of tuning in (that would inevitably lead to turning on and then dropping out politically). And in Naison's remembrances, it is clear that, for him at least, the seemingly apolitical music of Joplin evoked a personal politics involving relationships and even the innermost interior places where people are most alone, and hence most vulnerable. Perhaps the Austin authorities had reason to target Joplin as subversive, as radical in the sense of getting to the roots of things.

But drugs, music, and the counterculture did not turn people away from politics, which might tempt us to debate Gitlin's thesis about the duality of politics and culture. Politics turned people off politics—Nixon's politics, following Johnson's politics, following the Klan's politics. Although Port Huron was widely read, by 1968 the ideals of participatory democracy and the compelling values section of the document bore little relationship to the cynical politics of the times, as American bombers pulverized the Vietnamese and the FBI and the police hunted down the Left, especially the Black Panthers.

Gitlin in the interviews suggests that the Right won political power, while the Left won important cultural victories such as civil rights and a certain freeing of the spirit. Gitlin implies that the Left controls very little—a tiny slice of college curriculum and the tenured traffic in arcane ideas easily caricatured as wordplay. After the sixties, ex-radicals decamped into academia and took up the causes of multiculturalism and cultural theory, trading their broad-gauged and accessible literary style for the academic obscurantism that supposedly signals gravitas. This is an analysis consistent with Russell Jacoby's (1987) critique of academic radicalism in *The Last Intellectuals: American Culture in the Age of Academe*, an argument from which Gitlin draws.

The Right could achieve political gains and the Left cultural gains, neither of which are immaterial, because the decade was marked by conflict over everything: power, the military, the university, the environment, sexuality, race, gender (and now sexual orientation), music, sartorial and tonsorial styles, nation, the pace of progress, relations between the generations. These conflicts produced different outcomes for the Right and Left and hence different legacies of the decade.

Perhaps this is the way it always is: Culture follows politics, much in the way that Marx suggested that ideology (collective belief systems that falsify reality in order to perpetuate it) follows political economy, concealing it from view and placating people with false substitutes for freedom and subsistence. This is not to deny their complex interrelationship. Using the Protestant Reformation and capitalism as examples, Max Weber (2009) points out that ideas and social structures have a certain "elective affinity," arising together independently and then blending to the point of near identity. During the sixties, politics and culture both began even before the decade officially opened. The first civil rights actions occurred during the early to mid-1950s, which also saw the waxing and waning of the cold war. And SDS by another name (Student League for Industrial Democracy) emerged from the late 1950s. Buddy Holly, from the desolate plains of Lubbock, Texas, could be as much a link between the fifties and sixties on the cultural side as were Rosa Parks in Montgomery, Alabama, and the four North Carolina A&T students who led the Greensboro lunch counter sit-in on the political side. And as we learned from the timeline presented earlier, the first city bus desegregation effort began in Baton Rouge, Louisiana, in 1953. During that year, popular rockers included Bill Haley and the Comets, Chuck Berry, and the Drifters. Buddy Holly was born only three years before Tom Hayden.

Perhaps the new music culture prepared the way for subsequent political protests and actions. This suggests causality: Political disappointment pushes people away from politics and toward self-expression. But there is another equally plausible causality: Sixties protest music and protest culture politicized people, a topic that I pursue with Dick Flacks later. Buddy Holly, Elvis Presley, the Beatles, and the Stones—all of whom were borrowing from black musical forms—helped liberate consciousness, especially among the young. The music liberated people's bodies to dance as well as sing, suggesting that New Left and civil rights politics had their origins in the emerging antipuritanical tradition of rock-and-roll, which, like the women's movement, put the body on the political agenda. Although linear thinkers may prefer one causality over the other (politics/culture or culture/politics), I tend to think that both are true, or at least each represents how it worked for different people. For some, political disappointment led them to drop out; for others, the freeing music and "counterculture" jolted them out of the fifties doldrums and inspired them to join demonstrations and perhaps even resist the draft.

What about drugs? Certainly, drugs and music were linked for much of the decade, as marijuana smoke was commonly found wafting in the air at public gatherings starting in about 1965 or 1966. It is important to remember that there was an overt "war on drugs" that stemmed from a prohibitionist urge to deny pleasure. Possessors of pot could receive serious jail time because the police and federal authorities well understood that drugs might not sedate the masses but enliven them. The majority of pot-smoking kids whom I knew in high school and college did not become politically active. For them, getting high was equivalent to getting drunk, although perhaps it was cooler because it troubled parents and authorities. Drugs and music in themselves are not political, although they may spring from politics or perhaps even prepare the way for them. Or drugs can be just drugs, means of escape. In any case, the sixties, especially the second half of the decade, were times of militancy during which these issues of cultural politics, the draft, the building war, civil rights, and then Black Power were on almost every young person's agenda.

In this reading, music and drugs meant protest as well as a vision of utopia, of a better life. Protest mixed with hope slides into despair when the political forces of reaction and repression become too weighty, as occurred during 1969 when the movement decamped to upstate New York and became Woodstock Nation. Again, there was incomplete overlap: Many a frat boy read the notice of an

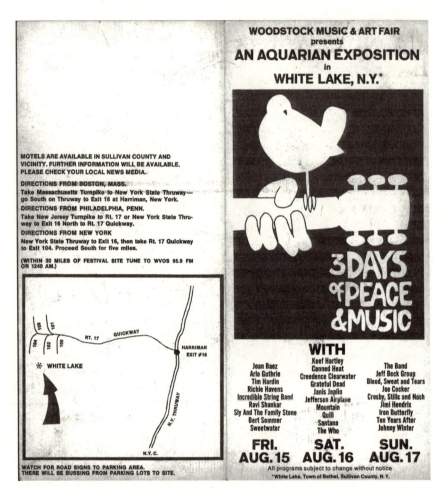

Woodstock, 1969, three days of peace and music. (Photo by Blank Archives/Getty Images)

upcoming concert in Bethel, New York, in the pages of *Rolling Stone* and planned a late-summer road trip before college classes began in the fall. These frat boys did not want to serve in Vietnam, but neither were they flaming radicals. Perhaps they were radicalized by events, but they did not have adequate organizational or intellectual means with which to channel their protest. So they partied in the mud, bought albums, slept around, and got high, habits that for many endured far beyond the end of the sixties as baby boomers entered middle age and experienced midlife crises.

Young women protested and partied as well. However, the New Left was largely patriarchal, with men dominating decisionmaking, even among movement people. The second wave of the women's movement had roots in the suffrage movement (Susan B. Anthony and Elizabeth Cady Stanton, among others), which urged legal equality between the sexes. Second-wave sixties women were also radicalized by their subordinate roles in the civil rights and anti-war movements, which contradictorily sought universal human rights but denied power to wives and girlfriends.

It is difficult to tell the story—many stories—of the sixties without commenting on the role of universities. Hayden and his early SDS cohorts argued that the large public "multiversity" was not serving their interests or the interests of social justice. Jam-packed into teaching-assistant-instructed classes in the hundreds of students, these kids were beginning to notice that their faculty were not asking the really important questions of "relevance," about poverty, racism, the decline of livable cities, the cold war, the nuclear threat, the environment, the role of women. Far from being left-wing firebrands, many older faculty during the late 1950s and early 1960s (and even today) were merely bureaucratically organized civil servants who punched in and out, refrained from rocking the boat, and published modestly on narrow topics that padded their vitae but did not change the prevailing paradigms. Hayden and his cohorts wanted to transform the university and make it a vehicle for social change. C. Wright Mills led the way when he criticized timid academics who did not occupy, or address, the public sphere.

Only during the later sixties did universities come alive with debate and dissent. The war in Vietnam was the primary issue, although civil rights and women's rights were also debated. Activist faculty embraced their roles as public citizens and did not pretend that their scholarship was value-free, as Weber (1958) terms it. Social scientists and humanists in particular embraced the New Left project, marching and teaching against the war and turning their classrooms into Socratic laboratories for democratic dialogue and cooperative education. This also affected education on the K–12 level, as people started free schools, using ideas and models provided by the Summerhill experiment (Neill 1977) and by Paul Goodman (1960). Paulo Freire (1970) argued for a pedagogy of the oppressed, and Ivan Illich (1972) called for a "deschooling" of society. College students and faculty applied ideas in the effort to bring about social change and build community.

For a brief period, during the escalation of the Vietnam War, beginning in about 1965 and continuing at least until Kent State in 1970, the American professoriate was largely of one mind: The university should play a role, if not necessarily a radical one, in

Tom Hayden back in the day. (Photo by David Fenton/Getty Images)

achieving social justice, particularly in stopping the tragic war in Indochina. Faculty contributed to "grade inflation" by giving their male students grades sufficiently high that they could keep their student draft deferments. Although there was division among faculty over the correct course in Vietnam and about civil rights, this division was generally more muted than in society at large, where middle-American "hard hats" like the television character Archie Bunker hated hairy hippies and peaceniks. Certainly by Tet in early 1968, when it became obvious that the public had been deceived by the generals and the White House, many American faculty members believed that they should contribute in their own small ways, via demonstrations, protests, and teach-ins, to stopping the war.

This period of faculty activism, especially on the part of younger faculty, stands in contrast to the somnolent state of the professoriate during the fifties and to postsixties developments in higher education. Before the Port Huron Statement and the first stirrings of the movement in the early sixties, the university was portrayed, even by liberal faculty, as a world apart, not as an integral component of the military-industrial-educational complex. After the sixties passed into history, universities retrenched during various national and state budget crises, and they were taken over by professional managers who run them as businesses. Meanwhile, sixties radicals earned tenure and wrote in the restricted codes (see Bernstein 1975) of academic discourse, as Jacoby (1987) laments.

The politicization of higher education during the 1960s, and continuing through the subsequent academic careers of "tenured radicals" who decamped to the university after the movement had withered, has been attacked and lamented from both the Right and Left. Allan Bloom (1987), Dinesh D'Souza (2007), and David Horowitz (2006) argue that American culture has been imperiled by a creeping Leftism, inspired by Karl Marx, Herbert Marcuse, and Jacques Derrida. On this reading, Left theory is often conflated with postmodernism, which supposedly celebrates absolute relativism and is thus amoral. It does not matter that "postmodernism is not what you think" (Lemert 1997) and that there are serious disagreements between Marxists and postmodernists. On this right-wing reading, universities are armed camps dominated by authoritarian left-wing faculty who indoctrinate pliant undergraduates and punish neocon naysayers.

The legacy of the sixties was the disappearance of the American Left, even though Rightist accounts of the 1980s and 1990s, hinging on the so-called culture wars, argue that academic life has been taken over by tenured radicals who pollute the minds of the helpless young. That account ignores the fact that academics lack power, are not homogeneous (think of engineering or business faculty members compared with liberal arts faculty), and have not influenced popular culture. The Right simply wants another excuse to purge the universities and turn academic life into a business, a project in which they have nearly succeeded, given universities' stress on grantworthy applied research in the face of eroding state support of higher education. Under pressure from well-heeled alumni who worried about their kids learning secular humanism in college, Harvard considered requiring students to take a religion course, a sure sign that the sixties had lost their hold on academia. The course would have been called "Reason and Faith." Subsequently, a faculty committee backed away and instead proposed a course called "Culture and Belief." The conflict between sacred and secular is not yet a settled issue.

Universities, often afflicted with bureaucratic inertia and organized along the lines of Henry Ford's division of labor, are perhaps inherently conservative. "Output" (grants, narrow publications composed in technical language) becomes more important than enlightenment and relevance. Academics lard their vitae instead of trying to bridge their scholarship and social activism. The war in Vietnam gave U.S. academics few alternatives to taking sides. Faculty either helped their students avoid the draft by maintaining grade-point averages sufficiently high to retain their student deferments, or refused to do so. Faculty either marched or supported the war. They either wore a peace button or plastered an American flag on their car window. There was no middle ground.

The Left critique of the university argues that tenured radicals are faculty first and political agents and activists only second. Tenured Leftists become more interested in their own career advancement than in social change. They lose the ability to be "public intellectuals," writing and teaching for intelligent audiences beyond the academy. Their writing becomes crabbed, technical, and self-referential. This critique of academic life is partly a critique of an academic capitalism that transforms the university into a private-sector business requiring faculty to conduct "funded" or "sponsored" research on issues relevant to corporations and the state.

Ex-radicals now teach "theory" in English departments, while more instrumental people wield power and run organizations. This version of theory is for the most part unconnected to actual political movements, because there are not any, at least by comparison with the sixties when millions came together in the movement. That the Right won power and the Left academia (or one small corner in it) is not because the Left's nerve failed. The Weather cadres were nervy to a fault. The Right won because it was more adept at repression. While Leftists were gamboling in strawberry fields, discussing James Baldwin while smoking dope, the Rightists were earning law degrees and MBAs. They were "straight," which now contains a double meaning.

It is easy to ridicule academic radicals, perhaps an oxymoron. Both Gitlin and Jacoby take the Left, including themselves, to task for lacking real political ambition and instead purveying turgid prose. American pragmatism has always valued action over ideas, which is part of the problem here. Today, there are few "actions" to join, except the occasional bicoastal demonstration against former president George W. Bush's war. The Right has moved political discourse so far away from the managerial liberalism of the New Deal that Democrats, to survive, espouse religion, family values, patriotism, and capital punishment, a recipe for oblivion given that Republicans sound genuine when they mouth those words. The Left, if it plays this game, will always lose for reasons that Marx well understood: The state is the executive committee of the bourgeoisie, and the ruling ideas are ideas of the ruling class. The Right has power over discourse and the imagination because it often holds power, ever the Marxist insight.

I concede to Gitlin that there may be a good deal of affectation among academic radicals, a self-importance that varies inversely with political purchase. I agree with him that the cultural studies movement often chooses superstructure over base, ideas and culture over the mode of production. However, the Frankfurt School (see Jay 1973; Agger 1992) suggests that the mode of consumption (and of information) must be taken seriously, too, if we are to understand how capitalism has outlived Marx's expectations of its demise. And we should probably also consider the mode of entertainment and modes of communication/connection, such as the Internet and cell phones.

All of this requires a rethinking of academia and of activism. The university has never been a world apart, a bastion of pure and objective scholarship. "A new left must start controversy across the land, if national policies and national apathy are to be reversed. The ideal university is a community of controversy, within itself and in its effects on communities beyond" (Port Huron Statement 1962). Universities respond to external pressures, and they sometimes create pressures of their own. The sixties demonstrated that the university, which is prone to bureaucratic inertia, can play a leadership role in social change, especially on the part of students and younger faculty who question both academic and societal convention. Academic purists—Stanley Fish (2008) comes to mind—who want to remove the university from political and social life are missing the point that universities are always already socially situated, whether they exist in the public or the private sector. As such, faculty and students cannot just opt out and pretend that their work, teaching, and studies are somehow not already infected/inflected by political concerns. Rather, they must address openly the contribution of universities to capital and culture, to profit and social control, on the one hand, and to enlightenment and emancipation, on the other. This is the role of universities sketched by Habermas (1971). To borrow a desideratum from the Frankfurt School, academics must engage in unfettered discussion and contribute to societal rationalization. "Any new left in America must be, in large measure, a left with real intellectual skills, committed to deliberativeness, honesty, reflection as working tools. The university permits the political life to be an adjunct to the academic one, and action to be informed by reason" (Port Huron Statement 1962).

In the interviews, we discuss the political impact of the sixties. Who "won" what, and what does it mean today? It is interesting that, apart from Flacks's comments about patriotic folk and rock music, few of the activists have much to say about the counterculture. They all focus on political outcomes, especially in the framework of Gitlin's hypothesis that the Left lost the sixties politically while achieving certain cultural, legal, and intellectual gains. Perhaps this is because they are all movement people, concerned with the role of activism in achieving social justice. Had I been interviewing sixties rockers or hippies, I might have received different answers.

The activists offer fascinating political and cultural sociologies that treat cause and effect complexly. They resist caricatures of the sixties. It is possible—indeed, this is my thesis—that the sixties both raised and dashed expectations. Even to explore the sixties archaeologically keeps the embers of hope glowing as it illumines identity—the people we have become. The sixties were a state of mind, but at times they felt like a police state.

RICHARD FLACKS

The Legacy of the Sixties

"This is going to be almost bizarre, but I think to a very great extent I would call the project of the sixties a democratization project. It's still an ongoing and viable living practice in the U.S. and in other parts of the world. That's a very simplistic way for me to articulate what I think because I've learned a lot. After the fall of communism, I thought we were going to see a tremendous burst of new thinking in Eastern Europe. It didn't happen, and it's quite sobering to see how, instead, a free-market kind of perspective became dominant, which was not what I had expected. And that's one source of very sobering experience in terms of who won what."

The Sixties Extending into the Seventies

"My impression of the East German dissidents who [were responsible for] the [Berlin] wall coming down, they were pretty New Left in their attitudes, and they were dismayed by the takeover of Germany by East Germany and that model of unification. Now, where are they? What happened to all those people? I have no idea. I haven't followed this, but the other sobering experience of the nineties down to now has been loss of a visionary articulation among American movements' spokespeople, in other words, the drift of American aggressive leadership, political leadership. I don't mean in the Democratic Party; I mean just the leaders of different organizations, of the think tanks and other places where the more Left side of programs and actions is being articulated. I was talking about this to my wife last night. Our local environmental activism, which in the seventies was very visionary, it wasn't just about protecting the turf of Santa Barbara from development; it was about a more global vision, most of [which] has been lost.

"People don't speak that language at all. They're much more technical. On the one hand, everything becomes a technical issue, and much more short-term focused in the battles that are waged. It's more like a resistance battle against encroachment by the Right than a visionary assertion, and that's very sobering. There are a variety of ways in which one could describe the Left as petering out, but they're not what [are] normally given us as the sources of it. In other words, I think there was a very strong left-wing current in the 1970s. It wasn't united, but it was strong [and more] locally based than in the sixties, and if you went around America and documented how communities of many different kinds changed since the sixties, in terms of who gained power and lost power. Let me illustrate this. In the early seventies, Santa Barbara was a right-wing bastion; Orange County, California, was a far-right-wing bastion; California was largely a right-wing bastion. If you fast-forward to now, the state legislature in California is controlled by liberal and Chicano leadership. The local government in many parts of the state is far to the Left of anything you could have imagined thirty years ago. It doesn't mean they have the ability to do anything programmatically. A lot of that has to do with the rise of the Chicano voting bloc, the rise of a new kind of labor politics in California that's aligned with the immigration wave. But many of the people who are leading all of this were sixties people.

"LA citywide now is more like, in certain ways, Santa Monica was trying to be in an earlier period. [It is] almost ridiculous for me to say these things because they're very difficult to institute, the agenda of reform, that the people who got elected to these have wanted to do. But that's not completely true. There are programs and policies instituted that were only on the horizon a couple of decades ago. There were several members of SDS who sat on the LA City Council for a number of years. They've been termed out. Some have moved on to the state legislature, not just Tom Hayden. It isn't [just people's experience with] SDS; it's the broader activist experience that people have. You know who John Wilhelm is? He's the head of the hotel union. It's the most dynamic organizing union in the AFL-CIO [American Federation of Labor–Congress of Industrial Organizations]. Well, John started in SDS in New Haven. He's slated to be the next president of the AFL-CIO."

The Winner in the Sixties

"I think it's more like a stalemate. You could say that nobody won the sixties. The right wing grew because of the sixties in large measure, as backlash, as resistance to feminism, to civil rights or racial equality. The complexity of the matter which Marxism can't encompass is that there is no single working class, no basis of working-class unity, at least in the U.S. There are racial-ethnic diversity and antagonisms, among other things, combined as that is with great occupational differentiation, great differences in life chances within the working class that are associated with race. How do you make that unity? I'm not saying it's never going to be possible, but it certainly hasn't been in these thirty years since. And so the model of the Left that unifies the working class and related groups [stresses] economic [and class issues], which is still what perplexes people. When they criticize the postsixties Left, they think, 'Oh, if only we would return to this universal model' that they imagine was in there; it was there before the sixties but never was there in the United States. We've never had that kind of Left in the United States. The Left has always been fed by race and ethnic identity types of energies as well as class."

Dilemmas of Managerial Liberalism
That Emerged from the Sixties

"The majority of American voters still support the Democratic Party, in name at least. It's the Democratic Party that cannot, given the complexity I'm talking about, figure out a way of sustaining a majority-based government nationally. I almost have to give my whole political sociology course; I can't even do it when I'm giving the course. I can't even make this clear because it's so complicated. In order to really accomplish the next step that would have to be accomplished, from a Left point of view, more power would have to be available than is available. You see what I'm saying?

"What the Left would want to propose economically has to do with a degree of control over corporate power, but the resources for that power aren't there. It isn't because we didn't do the right strategy since the sixties; it's because no one knows what strategy could actually countervail effectively. The power of multinational corporations for determining economic policy [is immense], and that's to a large extent why trying to restore the power of the Democratic Party in a progressive direction is so frustrating. No one really believes that if the Democrats could win control even of both houses of Congress and the presidency, what could be accomplished in that. If that happened, [what would the Democrats do] with respect to the problems of social justice, social equality, and so forth? I'm not saying nothing will be [accomplished]. The problem of our time which we didn't anticipate and I don't think anyone anticipated is the degree to which something we call corporate liberalism was dominant, and that was an alliance between state and corporation that would be in favor of domestic reform in order to maintain domestic legitimacy.

"There were all kinds of imaginations during the Johnson years of how we could have a domestic partnership between government and corporations to rebuild cities and how there'd be major investments in education. All of these things with the Left playing this kind of aggressive role that would keep this moving forward, but implicit in the New Left was this belief that the power elite is a responsible corporate political elite, by which I mean they wanted to run the society effectively. We were opposed to them, but we were opposed to them because it wasn't democratic, not because we didn't think they were trying to [improve society]. Kennedy and Johnson [epitomize] this kind of idea [in] that they had major reforms [on their agendas]. I don't think anyone anticipated the degree of irresponsibility of this government we're with now. This is a pure capitalist gang; it has no interest in the welfare of the system as a whole. I would rather talk about that than about the Left's inability to articulate appropriate strategies for the last thirty years. What's happened to elite responsibility in that time? Is that the fault of the Left or the sixties, or is there some other dynamic [involving the Right]?

"I have tried to understand why that seems more universal than that. Why does a Blair arrive at the same time as Clinton with the same neoliberal perspective and the same destructive attitude toward traditional left-wing vision and strategy and policy? Why is this happening [at the same time]? Remember in the seventies there was a tremendous amount of optimism about Euro-socialism, Euro-communism, new thinking of a left-wing nature."

TODD GITLIN

And the Winner Is . . . ?

"Small question. Okay, we're now leaving the minutiae of fact, and we're getting to the biggest political question of our time. My short answer is, for most of four decades, the Left won the culture and the Right won political power. What endured from the Left was the opening up of rights, civil rights, women's rights, gay rights, civil liberties.

"The Left upheld rights of the Enlightenment liberal project, and in their name implanted itself after the sixties; graduates of the Left implanted themselves in the institutions of culture, universities, the media, art museums, that sort of thing.

"The Right set out to take state power. The Left was ambivalent about power. This is something I've written about since. I summarize at one point with the slogan 'The Right won Washington, and the Left won the English Department.'

"If you look at the politics in terms of access to power, to national power, and obviously global power, this is something the Right set out to attain, and since Nixon, they've done it rather well—through 2008. The two Democratic presidents were white southerners; both of them had to act on the ground that had been staked out, actually less by Nixon, as it turned out, than Reagan. That was Reagan's achievement.

"The Right demonstrated that [it was] capable of winning national power, and the Left was marginal. What went on for decades was that the academic Left, at least, was satisfied with another objective, a sort of party favor or consolation prize. That's to put it dismissively, I know. But the Right essentially had the institutions of political power to itself after the sixties, while, until very recently, at least the critical mass of the graduates of the sixties have ensconced themselves in a niche that they can control or at least substantially contest as a sort of compensation for what they don't have in the realm of political power."

TOM HAYDEN

Why Has the Postsixties American Left Stalled?

"Social security would be even stronger, if all the money was placed in the stock market so that people would have even better health care and government programs. And [the Right has] a hard time with their agenda, but they know that one thing works, which is, in a country that is relatively middle-class like this one, people are afraid of too much, too fast. They're afraid of radical change, so they play on this fear of radical change, and also they need to discredit radical heroes. The best way is to have them simply disappear through engineered amnesia in the school systems. You know, who, after all, really remembers Tom Hayden? But they also need to have some lightning rods to refute them.

"I think there's more than political manipulation by Republicans there. You have to look at the whole picture, the effective achievement of disenfranchisement by discouraging more people from voting as opposed to officially banning them from voting, which was the original program. You've got a chronically depressed lower-income population. Secondly, the middle class has been effectively divided from the poor because middle-class people have material reasons not to want to send their kids to inner-city schools, however integrated, not to want to send their parents to public hospitals, however meritorious the idea may be on paper. So you've got these factors, more than Republican manipulation, I think, moving the Democratic Party away from its populist base towards a sort of confused middle class that seeks to be as wealthy as possible in their lives, and they want the best entitlements possible, even if they're privatized. And then you have also, within the process, the connections between Wall Street and municipal finance, being that the Democrats' criticism of Wall Street is not only threatening to campaign contributions, but threatening to how city finance is structured. And that has to do with areas that are under Democratic mayors and governed by Democratic Party officials for a very long time. So there're a lot of reasons that the party shifted to the Right.

"Reagan winning has to be included in the mix, absolutely. The Republicans finding new ways to spin their old remedies and call them new ideas, absolutely; the Republican development of wedge issues, absolutely; the Republican funding of think tanks, absolutely. But those are all the tactical creations of the Republican Right, but there're always underlying forces that are virtually bigger than all of us. So there was a time when to win as a Democrat, you had to move to the Right, or get out of the party, or pursue single-issue movements and not have so much investment in the electoral process. It may be turning around now. It's my thesis that the underlying forces now point towards the progressive populist majority.

"The Democratic Party, *New York Times*, the funded class—they missed, for instance, a couple of things that are worth mentioning. They missed the emergence of the biggest antiwar movement in anyone's memory, and I mean, missed it literally and haven't really recovered. That demonstration of one hundred thousand people in October of 2002 was missed by both the *New York Times* and the NPR [National Public Radio]. They both reported that it was a failure because of a very low turnout, and then they had to apologize a week later for having been off by a hundred thousand or so. And one wonders, they never gave an explanation; one wonders how a journalist, of all people, could miss the size of a demonstration. The second thing is they missed Seattle [in 1999].

"They didn't see it coming. Then it became 'Well, that's an isolated event.' But far from isolated, it undermined the momentum of NAFTA [North American Free Trade Agreement], CAFTA [United States–Dominican Republic–Central America Free Trade Agreement], WTO [World Trade Organization], and all of those trade agreements. So you're talking about the global capitalist economy and the war in Iraq. You're talking about the big issues here that have been missed. And I think that the movement, attributed to turbulence in the Democratic primaries, that gave momentum to Dean (Dean had to be eliminated for an establishment candidate), the turbulence is still there. Kerry may be too timid to exploit the turbulence. We'll see."

MARK RUDD

Is There Continuity Between Right-Wing Hegemony in the Sixties and Today?

"I don't know about direct line, but the current repressive policies are kind of a counterattack after about thirty years in which the police and security system has been under attack. In other words, I see it now as a reaction.

"You say there was a straight line between the sixties and now, and I'm kind of saying, 'Not exactly,' because I don't know how you define a straight line, but there was a period in which the security system was on the defensive. For example, there was a law that you couldn't go abroad to assassinate people. Now there's a reaction to that.

"I think that for me that would be the difference; the Right is better organized. I think, in terms of numbers, the numbers are maybe equal. The people who came out of the sixties here [have] a basically liberal or progressive orientation, but the organization is horrendous.

"I'll give you an example. In Albuquerque, New Mexico, if Amy Goodman comes to town—Amy Goodman has a radio show at Pacifica. It's broadcast on about one hundred stations around the country. It's called *Democracy Now*. You should take a look at it on the Web, www.democracynow.org. It's our main source of news. It's not NPR; it's more independent than NPR. When she comes to town, or when Noam Chomsky comes to town, they have to find the biggest auditorium in town, and still people can't—all the people who want to hear him—can't get in.

"In Albuquerque, [Chomsky] fills a twenty-six-hundred-seat auditorium, or in Santa Fe. And it has to be broadcast on the radio. If you could organize those five thousand or so people who listen, or maybe there's more than five thousand, it is really closer to twenty thousand—if they could be organized into some political entity—we could elect a school board. We could do anything. There are all kinds of [Leftists] still stirring.

"I think your generalization about the Right is correct, and the reason why they are so large and effective is organization, the ability to work together to get stuff done. It seems to me that the Left's biggest single problem is lack of organization or lack of ability to work together to get stuff done, to get people elected, primarily."

ROXANNE DUNBAR-ORTIZ

Evaluating Gitlin's Thesis

"I think politics versus culture is a false dichotomy. In that sense I agree with Gramsci. I think Gitlin is right, but don't think it's such a small thing, the cultural impact made by the sixties movements. That's the problem when your main thought is taking state power, especially a state like (although it's unique) the United States. The structure of the political system (Electoral College, winner-take-all, money buys power, etc.) makes it impossible for a revolutionary movement (even if we had one) to take power politically, and certainly not by force of arms (although organizing in the military is not impossible, and it is conceivable that the U.S. state could be toppled, but not likely or desirable, I think)."

Were the Sixties a Decade of Death?

"The sixties as a decade of death. I actually thought that at the time. It seemed to me that all the ecstatic dancing was a dance of death while we watched on television as the bombs wiped out villages, the blood streaming from the survivors, or their bodies seared by napalm. But by then I had become quite entangled with Mexico (I was married to a Mexican national) and thought that was good for consciousness in the U.S. to feel the effects of death. But there was the other side of it, as there is in Mexico, the pure joy of life, somehow in facing death being freed from fear of it. I loved the feeling of fearlessness I gained, and I still nourish it. When it wanes, I begin to feel imprisoned, suffocated.

"State repression had always been experienced by poor blacks, by the undocumented, by workers striking and organizing, by the imprisoned (all poor). But with the civil rights movement, middle-class white students and others got involved and experienced the brunt of state repression. I think the killing of the four young whites at Kent State brought the student movement to an abrupt halt, scared off any new recruits or really radical movements on campuses up to today. It doesn't take much repression in the U.S. to scare people. In other places it takes massive killing and regular torture, but not here. We need to get tougher: If we try to overthrow the state, the state is going to try to destroy us. States exist to be repressive, not always bad. Supposedly, they are organizing society for its own good, but the state also has its own interests and is guided by those who hold the reins of power. It's not that we should not expose and fight state repression. We must do so, but we need to put it in perspective and stop being so shocked, shocked that such a thing could happen as to harass John Lennon or MLK or me."

CASEY HAYDEN

Continuity in Right-Wing Repression Between Then and Now

"When I was in college, the House Un-American Activities Committee [HUAC] was my first taste of civil liberties abridgements, investigation of citizens' associations and thoughts. Many SDS members cut their teeth on the anti-HUAC campaign, long before SDS. Civil liberties and academic freedom were requisites for any political organizing; that was the first thing we had to learn. Laws now which investigate citizens for what they think or might do, which give the government the right to eavesdrop on them, and which condone torture are killers for real and intelligent political critiques of the government. Actually, we have the legal system now of a fascist government, although it is not being used to round us all up. The legal system is in place, however. And yes, I think this is all in a straight line, HUAC, COINTELPRO, Homeland Security.

"I think it's a good thing that at least in the universities, the memory of our work in the movement remains alive. We have to remember that these oppressive, quiescent times in between political uprisings are important times. In the fifties, many remnants of radical thirties organizations remained, and the people in them, in addition to laying the groundwork for the sixties, provided us with an orientation and with information, organizing know-how, and historical continuity. Liberal student religious organizations and publications were important and Left publications. I hope such are quietly at work now."

The Gitlin Thesis Reconsidered

"Todd's framing all this in terms of winning and losing is a bit tricky. It's not like there is ever a stable win. It's a dynamic. One thing leads to another, so you win one and then they win one, and then you win one and so on. For example, we ended segregation in the public schools, so the moneyed classes simply abandoned the public schools and created a private school system, a private-sector model which is spreading everywhere. So we don't want to dwell there in win-lose land too much. It is useful to decide what matters to one and go for it in whatever way one can, for the sake of the quality it gives to one's life. I was shocked when segregation fell, when the women's movement achieved at least a civic conversation on gender equality. I never thought initially that we'd be successful in those areas, and had I premised my participation on winning, I'd never have gotten into any of it. I did it because I loved living an authentic life. We all want to be happy. That is the great motivating factor in all of life, social change included."

In the next chapter, I address the origin of sixties social movements in the civil rights movement, particularly the Student Non-Violent Coordinating Committee (SNCC), which provided a template for

SDS. Necessarily, I address the transition from civil rights to Black Power after Selma in 1965. I also notice that early SDS and early SNCC shared a common commitment to consensus and an aversion to top-down leadership. Finally, I argue that Martin Luther King and other black leaders were committed not to a narrow legal conception of civil rights but to a broader poor people's movement that would have united black and white in the effort to reform capitalism, not only to redress racism.

ဢ Seven ଓ

Black Before White:
From Civil Rights to
Black and Brown Power
and the Women's Movement

Our objective is complete freedom, justice and equality by any means necessary.
                                                    —Malcolm X

Before you begin reading further in this chapter, go to YouTube on your computer and play one of the great songs of the era, "Sympathy for the Devil." Let it play over and over again. This will set the appropriate mood. Then listen to the YouTube rendition of U2's "Pride (in the name of love)." The Rolling Stones astutely recognize that the Kennedys were killed, at least metaphorically, by all of us. They issued the song in 1968, which witnessed the assassinations of Bobby Kennedy and Martin Luther King and the police riot at the Chicago Democratic National Convention. I presume the Stones are saying that the mean streets of America swallowed up heroes. I was thrown out of my high school English class when, in an open discussion about Bobby Kennedy's assassination, I speculated that America was sick and that Kennedy's assassination was not an idiosyncrasy. I was sent to the principal's office, affording me an insight into adult authoritarianism; after all, it was an open discussion.

Sixteen years after the Stones recorded their bitter indictment of America, U2, the Irish band admired by Tom Hayden in later years, recorded a paean to Martin Luther King, a doleful lament about what might have been. The thesis of this chapter is that, although the white Weather Left mouthed Marxist-Leninist lyrics, as it were, the civil rights movement, in the transition from civil rights to Black Power via the Christian democratic socialism of King, became the real socialists, blending black nationalism, stretching back to Marcus Garvey, and King's grounding in the writings of Karl Marx. Add to this mix Cleveland Sellers's and Jim Forman's socialist radicalism and the socialist feminism of Frances Beal, all of whom accelerated the move from the civil rights era to the subsequent era of Black Power.

SETTING THE STAGE: KILLING FIELDS OF THE BLACK BELT

> *They killed one nigger, one Jew and a white man—I gave them all what I thought they deserved.*
> —Judge William Cox on the light sentences he meted out to the killers of three young civil rights workers

In this narrative, the sixties are embedded in the rich red soil of the black belt of Mississippi. I have discussed the early civil rights movement, which had its roots in the forties when Jackie Robinson crossed baseball's color line and then in the fifties when Rosa Parks led the Montgomery, Alabama, bus boycott and other bus boycotts broke out in places such as Baton Rouge, Louisiana. The Little Rock school desegregation only increased the civil rights movement's momentum, even before the sixties began. The Student Non-Violent Coordinating Committee (SNCC) emerged from the 1960 lunch counter desegregation efforts early in that year, with Ella Baker spearheading this courageous movement of young blacks and then whites who refused Jim Crow segregation and insisted on their rights to occupy public spaces, rights they traced to the Constitution and other human rights manifestos.

The sixties were black before they were white, and they ended being black, albeit in death—King's death and the numerous lynchings, shootings, and burnings that defined daily life for civil rights workers, not to mention the razing of black ghettoes in American race riots toward the end of the decade. The white sixties overshadow the black sixties because the largely white media missed much of the early civil rights movement, overreacted to Black Power as civil rights gone bad, and focused on the effort of white kids to stop the Vietnam War in order not to die alongside black troops "in country." Suppressed rhetorically is the racially inflected term "in country," which is short for "Indian country," the name given by American troops to the dangerous and alien jungles of murderous Vietnam.

I struggle, as other historians do, over whether the black movements were successful or Pyrrhic—or perhaps both. A prominent black woman musician and civil rights worker refused to be interviewed for this book because she objected to my portrayal of the sixties, especially the black sixties, as a decade of death. She said that this narrative mutes the importance of civil rights–era gains, such as the various civil rights legislation passed during 1964 and 1965 that reinforced voting rights and various ideals of equal opportunity. Surely, these Johnson-era pieces of legislation would not have been achieved without the Greensboro lunch counter sit-in, the bus boycotts, and Little Rock. But to register these achievements does not deny that King's, Forman's, Sellers's, and Stokely Carmichael's dreams of a classless America in which blacks did not experience internal colonialism bit the dust as King was killed and the military/police apparatus killed off SNCC and the Black Panthers.

Whereas the white student movement began with a general critique of American society contained in the Port Huron Statement and, as the decade wore on, narrowed into a critique of the Vietnam War, the black movement began with civil rights and ended with Black Power and its implied or explicit socialism. This socialism drew on King's reading of Marx, perhaps even of early Marx, and connected class and gender to race, anticipating later themes of multiculturalism beginning in the 1980s. The young black and white civil rights workers who confronted the murderous opposition of the Klan and the police during the early years of the civil rights movement were radicalized, much as the peaceful Students for a Democratic Society (SDS), especially after the hellish year 1968, abandoned civil disobedience for armed insurrection.

The difference is that the Black Power advocates, even the Panthers, did not embrace a "red army," a people's army, as the solution to hegemonic capitalism in the "mother country." The Panthers' arming themselves was purely a defensive maneuver intended to thwart the lynch-mob mentality that had resulted in the deaths of three young civil rights workers, Andrew Goodman, Michael Schwerner, and James Chaney, outside of Philadelphia, Mississippi, in 1964 and other deaths later. The Panthers were Marxists, not Marxist-Leninists, much as King was subtly a socialist, not a social democrat. The difference between the Panthers' Marxist critique, which blended class with race (if not yet gender), and Weather's Marxism-Leninism is that the former did not view itself as a "vanguard party" in the style of the Bolsheviks. Indeed, the

Panthers viewed Weatherman as "Custeristic," in the words of Fred Hampton—essentially on a suicide mission.

Seen in this light, the end of the civil rights/Black Power movement, a product of its legislative successes and organized white terrorism highly threatened by those very successes, extinguished the dream of a humane socialism borne of King's Christian idealism and SNCC's increasingly sophisticated analysis, which linked class and race. Although the spiraling downward of Port Huron's equally sophisticated analysis and tremendous youthful vigor into Weather's masochistic Maoism played on a more visible stage—more visible to the white media—the demise of the black movement had more enduring consequences for the American Left. The missing link in this is King, whose death occurred on the brink of his efforts to broaden civil rights/Black Power into a poor people's movement, into class struggle by another name. Scholarship (e.g., Jackson 2007) on the emergence of civil rights into Black Power makes it clear that King was always sympathetic to Black Power, developing not only working relationships but also friendships with the likes of Carmichael. King struck a delicate balance between protecting his position in the more conservative and incrementalist Southern Christian Leadership Conference (SCLC) and also working with SNCC to achieve a powerful coalition that emerged at a time when the national white media were, through television, bringing the race war home to liberals in the North, especially to the Kennedys and Johnson.

King's death was tragic not only because a fearless leader was lost but also because the black movement, through King and SNCC, was on the verge of a major theoretical breakthrough—a racially inflected critique of capitalism that once and for all would have moved the American Left beyond its original moorings in a color-blind and gender-blind liberalism. Much as I am convinced that the early Port Huron leaders of SDS, especially Hayden, were influenced by the early Marx, at least via C. Wright Mills, so King's formation as a student of Marx and Carmichael/Forman/Sellers's reformulation of civil rights as Black Power was a crucial moment in the broadening of racial politics into a broad-based interracial radicalism. This is easy to miss precisely because the rhetoric of Black Power seemed to narrow civil rights into separatism, read in the expulsion from the organization of die-hard white SNCC activists such as Bob Zellner in the name of black pride.

No matter how militant the Panthers were toward decade's end, brandishing shotguns and marching in paramilitary paraphernalia, they were pacifists compared with early Weathermen who blew themselves up trying to make antipersonnel bombs for use on domestic military personnel. I conducted one of the most interesting interviews for this book with a former Black Panther leader from Eugene. Tommy Anderson (now Jaja Nkrumah) reflects on the blind spots of the Panthers, acknowledging their untutored bravado and brashness. He comments on the role my father played in counseling the local Panthers and black militants, reminding them that they were outmanned and outgunned by the martial state. He remembers my father fondly for his refusal to mince words in giving honest advice to the Panthers, whose project of black pride and militancy he certainly supported. No groupie, my Dad worked with the youngsters who grew up in hardscrabble Compton, California, and who came to white Eugene in search of a college education. The Panthers listened, whereas the Weathermen were not accessible, lost in the mania of true belief.

In evaluating Black Power and even the Panthers positively, by comparison to the self-defeating Debrayism of Weatherman, I risk the same idolatry of blackness that bedeviled the Weather kids, who were distraught about their "white-skin privilege." The Weather kids tried to outmacho the Panthers in order to win their approval, a dynamic played out in Chicago during 1968 and 1969 as Weather held discussions with the Panthers and tried to forge an alliance with them. This is not to deny that there was a great deal of macho posturing by the Panthers and other black radicals. Sometimes it seems that the only sane and balanced people during the sixties were the women—SDS women such as Casey Hayden and SNCC women such as Fran Beal. A persistent undercurrent beneath racial and peace politics was gender politics, which, as Hayden and Beal tell it, emerged from Left women's dissatisfaction with their macho boyfriends. (See Box 7.1.)

─────── ℘ **Box 7.1   The 1961 New Year's Eve Party** ◌ଞ ───────

A story is told about how some SDS women in Ann Arbor, Michigan, on New Year's Eve, wanted to party with their boyfriends, who were involved in a lengthy and tedious discussion about theoretical details. I have heard different versions of that party, including from two people who were present: Casey Hayden and Mickey Flacks. The party was held on New Year's Eve 1961, at Tom and Casey Hayden's house, which doubled as Ann Arbor SDS headquarters. Mickey Flacks remembers that the women were in the living room setting up food and drink, while the men caucused downstairs. Eventually, the women protested that the men were not upstairs helping out; they were segregated, perhaps offering a paradigm of subsequent gender politics. According to another version, Casey tried to drag Tom, her then-husband, away from the fray and get him to get the guys to socialize on this symbolic eve. According to that account of events, he got mad and insisted that the male discussion was more important than a celebration of the new year.

Was the main issue that women were serving the potato chips while men theorized? Or that men did not value relationships? That their theory ignored the personal and interpersonal? These were, after all, not just SDS girlfriends or wives: They were the future leaders of the women's movement. My hunch is that the women's movement gathered significant momentum on that eve, as Casey, Mickey, and others were radicalized in the context of their own everyday lives. History—with a capital H—is made up of the minute moments in which tipping points are reached and centers do not hold. In the interviews to follow, the participants tell their own stories.

At stake is memory of distant but meaningful events. We inevitably bend history to suit our purposes, not deliberately, but from the vantage of who we have become in the meantime. There was no "New Year's Eve party" apart from people's accounts and memories of it. That risks a postmodern relativism; the party actually occurred. But the meanings of the party are multiple and depend on people's subject positions—the selves they have become. That is what makes a single "history of the sixties" so difficult—indeed impossible—to write.

Also at stake is the status of personal relationships, which were an important issue for SNCC in the South and early SDS in the North. Subsequent feminists termed this "the politics of the personal." People at the party and participants in the larger movement had, and have, different perspectives on the dynamics of gender and race, and on North and South, that flow from their memories and interpretations of such events. I discussed these issues with Mickey Flacks, Wesley Hogan, and Casey Hayden. I believe that, even though there are disagreements among them, we are able to arrive at a complex, nonlinear truth about how personal relationships were the foundation of the early antiwar and civil rights movements. Both SNCC and SDS were trying to change the world, but only via the small gestures in everyday life that tie people together. What happened on that distant New Year's Eve shows the importance of relationships and of memories. It also demonstrates the power of the dialectic, about which I have written earlier.

Wesley Hogan (2007), the author of *Many Minds, One Heart: SNCC's Dream of a New America*, offers a nuanced interpretation:

> My interpretation [is] that these dynamics (which happened repeatedly over the fall, not just at New Year) were a reflection of Casey's clarity versus the insecurity and lack of clarity on the part of Tom, Dick Flacks, Bob Ross, etc.—those men who were very analytically sophisticated but simply hadn't engaged in action, the way Casey had in the South. Casey had learned in the civil rights movement that you needed to build and maintain strong relationships in order to act politically; Tom et al. thought you needed the "correct political analysis" to act. So women in the northern movement were more astute about this because of their gendered acculturation, but many black and white men in the southern movement had learned it as well, through their own experiences. So in your paragraph, I don't think it was just about trying to pull the guys away to socialize, it represented a different understanding of how political change happens, and a more experientially grounded understanding of the importance of cohesion, camaraderie, and play to that political action. Mickey Flacks, however, did see in this exchange the early feminist movement, early consciousness raising of the fact that "the personal is political." (Personal correspondence)

I respond that Tom Hayden spent time in McComb, Mississippi, in 1961 getting beaten up for his troubles. Hogan clarifies Casey's views this way:

You're right that Tom Hayden (and Al Haber) did go South, and did get involved in some direct action. But compared to those in SNCC, their experience was very minimal in 61–62. It did not produce the same insights that living and working in the South did, over months or years. Tom Hayden had those kinds of experiences four years later, when he worked on ERAP [Economic and Research Action Project] in Newark. But that was '65–'68, much later than Casey. I'd like you to clear up my comment on experiential knowledge versus analytical sophistication to reflect this: it wasn't that Casey, Bob Moses, Martha Norman and other people were necessarily smarter than the northerners in 1961–62, it was that their experiences in the south had forced them to understand national politics (and personal politics, inside-the-movement politics) in a much more nuanced, sophisticated way. In many instances, they felt like their lives (and the lives of their peers) depended on it. Not so for Hayden, Flacks, et al. until later. (Personal correspondence)

Casey Hayden extends the dialogue, addressing the complex relationship between North and South, white and black, the political and the personal and interpersonal:

I'd just come from the South, influenced by SNCC, and SNCC folks loved to party. The bonds of close social engagement were important in the Southern black community generally, but especially so among the young activists there. I think to some extent it reflected a more relaxed attitude toward their own role, decision making, and choice of tactics. SNCC was clearly the cutting edge of social change, so right action in SNCC was, finally, whatever SNCC decided to do. The personal interactions created the bonds of support, identity, and physical safety that to a large extent made the actions possible.

Northern white left intellectuals were almost all male, and the women who were involved tended to be quieter and more reticent than women in SNCC. The guys tended to be a bit more uptight generally, in my experience, than the SNCC folk, and more unclear about their political roles. With good reason, as to all intents and purposes they were the ruling class/gender/race, so they had to find a way to break through that both in their social analysis and in their own actions. Hence the deliberations on right action were subjectively as well as objectively called for, they were very invested in the intellectual discernment that was the heart of their deliberations together. Finding the way to break out when one is inside the belly of the beast demands intellectual (that is, objective) and emotional rigor. So the dedication to that meeting that night, and the sense that a party was too light hearted for the demands of the political situation, had its roots, I think, in both the exterior and interior aspects of the new left cultural style, i.e., both the actual and the felt need for critical analysis. (Personal correspondence)

Mickey Flacks worries about the North/South distinction because her own husband, Dick Flacks, a red-diaper baby whose parents were fired from their northern teaching jobs for having radical political views, certainly lived a radical personal politics. She also notes that personal relationships mattered greatly to northern movement people, and she offers an example of how she and Dick would attend Saturday afternoon University of Michigan football games, sometimes provoking astonishment from movement people who perhaps did not share their view of the importance of keeping life normal and building relationships within it. Mickey notes that she and Dick have been married for fifty years and are still active in radical politics.

Had the guys at the Haydens' house in 1961/1962 helped out in setting up the party, leaving aside their doctrinal debate for the time being, the dialectic might have been delayed. Taken-for-granted gender roles, even among these progressive Michigan intellectuals and activists, forced the issue: The party that distant New Year's Eve radicalized Casey and Mickey and even some of the guys. Not only did the celebrants ring in the new year; they also gave birth to the women's movement, which emerged dialectically—again, that term—from the male-dominated movement in which the guys did the talking and the women set up the parties.

———————————————————— ✄ ————————————————————

One of the things I learned in researching this book was that Casey Hayden was one of the most important neglected figures in official (male!) accounts of the decade. The party I just described took place at her and Tom's house in Ann Arbor. She and Mary King wrote an early feminist manifesto critiquing not SDS but SNCC for its embedded male chauvinism. I corresponded with Casey about this, and I discussed this with Cleveland Sellers and Fran Beal. As with anything that happened a million years ago— and the sixties are so distant because our times are so different and yet so similar, as I am arguing—memories fade and distort. They cannot be trusted fully. Yet it is clear to me that the women of SDS and SNCC were extremely important in doing much of the dirty work involved in social movement formation and in sheer

Tom Hayden and Casey Hayden at the former SNCC freedom house, Mississippi, 1987. (Photo courtesy of Tom Hayden and Unita Blackwell, photographer)

everyday living, and they were also important in unofficial and often unacknowledged leadership roles, out of which emerged the feminist movement. Both Hayden and Beal notice that gender, although connected to race and class, is somewhat independent of them. In other words, women on and of the Left were still sometimes treated as subordinates by the very men who dedicated their lives to ending subordination, an irony not lost on the mid-1960s feminists who began a movement that changed the world.

Class, race, gender, and peace politics were clustered together, twisted into strands that overlapped and formed a tapestry of difference within unity. Here is the way I tell the story: The civil rights movement provided a model, especially in the work of Ella Baker and Bob Moses, for the white New Left, which at Port Huron conceived a whole new world based on participatory democracy and economic leveling. In this sense, race preceded class. And yet the civil rights movement and the white New Left were blind to their own gender politics and inadvertently gave rise to feminism, which doubled back and enriched racial and class politics with what sixties feminists famously called "the personal." Casey was complaining on that distant New Year's Eve that the guys needed to be in touch with their personal sides, their everyday humanity, which played out in their relations with their women sisters and lovers as well as in their relations to their own bodies, their children, nature, even animals.

Admitting that the personal is political does not reduce politics to small gestures. This is something that the early civil rights workers and early SDS knew as they went door to door in recognizing that the street corner is a microcosm of the bigger polity and social structure. There is also a politics of large gestures. The mass marches are necessary, too, as is the use of national and international media. Compared with established political systems and structures, the male New Leftists, both black and white, were already oriented to everyday life, just not in a way that made gender exclusion thematic. We cannot really blame guys who had been raised during the forties and fifties in nuclear families in which the mother traditionally did not work outside the home, obeyed her husband, and refrained from engaging in politics. These are just the ways in which people were taught to live, the New Leftist no less than traditional men who went off to work and to war.

Writing this book has convinced me that even to talk about gender, race, and class as if these were separable entities is a mistake, especially as we tell the stories of real men and women, of many colors, who tried to make a new world both in the public world and in their own miniature worlds. SDS, before it spearheaded the antiwar movement, went into northern cities to work with black and poor people, both women and men, in helping them help themselves to crack open the political process and improve their own lives. The white New Left used Bob Moses's architecture of voter registration and freedom schools as its model, whites learning from blacks how to teach other blacks about what we now call "empowerment." And in doing this work, both white and black men tended not to notice that they were giving many of the speeches while the women ran the mimeograph machines and did the cooking, dialectically producing the women's movement as a negation/continuation of the SNCC/SDS movements to improve the world by reformulating everyday life—except for the roles of women.

This chapter, then, includes the voices of women as well as men, of women both white and black, as they remember their closeness to and distance from the male movement. At the time, people were not thinking about such issues in large conceptual ways, but they were getting up in the morning in Mississippi or Newark and figuring out how to get breakfast and then to formulate an organizing plan for the day. Only during quiet time, and through the clarity of hindsight, did some of them, usually women, figure out that New Left ideals did not always carry forward into the intimate lives of its members, which may be to acknowledge only that people are complexly contradictory and have blind spots.

We cannot leave out minorities who were not black. In this chapter, we hear the voice of José Angel Gutiérrez (1998), a pivotal leader in the Chicano movement who confronted all of the issues discussed here. Militant Chicanos like José had in common with many black leaders and activists an underprivileged economic background, which certainly contrasts with the comfortable upbringing of many of the white New Left leaders. The story José tells reproduces the anger and activism of members and leaders of the black movement and even of segments of the white movement. For this reason, I resist the tendency, afoot since the 1980s and the rise of multiculturalism, to assume that each racial and ethnic group's "story" is irreducibly unique and cannot be translated into the stories of other groups. This seems to privilege a biological concept of racial identity in much the way that the Weathermen despised themselves because they were not black and could never be. In my other writings (Agger 1993, 2002), I have argued for a perspective on the social construction of racial identity that "allows" black people to be white (think of well-educated and affluent black people who straighten their hair and send their children to Jack and Jill, an acculturating/integrating organization) and white people to be black, depending on their experiences and perspectives.

As my interviews demonstrated earlier, Hayden (2001) makes much the same argument when he claims his Irishness and indeed views Irishness as a type of blackness or darkness, an Othering by white Protestant culture. Anyone under threat can be a victim, as the multiracial deaths during the civil rights era perfectly demonstrate. Anyone can be lynched or murdered. SNCC wrestled hard with its decision, as the civil rights era flowed into Black Power, to expel whites such as Bob Zellner from its organization. In retrospect, this was a bad move and obstructed the multiracial poor people's movement that King came to advocate. But in the moment—by 1965 at the latest—life for blacks in the South and increasingly in the North had become so murderous that blacks needed to develop a collective pride that would lead them to mobilize in self-defense. No offense was intended to whites who were left on the sidelines. Indeed, I have read speculation that Stokely Carmichael gave Tom Hayden the idea for the Economic Research and Action Project (ERAP)—whites organizing poor whites and blacks in northern inner cities, modeled on SNCC activities in the South—anticipating that the black movement would increasingly work parallel to white radicalism. No hard feelings; this was a necessary division of labor, or so it was thought at the time.

Hayden denies that the idea of ERAP came from any SNCC person. He says that ERAP "certainly flowed out of events such as [ongoing] community organizing in the South." He also indicates that Michael Harrington's (1962) book *The Other America: Poverty in the United States* inspired ERAP because it put urban poverty on the agenda. He suggests that the Johnson administration's War on Poverty, spearheaded by Sargent Shriver and crystallizing in the 1964 Economic Opportunity Act, played a role in inspiring ERAP. The Economic Opportunity Act provided the means for what some called a "domestic peace corps." The so-called War on Poverty was also influenced by Harrington's book. Finally, Hayden indicates that the initial ERAP initiative was funded by the United Auto Workers. It is clear that the focus on American poverty, spurred by Harrington, took both mainstream (War on Poverty) and radical (ERAP) forms, demonstrating that the domestic policies of the Kennedy/Johnson years were not that far afield from the concerns of SDS and even SNCC. SDS abandoned ERAP as SDS became focused on stopping the Vietnam War, one of Lyndon Johnson's other enthusiasms.

The story I tell is not a brief for integration as a strategy; by now, blacks and whites have been resegregated into an economic Jim Crow, with whites enjoying the fruits of socioeconomic skin privilege and blacks swelling the ranks of the permanently unemployed.

The radical who refused to be interviewed because I emphasize death and defeat over life and victory certainly has a point that the civil rights era ended with real legislative successes that still endure. However, for the most part both civil rights and Black Power failed to achieve economic leveling, which was not for want of trying. Carmichael, Floyd McKissick, Forman, and Sellers had an acute analysis of the class bases of racism and of the racial bases of class inequality. With King's death, however, coupled with the rampage of the Rightist counter-revolution in the South and North, the black movement came to an end, only to be reinvented culturally with rap and hip-hop, which barely dent the dominant system of race and class.

What happened during the sixties was that people began to realize that the Bob Zellners and Bob Aggers, both supporters of Black Power and pride, were actually black on the inside—not just fellow travelers, but brothers. This is why those who turned SNCC in a radical direction as the death toll climbed and Gandhian resistance seemed futile and even suicidal do not defend black nationalism as a panacea; they simply observe, as they did then, that America was hopeless and that they might as well turn to Africa for "Afrocentric" inspiration and succor.

Singer Harry Belafonte sponsored a SNCC trip to Africa in 1964, which began a real turning away from civil rights and toward Black Power and black nationalism. During the trip people such as Bob Moses met Sékou Touré, the impressive black leader, and were inspired by pan-Africanist pride. They also crossed paths with Malcolm X, who was touring Africa himself. Malcolm was already convinced that the future of the race lay in Africa, not in America. Thus was contemporary Black Power born, a seed that was fertilized by the bloody politics of the South and North as the white power and police structures fought fiercely to turn away King's army of peaceful protesters. Black nationalism had an earlier provenance in Marcus Garvey's pan-Africanism.

The joining of the leaders of SNCC, the Congress of Racial Equality (CORE), and SCLC in 1965 to march from Selma to Montgomery, Alabama, in protest of the brutality of the Selma police, the state police, and the Klan marked a turning away from civil rights and toward Black Power. We know now that King supported this move privately, convinced, as were Carmichael and McKissick, that power comes out of the barrel of a gun—a gun aimed by a black person in self-defense. This was not pure theory: Black residents in Alabama rural areas such as Lowndes County were already arming themselves against the Klan nightriders. The Black Panthers were conceived in Lowndes County as Carmichael led

Floyd McKissick and Stokely Carmichael marching from Selma to Montgomery, Alabama, March 21–25, 1965. (Photo by Vernon Merritt III/Time & Life Pictures/Getty Images)

local activists and residents to form a distinctive political party be-holden neither to Democrats nor Republicans. The party was orig-inally called the Lowndes County Freedom Organization. Its sym-bol was a black panther. Later, Huey Newton and Bobby Seale, among others, founded the Black Panther Party for Self-Defense, borrowing both the idea of armed self-defense and the black panther logo from the rural Lowndes County organizers.

Seen this way, black self-defense, which was essentialized by the white Weatherpeople as the epitome of committed manly revolutionaries, was a dialectical negation of the bloody rampage of the police and the Klan against the civil rights movement. After all, why would the Dixiecratic establishment give up political and economic power without a fight? And fights have a tendency to reproduce themselves when victims arm themselves and do not go quietly. One could read Weatherman, in this light, as an outcome of an outcome—the extrapolation of black self-defense triggered by state-sanctioned killing of white and black civil rights workers. Of course, Weatherpeople took this a serious step further. They decided that self-defense could lead to the formation of a white revolutionary fighting force, as they called it. Self-defense in Lowndes would somehow lead, through the crazy circuitry that we call history, to the streets of Chicago in October 1969 as football-helmeted Weathermen busted windows and heads in their imitation of Chinese and Cuban revolutionaries. They thought that this would expiate their white guilt about not being black, perhaps even earning them honorary membership as Panthers.

Weather's militancy was not sheer idolatry or imitation. Violence was in the air, and it was started by the martial forces of the right-wing state. The state-sanctioned killing of the three civil rights workers outside of Philadelphia, Mississippi, and the killings in and around Selma (and many other places), all of which precipitated black armed self-defense, had their equivalent in the murder of Fred Hampton in Chicago. SDS dissolved and went underground. This was not a result of reading done by Mark Rudd and Bernardine Dohrn; it was a pragmatic reaction to the police decision to raise the ante and to murder Panthers without provocation.

Let us follow the story closely: Murderous behavior in the South galvanized Lowndes's blacks to form a party that bore the name and image of a black panther. National Panther leaders transported the idea and icon to California. Panther chapters sprang up everywhere, including Chicago. Hampton was charismatic and dangerous. Southern murder begat northern murder as police violence provoked black self-defense and political mobilization, which provoked more murderous repression. This dialectic was not from the pages of a book, say by Marx, but was enacted in the streets of America and in its hinterlands as blood soaked the streets and the earth. Even more than the violence done in Vietnam and to American soldiers there, many of whom were black, race aroused incredible passions and pathologies. At stake were slavery, economic bondage, political disfranchisement, and a psychosexual demonology that led white men to protect white women. During the SNCC Summer Project in 1964, Moses cautioned the black and white civil rights workers not to have sexual relations lest they arouse the sleeping beast of racial savagery, a beast that was already aroused by the mere sight and sound of uppity voter registrants.

Most scholars of the sixties observe that local and national police apparatuses dealt with the Panthers even more harshly than with Weatherman, even though the Panthers were not trying to form a people's army and seize state power. As soon as the police and state saw the image of the panther, a dangerously unbridled beast of prey, and then the paramilitary posture of the Oakland Panthers, armed and dangerous, they took aim. The nerdy college-age civil rights workers from the North were child's play compared with Hampton, Seale, Eldridge Cleaver, and their armed brothers. The martial state recognized that these firebrands were more dangerous to them than were white liberals, as we/they were called at the time, who worked the system, believing that compromise is necessarily more virtuous than the zero-sum game of us against them. The Panthers were playing to win, even if "winning" simply meant protecting black people from lynching and police murder.

Death rained down on black movement leaders and activists because race was a more explosive issue than war during the sixties, and arguably still today. As the Panthers, Malcolm, and other theorists of race insisted, America was founded on slavery and needed to protect economic slavery and its accompanying political disfranchising to staff dead-end service-sector jobs. Now, illegal aliens from Latin American countries, and especially Mexico, join blacks in forming this lumpen proletariat of dead-end workers, where there are even jobs to be had.

This raises the question, which remains devilish, of the relative priorities of race, class, and gender. I say this about the sixties: Fear of the black man, girded in self-defense, explains much of the martial behavior in both South and North, the lynchings, murders, burnings, and incarcerations. This is not to deny that race has an obvious economic dimension—think of slavery—but this economic component in itself does not explain the incredible intensity of emotion surrounding black/white relations.

As the noted jurist Ken Johnson describes in an interview in these pages, he served with distinction for four years in the U.S. military during the Vietnam era. He was one of the first lawyers to be admitted to the Judge Advocate General's Corps. He had already been active in the civil rights movement as a student at

Southern University in New Orleans. On his first day stateside in 1966, after returning from the Asian theater of war, he was called a "nigger" by a white woman. I ask Johnson how he could have remained a patriot after this, and he responds that his patriotism is grounded in the belief that the country is "unfinished"—a very charitable construction. He also admits that he has never stopped thinking about that incident because it sums up so much of the agony of the black experience in America.

And so race had a dual significance during the sixties. On the one hand, race was somewhat independent of other dimensions of social, political, and economic inequality; armed black men posed a special threat to the establishment and thus were targeted for special wrath. On the other hand, blacks and whites joined forces in the civil rights, antiwar, and women's movements, in spite of frequent misunderstandings and violations of territory. In addition, black protest preceded white protest and, in the form of SNCC, provided a model for SDS of existentially committed activism. These are complicated connections, and they reflect the complexity of the relationship between race and other social forces in America. I remain convinced that one cannot understand American society without understanding the foundational role of slavery and its legacy. This legacy produced insurgency that has provided a model for the white student movement and the women's movement, perhaps demonstrating that the white establishment always understood that the freeing of black folk would have revolutionary consequences for society as a whole. And this is why the establishment worked so hard to protect segregation, which has morphed from officially separated public institutions such as schools and restaurants into the de facto segregation of impoverished inner cities and affluent suburbs.

My family recently returned from a driving trip through the Deep South. It was quickly apparent that the races were still separate and certainly not equal. Although large Texas cities such as Dallas, Houston, and San Antonio are not without overt racism and socioeconomic inequality grounded in race (and reinforcing overt racism), there is a sense in these cities that the races intermingle and even blur. Our children attend school with many kinds of children of color—black, brown, yellow, and mixes of these. In Mississippi and Alabama, we rarely saw integrated groups of people, whether in fast-food restaurants, in the malls, on the streets, or in hotels. New Orleans after Katrina appeared utterly devastated, especially in the poor black sections. George W. Bush and the Federal Emergency Management Agency allowed New Orleans to become a site of shattered dreams, a monument to the unfairness of a capitalism that spares the well-off and to an antebellum racism that never seems to quit.

With the passage of time, the South has become hip. NASCAR is one symbol of this, as is country music. To be sure, northern racism and racially inflected inequality are no less virulent than the southern varieties. However, it does make a difference whether states were blue or gray. There is a sense that the South and southerners are unrepentant, which starkly contrasts with the collective guilt and shame of younger and even some older Germans. One of Weatherman's platforms was that Americans during the Vietnam War should not become "good Germans," people who acquiesce to the Final Solution. The South has been glamorized as college students proudly fly the "rebel" flag from fraternities and embrace the gridiron gemeinschaft of "Hokie Nation" in the wake of the 2007 Virginia Tech campus murders.

To be sure, Seung-Hui Cho, the troubled gunman acting out his rage about his own marginality, was not only a victim of "the damaged life," as Theodor Adorno (1974) terms it. He also authored his own damage, abundantly so. And yet social amnesia suppresses our collective memory of the Klan-inspired lynchings and murders that stretched from the 1700s through the 1960s. As Robert Moses indicates here, there is as yet no adequate commemoration of the triple murders of the three young civil rights workers in 1964. This is not to compare Cho's horrors to those of the Klan, but to notice that there has been no esprit de corps, school spirit by another name, around the celebration of those who died during the civil rights era in the struggle for social justice. One of my main themes is that the decade of death needs to be narrated, with the names spoken and remembered of those who went to their deaths needlessly, simply because southerners and racist northerners dug in to defend a society in which some people are chattels.

Yes, the civil rights movement made progress, enacting important legislation. Yes, the early civil rights movement became a model for the white New Left and feminists as they created a prefiguring beloved community; they put into practice in their own lives what they sought for everyone. But the legacy of slavery haunted the sixties, in which the state and police meted out tougher justice to black people and civil rights workers than to the cleaned-up kids, me and my friends, who leafleted for Eugene McCarthy. I remember a night in April 1968 when we organized for McCarthy; as usual, I was combining my political projects with my fondness for a girl named Karen, who was at my side. Some toughs in a pickup truck threatened to kill us if we did not leave by the time they returned. And they might have, if they had had the nerve to return. But this was not equivalent to the terror faced by civil rights workers in the South who could be shot or lynched at any moment, especially after sundown. We could always return home to our middle-class existence; the political workers in the black belt were shadowed by the Klan at every turn. There was no going home for them.

Even in Eugene, civil rights segued into Black Power. I include an interview with a Eugene Black Panther then named Tommy Anderson. He changed his name to Jaja Nkrumah to reflect his changed identity since the sixties. Other Eugeneans changed identity: Bobby Moore became Ahmad Rashad, and I became a Canadian. The times drove us away from home or toward new homes. I knew Tommy and his brother, Howard, as leaders of the Eugene chapter of the Black Panther Party. My dad was very involved in CORE and then informally advised and worked with the Panthers, some of whom took his political science classes at the University of Oregon. It took months to track down Tommy, which I did by posting a message to a Black Panthers Web site. When we began the interview, he did not realize that I was Bob Agger's son, but that quickly became clear. He became suddenly open and exuberant as he remembered the past.

The Eugene Panthers discovered natural alliances with poor white people, who suffered many of the same economic injustices as black people. They had "working relationships" with local white people, both in the community and at the university. After all, Eugene had a very small black population and the Panthers needed to work within the context of a mainly white and rural state. In this sense, there were some similarities in approach between the Eugene Panthers and early and later SDS, when their activists went into urban communities and worked among the poor in order to organize them and help them solve their own problems (both through the ERAP initiative and later with Weatherman's urban cells). These multiple involvements suggest that it is an oversimplification to talk about SDS primarily as an antiwar movement and the Panthers as totally bound up with black issues.

ROBERT MOSES

Was Bob Ever New Left?

"Actually, I didn't ever really consider myself part of the New Left. That was a term I saw [first] in *Newsweek*. . . .

"They had a kind of mixed metaphor on the cover of one of their magazines and they said, 'In Orbit on the Left.'"

Robert Moses. (Courtesy of The Algebra Project, Inc.)

Radicalism as Getting to the Root of Things

"And the idea that you were orbiting in some kind of elliptical fashion like a planet but that you were orbiting on the Left struck me as not really that useful, but I thought, at the time, while I'm not in orbit on the Left and Ella [Baker] has the idea of being radical. She said radical men go down to the root cause of things, and so I think that was more a sense in which, looking back, that would characterize both our actions then as part of SNCC and working in the [Mississippi] Delta around the right to vote and the work that I've been doing now for the last quarter century working with the grandchildren in Mississippi and great-grandchildren of the sharecroppers around math education.

"I don't think of [my work to enhance math literacy] as a continuation of the Summer Project but as a continuation of the work that we did with SNCC in Mississippi, particularly which I characterize as, and again in this sense of radicalness, what I think about the work was that, on the one hand, it was organizing work, so the example of that for us was the Freedom Democratic Party and the concept was one which I take over from Ella when she helped SNCC to come into being, she acted as an organizer to help the student sit-in leadership form something that could carry forward their movement, but she wasn't going to be the leader of it. She stayed on as an adviser, but she was helping something come into being that she wasn't going to be the leader of, and I think of that as one of the ways to distinguish leadership from organizing.

"So our example, which we carried into Mississippi, was the Freedom Democratic Party because we didn't have standing to be members of the Freedom Democratic Party, but we certainly were helping to organize it. So I think the radicalness of it is getting the people whose issue it is to actually be an integral part of the whole strategy, from the meetings, the policy, the actions, everything. Dewey has a comment in which he says that 'a lot of work for the common good is neither common nor good.'

"It's not good because it doesn't actually involve the people that you are trying to help and not common because they don't really participate in the whole strategy-building process."

Camus as an Inspiring Philosopher

"The main thing I took from Camus was the idea that in this struggle for human betterment, you had to walk a fine line so that you were neither a victim nor an executioner. And that, really, was very helpful going through all of the different twists and turns of the movement in the sixties."

Bob's Relationship to Tom Hayden and SDS

"Those early days, there weren't many who were coming south. Tom was one of the few who ventured south. I think I remember having a conversation with him in Jackson, certainly after I had gotten beaten up. I remember that. And then after that pamphlet SDS put out, 'Revolution in McComb'? And so that was really a long interview that I remember with him. That would have been either late '61 or early '62 after we got out of jail in McComb, and I think while we were in jail is when Tom came down and got waylaid there.

"In those days we were pretty surrounded by the Delta and the black belt. We had some interface with Justice Department people. We had some interface with small northern SNCC groups that were starting, but up until 1963 and the March on Washington we got out to DC and the National Council of Churches. I'm trying to call up the name of the person who was the national director who came down and began to pull in the National Council of Churches. Up until that time we were pretty much isolated. I don't remember having much interface with SDS groups or other groups."

On Sellers's Distinction Between Hard-Line Materialists and Existentialist Free Floaters

"I don't know if that's his distinction [laughter] or not. I don't think much of it. It was an attempt to try to build a basis for the decisions that were being made to structure SNCC, and so we were faced with really not understanding that; it's better understood now, I think, in terms of decentralized structures. I think there's a much better understanding of networks, and, of course, there's a much better understanding because there's a technology that really supports networking.

"So we really had evolved a structure which was much more of a network structure for SNCC, and SNCC didn't have money to pay staff, and staff were still in life-threatening situations. So it's kind of hard to think that you're going to have a central command where you are sending or really structuring a kind of central operation in which people in the field are facing the life-threatening situations and where you don't have any real support structure for them. People have to find their own place to live and find food to eat and so forth. So I never could make much sense of that distinction.

"That also doesn't really help me much because if you think of someone like John Lewis and the national crowd, they were the ones within the early sit-in movement who would like to talk in terms of Christian idealism and the beloved community. But they weren't able to take hold with that concept in Mississippi. If you remember after the Freedom Rides when the Freedom Riders got out, some of them tried to start a nonviolent movement in Jackson, but they didn't have any space, and they weren't willing to do what people in South Africa did, like face twenty, thirty years in jail.

"So in some sense Jim Lawson [the inspiration of much of SNCC's strategy of nonviolence], who was their spiritual leader in Nashville, wasn't available. He had entered into the Methodist church and was in Memphis, and so the young people from that orientation were trying to figure it out more or less on their own in Jackson. So they didn't have any legal covering, but what made the difference between that orientation and what actually happened around the vote was that the 1957 Civil Rights Act allowed the Justice Department to get us out of jail, so Mississippi would lock us up, but the feds would get us out.

"And so we didn't have to have a whole legal apparatus because there was none. So without any legal apparatus and without any middle class to set bonds, you were subject to what happened to the nonviolent movement people in Mississippi. Either you were going to jail without bail, or you were going to fold up. So they weren't able to actually sustain that movement in Mississippi. You can't think that the movement that actually took root in Mississippi, which took root based on Amzie Moore's insight, and Amzie certainly wouldn't think of himself either as a floater, a hard-liner, a materialist, or a Christian idealist, and it was his insight that we moved on, that the key to unlocking Mississippi would be organizing around the right to vote. And so the organizing around that took place basically by understanding that the tool to unlock the energy of the sharecroppers was the meeting places and crafting ways for them to meet so that they could field their own agency, and tackling small problems and then finally coming together around their representation as a political voice. So those had nothing to do with floating and hard-line or Christian idealism and materialism. Those categories really don't serve well what happened in Mississippi, and after we got the nation involved with students from all over, we were left with an issue of how to proceed, and we just couldn't figure that out."

The Role of Charisma in SNCC

"What actually happened, what actually got put in place, wasn't able to sustain a movement. I think one thing to really understand was that once SNCC got a charismatic media person, Stokely and then Rap, the dynamics within the organization shifted because you can't really run an organization there, the young people are very impressionable, where you are focusing on them as organizers and their eyes are on wanting to be like a certain charismatic leader.

"Fannie Lou Hamer emerged from [the 1964 Democratic National Convention] as a grassroots media person. Nine of us entered into history in that way, but that meant a lot of discipline about it, and so this is hard for SNCC because they also need to raise money and so to raise money you have to project yourself in the country; so these were big questions for Jim Forman.

"What happened was not moving away from a leadership position but really moving away from SNCC. So it would have been hard to stay in SNCC and not be in some kind of leadership position. That wouldn't have made any kind of sense given the history of what had happened. So it was like watching this play itself out because this certainly was part of what Jim needed at that time and was asking for a kind of media personality to emerge from within SNCC, and so that certainly wasn't something I agreed with, but that was part of trying to figure out a structure.

"I think what you have today, if you're looking at organizations and networks, there's a much more sophisticated understanding about organizations and how they might structure themselves. We have tried to take the lessons learned from SNCC into the Algebra Project, and so . . . you can go so far, like over the last twenty years, twenty-five years, we've managed to create a space for the young people that I was teaching who were middle-school students in the early eighties to develop and own and run their own organization. They call it the Young People's Project (YPP) to the point where they have their own board and have recently received major funding from the National Science Foundation in formal living divisions for a five-year period. But they have about one hundred youth math literacy workers that they work with in Chicago, Boston, Cambridge, and the Jackson, Mississippi, area."

Was SNCC Democratic Socialist?

"Democratic socialism doesn't mean that much to me. I think people have to work. And when you say, 'Welfare state,' I never quite understand what Bayard [Rustin] and some of the other people were talking about. We are entering an age where people won't have to work, so you can just give them welfare or money or something, because people really need to work and they really need meaningful work, so how work is distributed and how meaningful work gets distributed so that people can support families is a big, big issue. That's how I try to think about what the Algebra Project is trying to do [is] that in this transition into information age technology, quantitative literacy can be an opportunity structure. In other words, the kids who really master the knowledge, the shift in how you acquire and use knowledge, and the idea that knowledge is driving the work. What I'm really trying to see [is] how we can establish that for the targeted population, the bottom quartile of the kids at school now."

The Invisibility of Early SNCC in Narratives of the Sixties

"It's interesting because the sixties that I was part of has never really been a part of the national perception of the sixties. Because on the one hand, part of the national perception of the sixties is the SDS. Okay? The other is the more radical turn of SNCC, Black Power, and Stokely and Rap, Black Nationalists. . . .

"I think part of the issue there has to do [with the fact that the early civil rights movement] didn't have a home [in narratives of the sixties]. It couldn't have a home within SNCC because of the infusion of the volunteers into the summer programs. When you see John Lewis in the papers on the front page of the *New York Times*, with Hillary Clinton and Barack Obama and ex-president Clinton, who is he representing? In other words, which part of the movement is he representing? Because he really embodies a certain piece of early SNCC. Right?

"But when he's there, that's not what he's representing. He's representing a sort of abstraction, the movement, getting the right to vote, and the march is associated with King and SCLC. It was associated that way when it happened and associated that way within the history.

"But John was the piece of the march that refused to stop when they [were] told to stop. Right? So that certainly is the Freedom Rides; it's the sit-ins; it's MFDP [Mississippi Freedom Democratic Party] in some sense; it's the sharecroppers going for the right to vote. So none of that has gotten owned by anybody.

"That's not a story that's told, and what is more glamorous, and in some sense it reaches into a different sensibility for black people, is the defiance of the Black Power movement. And there was no commemoration for Goodman, Schwerner, and Chaney anyplace in the country. The country has no way to really commemorate them, and even in Mississippi the commemoration there doesn't encompass the movement that actually brought them there. And so there are really deep divisions over how to commemorate the movement, and only recently some of the Mississippi civil rights workers from that time have tried to regroup as a group and figure out how to talk about their history.

"The top leadership of the country was eliminated during the sixties. If you think of the two Kennedys and King and others that were eliminated and died mysteriously, including Luther and Stephen Currier, who was on nobody's screen, being hidden up there, the head of the Taconic Foundation, which was managing all the money going into the movement to the voting. But I don't think of it that way. I think of it more in terms of the way in which it was an overthrowing of Jim Crow, and it was the sit-in movement that did that, and so that takes you all the way back to Reconstruction and the setting-up that was overthrowing of almost one hundred years of political structures that had been reestablished for white supremacy."

CLEVELAND SELLERS

What Did New Left Mean to You?

"It means a kind of progressive belief in social change. It means trying to address the issues that ordinary people face: those issues of poverty, discrimination, hope, all of those kinds of things. It means trying to work toward a system that would, in fact, be inclusive of the voices of those who are marginalized and currently disenfranchised. It means developing a social system that would have a degree of equity in it, that would move away from the rich top 10 percent and begin to address the issues of redistribution of some resources; probably wealth could be included in that. It means a system that is equitable and a system that is inclusive. It means a system where we can have those resources available to those who are in most need of those resources: health care, education, employment opportunities."

Does Socialism Have a Role in Black Struggle?

"I do not know the answer to the question, and the issue is, I think, more about whether or not we have exhausted the discussion of the economic system itself first. And I am saying that there are those who still buy into that it will in fact reform itself enough to accommodate, and not enough discussion about what are the alternatives. When we get to the kind of demise of the 1960s era, freedom struggle, we are at the point where that discussion is being held. I think that discussion continues in the African American community, and it is still an ongoing discussion. It is ideological, and so when we talk about the demise of the movement, we generally do not factor that in as being one of the items that created the kind of atmosphere where you could not go any further. If you were to read Dr. King's 'Where Do We Go from Here: Chaos or Community?,' he began to address that issue."

King's and McKissick's Relationship to SNCC

"SNCC was more an organization that believed in organizing and organizing your way out of a job, so you would organize communities to empower them so they could take over and be in control of their own kind of little political organization. SCLC was more about mobilizing, and they were more about applying pressure. True, the political parties and that labor-liberal coalition that by the time you get to 1965, it has pretty much disintegrated anyhow. Over the

Cleveland Sellers. (AP Photo/Mary Ann Chastain)

war in Vietnam, SNCC came out with this statement in January 1966, and most of the leadership in the civil rights movement, including Dr. King, were opposed to that war in Vietnam, but our job within the movement itself was to raise those contradictions among the other civil rights organizations, primarily Dr. King and

SCLC, and so about one year later you have Dr. King do the same thing; that is, take a position against the war in Vietnam. Now his is based on a different analysis, and that has to do with orientation of his organization and his own orientation, but the fact that he was willing to make that step, I contend, was very much involved with our discussions and debates with him and how we began to get him involved in having those kinds of discussions.

"McKissick [of CORE] was one of those who we had to push also. Now if you go back to the mentions of Black Power, there were some discussions and debates to get McKissick onboard with the Black Power item, and I think that if you read 'Chaos or Community?' by King, you will see that even the issue of Black Power, he addresses it in a different way. He said that there are some people who articulated in a very negative fashion and there were others, but he was never, after the summer of 1966, critical of Stokely . . . using that term.

"And that was because that kind of relationship still existed in the movement. As a matter of fact, when Dr. King was going to make his statement at Ebenezer [Baptist Church] on the war in Vietnam, Stokely was one of the people he called up on the phone and told him to come to Ebenezer that morning.

"Now you have the press and you have COINTELPRO, both things interfacing and playing a role in this whole process, so they wanted to create those divisions, and even though those debates were heated at times and there was, in fact, a struggle, it was intellectual and based on ideas rather than on personality and that kind of thing. So it never disintegrated to the point where people were being very petty. There were people around the edges that would say things and appear to be very negative, but that is not the way we looked at it, and that is not the way we tried to deal with it. We tried to get through language and those other barriers to hear the idea."

Hard-Liners Versus Free-Floating Idealists in SNCC

"And the reason why I am developing this particular thought process is because I am getting to the point that when SNCC began to travel and look at Africa and one man/one vote even more recently than it did early on, that we began to see that America's relationship to Third World countries and liberation movements and that whole analysis, the whole thing of the octopus, I think, is the animal that even Dr. King uses to talk about how it, with its tentacles could actually corral colonies and create all of these colonies around the world and have that kind of control. Now what I am trying to suggest is that the movement, the internal workings of the movement, the people who are on the ground, [were like a] university without walls, and these discussions would go on on a continuous basis. We went through Camus and Sartre and the existentialists, and we went through Bertrand Russell, and we went through Frantz Fanon, and we went through Debray, and we looked at Cuba and had discussions around the writings, and the workings, so it was always a process of learning more and creating information that gave us a tool for a better analysis of what we were facing as minorities and young people in America. That was a continuous kind of thing. I want to probably take some credit, not myself, but as young people in and around SNCC and Highland[er School], for helping shape the conclusions that Dr. King had arrived at about the kind of democratic socialism that he suggested."

"So I think the split down the middle in terms of the differentiation between who fit in which group was probably those who were more of the kind of Christian idealism as a philosophical base, which Camus and some of the other existentialist philosophers fit in. And the hard line would probably be more materialists in the sense of let's work on some basic kind of structural change if we can begin to do that, at least move in that direction to begin to have that discussion."

SNCC Growing and Becoming Bureaucratic

"Now the other part of that comes with 1964 and 1965 with the Mississippi Summer Project, SNCC went from an organization that was probably about 30 members to about 130 members. It went from a predominantly black organization to a majority white organization in a very short period of time.

"When it ended, by the time it ended, we are talking about how there were a lot of volunteers who had come and decided that they were going to stay and SNCC allowed those volunteers who were staying on projects in Mississippi to become members of SNCC.

"SNCC bought automobiles because we had a number of automobiles that were donated, but they would not last that long and so we bought . . . twenty-three or twenty-four new Plymouth automobiles, and so we began to take on these resources, and so coming out of the summer, we were a different organization. We had personnel, so you had to have some kind of structure, you had to deal with personnel, you had automobiles, so you had to take on the responsibility for that, you had insurance on the automobiles, you had upkeep and . . . so you had to have . . . some of the awful bureaucratic systems made into your organization, okay? Somebody had to do it.

"It was on my watch that that came up. And so I didn't mind it, but we began to see, if you are talking about social change and revolution and liberation and all of those other kinds of things, we saw those resources that we were gaining as important ingredients to help that process through, and you just had to manage it. You could not just leave it out there.

"The other example was we decided that we needed to have a printing press, and so when you get a printing press, you have to have printers, and you have to have mechanics for the printing press, and you had a photography operation, so you needed darkrooms. All of that cost money, and all of that meant that you had to raise money, you had to budget, so you have to have a degree of organization. I could not be 'Today we'll be printers, and tomorrow we'll be in the field doing certain kinds of work.' So it did cause a delineation between what people were doing, and it did cause the organization to take under consideration what people were, in fact, doing. So we had an assessment to find out who was where, and that was all because we were no longer the small group, that we did everything."

The SNCC/SDS Relationship

"Bob wasn't there. But my point is that there was always a kind of working relationship when Hayden was up in New Jersey. At the time he was up there, I think we were still up at Harlem, and so that was a referent for us. That is when we went up to New York in that area, we would go up and take a look at ERAP.

"We would always kind of go through and see what, in fact, was going on with that project. There was always that parallel even though we were working more deeply in the South, and some of the SDS folk grew out [of] what was called the 'northern student movement,' which was headed by Bill Strickland, and that was merged in with SNCC. And the friends of SNCC saw a lot of the activism as it began to move off the campus, and that is one of the reasons why you see a spinoff in ERAP, in fact, evolve because students wanted to go and commit themselves much further than debates and discussion around the campus. They wanted to be actively involved. ERAP comes on for that purpose."

SNCC's Northern, Urban Roots and Theoretical Sophistication

"The student movements in Nashville and Atlanta have been written about by scholars, so you see a kind of Christian idealism that undergirded those things, but if you look at the student movement in Howard, you got a different set of circumstances. It is in an urban community; those urban issues are more connected to these students. We did a rent strike and desegregation of the buses in DC, and we also had a fight with the university to have Malcolm as one of the lyceum program speakers during that period of time in 1962, 1963. And we also had that same fight over Bayard Rustin, who the university saw as a kind of socialist, and they were reluctant about having him speak, but we organized our campus, we had the political courage and fervor that you found in the student movements in Nashville and you also had much more than Howard University students represented: Maryland, the University of Maryland, Georgetown, George Washington, and the schools around the District of Columbia. They are no longer there now, but there were a couple of black institutions there."

"When we were in our intense studies themselves as the movement began to evolve, certainly after 1964 and 1965, we looked at Marx and Mao and everybody else, so the analysis and the readings were very much a part of the curriculum for movement folk during that time. We had people like Jim [Forman], and so we had those discussions and that debate, and we had others who came in who had prior experience, and so the discussions and debates went on endlessly to try to find a way in which we could actually continue to move the movement forward and make it even more progressive. Now one of the things that we obviously had to recognize was that we were not going to be able to go but so far, and that is because you need to have that ideological discussion. Most of us came into the movement probably naïve of a kind of ideology and what it is, and as we began to evolve and began to raise these questions and do this reading and studying, we began to become much more clear, but there wasn't the time or the process. In SNCC we worked on having an internal educational program. That was one of the things that Jim insisted on. And we began to do that probably around 1966 by getting some property over by SCLC so that we had a resident educational center to which we were going to bring staff periodically and update them educationally, and as we brought new people in to become a part of the SNCC staff, we could do an orientation and bring them up and share with them the experiences that we had for the prior years. When you talk about Charles Jones and the others who were some of the originals in SNCC, you could stay in SNCC probably about two years. After that time, because of the intensity, the kind of horrific violence and those kinds of things, you had to find a way to step off the treadmill and find some other kind of activity to engage yourself in."

Bob Moses Shrinking from a Public Leadership Role

"Bob became almost the leader of Mississippi, the single person who was [the] philosophical and idealistic and material leader, and he did not wish to have that kind of role and that kind of position, and he wanted people to continue not to come to him to answer all of the questions and to resolve all of the issues and the conflict, and I think the Mississippi Summer Project was so effective that people used to look on him almost as a sacred kind of person."

SNCC's Beloved Community

"And so that's why he began to pull away, and then like all of us, after a while you have to take that step out, but it's almost like coming into the beloved community or the almost perfect community and you have to go away from it. We all left individually. We didn't go out in groups, and so it was extremely difficult the first two years after you left SNCC trying to find a community that was that nurturing and that intellectual and that scholarly and that committed to doing work and having that kind of political courage.

"The beloved community began to expire as people began to move away from SNCC, but the beloved community was the SNCC itself. And you begin to see people peeling off. When you get to the point where people are talking about the elimination of whites in the organization, you are at a point where there are probably not any more than maybe five whites or six whites in the entire organization, and then the group that actually votes on it is not even the people who were the advocates of Black Power, but a new generation that had come in and probably had any number of agendas.

"That was after Selma, but that was a group that came in and was assigned to Atlanta. That was a group of folk that came out of Philadelphia and was probably sponsored by some of the more narrow nationalist kinds of groups that came in, but they were convenient because they drafted up a statement on Black Power that was never endorsed by SNCC, but managed to find its way into the *New York Times*.

"Think about CORE if you want to think about the history, and you remember what happened to CORE: Roy Innis took it. There were always groups coming in because of the way SNCC was structured. They didn't see the organizational structure, so they figured that they could come in and actually say a couple of things to SNCC and talk about how slick they were and we were going to be gullible enough to kind of fold into whatever it is they are doing; certainly Ron Karenga and us, they came. Certainly Eldridge Cleaver, not even understanding our history and relationship to the Panthers, talked about a merger of SNCC and the Panthers. So there were other nationalist groups that also said that 'oh these folks are beginning to talk about this.'"

SNCC's Relationship to the Black Panthers

"The press had a merger of SNCC [and the Panthers], and Eldridge was saying that he had gotten the word from Stokely, but Stokely was the chairperson of SNCC. He could not make a decision about SNCC merging with anybody. Everybody in SNCC knew that, so we couldn't figure out why it was that Eldridge was moving on that, but he was, I think, to that extent trying to align and co-opt SNCC and make it folded in up under, so that would be a certain authenticity to the Black Panthers.

"I was program director when Stokely came in with the plan about organizing in Miles County and Wilcox and Green County and Dallas County in Alabama, and Jack Minnis was down in the research department, and he was putting together and looking through and seeing how that could happen. At this point, we are certainly disappointed with that liberal church coalition that failed us in Atlantic City. We were real frustrated about the fact that we had done all of the appropriate kinds of things, but when our interests did not match the interests of that coalition, then we were the ones on the out, so we were looking for alternatives to the Democratic/Republican Party. So there was a kind of choice between the Urban League on the one hand and the Panthers on the other.

"Now, see, where a lot of folks miss out on this whole process is that the Panther Party is actually the Lowndes County Freedom Organization. And so we put the money in to get Jack Minnis to sign the law that allows for an independent political party in a county in Alabama, part of the old Confederacy. When they put in those laws, they had it in there so a person could actually organize an independent party because there was some concern about the Republican Party and the Democratic Party, and if something comes up, they wanted an out, so they put that in. We said that we certainly are going to be organizing in the black belt because we had no success with organizing in the white people's project in 1964, and we had no success in organizing in any white communities anywhere we had been, and if we took an assessment of the movement, we had no success organizing whites during this era of civil rights.

"And so they picked the Black Panthers. Now the Democratic Party was upset with us for doing this kind of thing, and when

*Lowndes County Freedom Organization becomes the Black Panthers, and Jesse Favor runs for sheriff.
(AP Photo)*

there was a time to publicize the Lowndes organization, they publicized it as being a very narrow nationalist organization with a
symbol called the Black Panther. That's where the Black Panther
name comes from. We were able to get a lot of young people involved during the time when the elections went on in Lowndes
County and the other counties down there, and so we had a lot of
young people come down from Philadelphia and New York, and we

used the same structure that we used in SNCC, and you will see that people changed the name or the acronym, but actually had the same kind of thing, so we called those groups the Friends of the Black Panther Party. Some of those folks came from California. Some of them came from Philadelphia and Chicago, and when they went back, they had little Black Panther parties up in these areas. The one that kind of caught on was the one out in California.

"[Neither Newton nor Seale was in Lowndes County,] but some of the original folk were in Lowndes County. I'd have to go through and tell you who those people were, but now once they got started out there, then something happened with some of the SNCC people. This is in '67, and that is when Kathleen [Cleaver] decided to go to Oakland, and so did Faye Bellamy move from Atlanta to Berkeley, and one of the things that they were going to do is lend some of their expertise to the organizing of the Black Panther Party for Self-Defense, but we always saw it as being a kind of appendage, not quite a stepchild.

"At that point we were talking about independent political organizing in the movement, and we knew it had to be in a black community because that's where we had the numbers and we could actually effect change in those areas. And the other part of that is, if you look at the demographics of Oakland and the demographics of Lowndes County, they are a lot alike, 60-something percent African American.

"So that is the offshoot, but you know children grow up, and when they grow up, you know what happens with that. The other part is that Stokely always felt like he was going to maintain that relationship and he did, and so the Panthers decided they were going to have a whole hierarchy in the organization, and they selected SNCC people; Jim Forman, Rap Brown, and Stokely became ministers of justice and all that kind of stuff that went along, but that again was a way in which the Panthers could get some authenticity.

"I don't think that was a mistake; that was fine. I don't think it's a mistake, but what came was that at some point Eldridge decided that he needed to, especially when the heat came down from the confrontations, that he wanted to talk about a merger with SNCC, and that never happened, so that wasn't a mistake. One of the things that got me kind of booted out of SNCC was, the issue of organizing for the Black Panther Party that came up in a meeting and we're talking about now '67, '68. And the whole issue about liberation movements or paramilitary groups, and there was one in Cairo, Illinois, there was one in Memphis, there was one on the West Coast, they were popping up all over the area. And they were in major metropolitan areas, and the question came up whether or not we were going to organize for the Black Panther Party. My position was that I was not prepared to organize these paramilitary groups. . . . What is the ideology? What are they trying to do? What are they trying to change? All they are going to do is walk around with guns, and so I voted 'no.' I wasn't inclined to go with any of them. SNCC should just go back to grassroots organizing.

"And they were also anarchists, and there was something the Panthers called 'revolutionary suicide,' which flew in the face of what we had always been about—you're killing yourself. You're trying to build a community; you're not trying to kill yourself. Revolution and suicide are just contradictory."

Pan-Africanism and Patriotism

"I think that if you look at the experience of African Americans in America, you have had movements that have talked about expatriation and back-to-Africa movements and those kind of things, but I think one of the central themes has been based on love of country, and that's the idealism of democracy and all of those other things that go along with that, that folk here maintain over a long period of time and through that have generated a certain faith in those principles, those ideals. I think that is what many of us talked about and thought about when we talk about revolution and liberation and change, however we articulate what that is. At the same time, I think that for African Americans, there was and there is again an issue and area about identity, and I think that Black Power helped us begin to address that issue, and so that's where the whole inclusion of a kind of pan-Africanist perspective [came from]. We are still in the throes of actually collecting this history and getting it so people will understand the origin, and that is all important for any kind of collective, but I think there has to be a kind of internationalism that tops out all of this very narrow nationalism in terms of the nation-state syndrome. We look at our condition as being a part of the world community, and we end up being in a geographical area where we have some issues that we have to address."

Identity Politics and Pathology
Among Young Blacks Today

"I think you have to go through answering the question about identity and culture. That's because of how African Americans get here. That is a unique kind of arrangement and not only how we get here, but how we get here and then into slavery, the kind of stripping of any sense of humanity and then building through that and then having the rights stripped from you; you know you get some degree of humanity back, but you're still limited with your rights. So those are issues that certainly need to be addressed.

"And that's one of the reasons why they have all of this pathology of self-destruction and suicide. They have no idea who they are. They don't have any kind of identity, and they certainly don't have any faith in anything or anybody, and so when you get to that point, it's 'I'm a dead person walking, and I might as well carry somebody else with me,' and that kind of pathology is just in all urban cities right now. We have a problem here in Columbia [South Carolina] where almost every week there is a fifteen-year-old that is getting shot, and that's the same thing happening in Los Angeles. The same thing happens in Philadelphia. It's all over, and so there is going to be a movement back in that general direction. It will come out of necessity.

"I think you have to be able to separate it out. The genre is okay and that's what we have to understand. Now there is a difference between hip-hop and rap, and I think rap is the genre, and what we have is an industry who has co-opted and created this new thing called hip-hop and then gangster hip-hop and this misogynist hip-hop, and we haven't been able to turn that off, and one of the reasons why is because we don't control either the resources that go into keeping that alive; neither do we control the imagery that goes into that whole process, so the hip-hop generation and those who are purchasing this garbage are basically young white Americans.

"So what is going to have to happen is that African American youth are going to have to come together and talk about rap and what that is and be able to distinguish so you can get people to understand how they buy into continuing a very sleazy depiction of African Americans, and it is unreal and it also creates the kind of symbols that are inhumane and shows a very negative stereotype of a people who have been fighting for a very long time over the issue of how the renaissance was the New Negro; even the civil rights movement had a pushing of the New Negro. That becomes the black person, and then that becomes the African American, and then you have to deal with gender and being a man and being a woman. What are those things? That's identity. When I talk about identity, it goes beyond just race. And we are not trying to create a superior race, that's not in it, but you have to know something about your origin and your history and where you come from. That does not fly in the face of any kind of internationalism, I don't think."

Casey Hayden and Mary King's
Critique of SNCC Sexism

"I didn't think it was on the money, and I think that Mary and Casey at a retreat in 1980, but it was probably later than 1980, at Trinity College had a kind of awakening [as did] many of the women in SNCC. And there are a couple of things. One is that while chauvinism and sexism played a role with many of us, and people like myself always assume that SNCC was actually run by women.

"There is a role for women, but when we got out there, there were people shooting at you, and it didn't really matter about gender roles. You wanted somebody who was competent, and you wanted somebody who was committed, and you wanted somebody who was willing to step up when the time came to step up. That's what you wanted.

"The origin of women's liberation was supposed to have come out of SNCC; when the women in SNCC felt like they were dejected, they went on to begin to formalize and formulate. And that's been one of those histories that has come forward. So that's what she was doing; she was trying to make the connection between that, and, you know, I love Casey to death and Mary, too, but I think there was a shaking out that occurred at Trinity in which many of the African American women talked about the fact that even talking about Stokely, and that whole thing about the role of the woman as prone? He was not considered a conqueror of women. He was considered to be a kind of neophyte, and so he is talking about the role of the woman as prone. What does he know about that?

"[Fran Beal] will shed more light on that for you. And I think that we were able to transcend some of those and not only for us, but when SNCC came to a conclusion about a direction, then we went out and made sure all of the other segments of the movement would also do the same thing, but I think that it all shook out, and there is a book [by Wesley Hogan (2007)] on the rise of SNCC women that will probably address some of those things. There was a woman by the name of Annie Pearl Avery. Everybody wanted her to be with them when they went out on the line. Everybody. Every single person there was.

"That's an important part because a lot of times that is left out, but let me just share with you that we have not been treated very well by scholars. I would just say that I would try to help where I could, and when I found out that somebody had misrepresented it, then I would try to do everything I could to make sure that did not go where it needed to go. People like Michele Wallace, one example. She will never come off of our not-to-read list."

Beyond Civil Rights Today

"That's what Bob has said [about] the way he set up the math literacy, the Algebra Project to do that kind of thing, organizing local people and demystifying algebra, so I think that has some validity. There are a number of areas that we still have to work in, but one of the things that I have arrived at and I think other people are going to have to arrive at is that the civil rights movement ended probably around 1970, 1971, 1972. Now there is a protest tradition that runs through the African American community that has been around for a long time. But the abolitionist movement ended, and then you had the movement of people around the Reconstruction and after Reconstruction and *Plessy v. Ferguson*. You also have the New Negro movement, that was the Harlem Renaissance, the renaissance in Chicago, Philadelphia, and some other metropolitan urban areas as a result of the migration and the political change that occurred which had blacks elected to office. And then you had the civil rights movement, and so I know that there are those who wish to hang on to that, but that's gone. So any kind of new effort now will be different from that effort.

"Adults are not on the political playing field, and that has a lot to do with why you don't have that kind of activism and the raising of questions and drawing out of these contradictions and responding to those. One of the things that happened with us as we were coming along is that we did have Ella Baker and we did have Jim Forman and even Malcolm encouraging us to do things and to be involved and get involved. We cannot get people to use some of the tactics from the 1960s right now because they see it as being a different point in time and history, and they are right. So what we do is we have to go out and we have to educate, we have to have these seminars, begin to raise the kinds of questions that we need to raise, and I think students are beginning to take note. You have a new generation coming along now, and they are beginning to ask those questions. That's what we have to do. And we also have to find a way to share with them those experiences. If you look at most of the material on the civil rights movement, it will be centered around Dr. King. Well, that's okay, but what about Ruben Bridges? What about the four little girls in Birmingham? What about the kids in Mississippi, even Tom Hayden being a kid down in Mississippi trying to bring about change? What about their stories? What were they concerned about? How did they get motivated? When are these stories going to be told and made available?

"We shouldn't expect anything. We haven't done what we were supposed to do in terms of sharing the legacy. We know the legacy, but all of us haven't stepped out there; so now we are still trying to encourage people to step on out there and talk to these young people because they are asking, 'What do you want me to do?'

"And we are saying, 'Well I don't know; ya'll ain't doin' nothin'.' Well that ain't no answer, so I think that's what we have to do. We have to make sure that the literature changes, and we have seen some changes over the last ten years where you begin to talk about the movement as having a kind of indigenous orientation where there were ordinary people who did extraordinary things."

Civil Rights Successes and Failures

"When I talk about the demise of the movement, I talk about successes as being one of those things. When you get the 1964 Civil Rights bill, the 1965 Vot[ing] Rights bill, you have addressed fundamentally those issues of civil rights, but when you get widespread desegregation, you get a model for social change that can be used by other groups, women and those kinds of groups, and you empower them to go ahead and do that. That's another thing that created the demise. When you can get people's attention around the war in Vietnam and certainly the civil rights movement, and you can change the perspective. It's not just those little peaceniks over there. [You get] frontline, mainline people to be against the war in Vietnam, so you effect that change, and you effect that pulling out and withdrawal from Vietnam. So these are the things that created the demise of the movement. Certainly COINTELPRO was another one of those things. People always want to say that the movement's demise was the bullet to Dr. King's head. I don't use that one because what it says is that if you want to kill a movement, all you have to do is shoot whoever it is that is considered to be the leader of that movement."

FRANCES BEAL

Civil Rights, National Liberation, and Patriotism

"We have to go back to the sixties and even the fifties in terms of the civil rights movement in order to answer that question [about patriotism], and we also have to take a look at what the world looked like at that particular time. People forget that McCarthyism still had an ideological and political hold on the country.

"And it was breaking down, but it really was the civil rights movement that smashed it. Because people know about COINTELPRO as it relates to the Panthers, but it also impacted the whole civil rights movement: Martin Luther King, SNCC, everybody who was involved in that. One of the things many people don't know about SNCC was that like many other organizations, [its members] were asked to sign a loyalty oath, which was common at the time, and they refused to do so.

"I worked for ten years for the National Council of Negro Women after I was in SNCC; they had signed it, as did organizations like the NAACP [National Association for the Advancement of Colored People]. But SNCC didn't because it was very conscious, at least certain of its members, like Jim Forman. They were very conscious of what that meant, particularly as it relates to labor struggles and other struggles like the civil rights movement. So I'm saying all of this to say that the civil rights movement and then the other social protest movements broke the back of McCarthyism. We didn't know it was weakened by that point; the civil rights movement was the one that really broke the back of that reactionary grip on the nation. People had been more or less beaten into submission to where any struggle or any criticism of the United States, its policies abroad or at home, was perceived as communist-inspired.

"The point I was trying to make was that in SNCC there were those who saw Black Power in terms of its relationship to some of the national liberation struggles that were going on all around the world. That's why an identification with the national liberation struggle in Vietnam emerged, both because of race and because of the U.S. policies. So I think that progressive internationalism is that which saw the United States as an oppressor of people of color all around the world, and that our responsibility of solidarity with those people was to oppose those foreign policies that were oppressive. The other aspect, of course, was we saw our own interests impacted in terms of the money and the militarism that was going on abroad and the lack of support for social programs here at home.

"I do believe that you can use the democratic impulses of the documents that have made up U.S. history in order to support a progressive form of democratic patriotism: patriotism that talks about freedom of religion, patriotism that talks about a struggle for national liberation against an oppressive colonial power, which people often don't remember at all, or a Constitution that essentially was written in response to the oppression of the immediate historical period that preceded it. In other words, certain things in the Constitution had to do with not just an abstract ideological belief in freedom, but the fact that certain repressive policies existed under British colonialism that they did not want to recur in the new U.S. nation; therefore they wrote certain freedoms into the Constitution as guaranteed rights. Remember, during British rule they used to house British soldiers in people's homes and there was taxation without representation. All of those freedoms flowed from opposition to specific aspects of the repressive policies that had prevailed in the thirteen colonies under British colonialism.

"Now naturally, it was a flawed document in the sense that it did not destroy slavery or grant rights to women or to men without property, but that does not mean that the document as a whole did not have an overall democratic underpinning. In that regard, we can try to hold the government not hostage, but accountable to uphold the democratic liberties enshrined in the Constitution and the Bill of Rights, and many of us in writing that articulated a critical assessment of U.S. policies in this last period did precisely that. We tried to hold the U.S. government accountable to the U.S. Constitution and relative to all of the inroads and chipping away at the Constitution that the Bush administration tried to do and did accomplish during this period. In this regard I think the ACLU [American Civil Liberties Union] has played a really significant and important role in trying to protect the U.S. people from those inroads."

Was Civil Rights Socialist?

"I think there's a danger in trying to find ideological labels. It is better to look at the actual policies, to the actual unfolding of history in order to kind of grasp it, rather than finding a label for it. But let me just say that the initial stages of that were not ideological. It had to do with racism and racial injustice and the fact that many soldiers had just come back from fighting the war against fascism and the Holocaust. That's a very important part. And then for them to come home to this type of racism here was an intolerable type of situation.

"So that was the international aspect. The other thing was that the United States was already engaged in the cold war and holding itself up as this great democratic alternative against the tyrannical communists. So to have at home obvious racist discrimination and terror was uncomfortable from a worldwide perspective and U.S. interests internationally. That's another important aspect. This explains why you had the break in the white united front, and northern politicians as well as the economic system said no, this form of racism was not advancing U.S. interests abroad. Because, don't forget, this was not only the diplomatic and political contention with the communists, but that one country after another in the fifties to the early sixties and in Africa was becoming free from colonialism."

SNCC and Pan-Africanism

"When SNCC went abroad to Africa, there was a lot of concern about that, because here were black voices, and SNCC was one of the first organizations to get NGO [nongovernmental organization] status at the United Nations.

"I think that that trip helped certain people, and there were already other people who were concerned about Africa, particularly what was going on in the Portuguese colonies and in apartheid South Africa, and also what was going on in Africa itself. And that trip helped internationalize our consciousness about the struggle for racial justice. On that level I think there was a link. But don't forget, part of the movement for racial justice also included in it a desire for understanding our history better, and there was a problem in terms of the white interpretation of history. People began to review and research our own history, reading about leaders like W. E. B. Du Bois and Paul Robeson as well as others of that type. It was all of those things, so I think you should stay away from one incident giving life to some other.

"This was the basis for my own founding of the SNCC Black Women's Liberation Committee and eventually the Third World Women's Alliance. But within SNCC there were some who were saying 'Oh, our oppression is purely a race thing.' That's the basic SNCC thing. And there were others who were trying to figure out how class and race intersect here within the phenomenon of what we were dealing with in terms of racial justice. And there were others saying, 'Well, we come from an African background, and, you know, Africa is the foundation,' and others were saying, 'Yes, but we were also born in America, and that has influenced us.' So there were enormous ideological and political debates and discussions going on [about] how to interpret our historical experiences at that time."

SNCC's Bottom-Up Organizational Structure

"Insofar as the floaters versus the [hard-liners] . . . I think that [Sellers is] talking about an organizational dynamic. There were people within SNCC who were struggling for new forms of organization in the way that they took up the struggle against racism. So the very foundation of SNCC in many ways was an oppositional form to the hierarchical way SCLC was organized. Because that is very much the way the church was set up. And SNCC in this sense emerged in opposition to that type of structure. I went to a meeting in Atlanta in the late sixties—my biggest meeting, my longest meeting, it was like a twenty-four-hour marathon because we were trying to reach consensus. I don't even remember what it was about at this point. I realized years later in some ways it was not democracy because it was the people who could stay awake the longest who became the winners.

"Who would win the argument? So there was always this tension between what form the leadership should take and could we have no leadership whatsoever. Do we have, for lack of a better term, a true democratic sense to this organization? Not the way that the communists did it when it was all centralism and no democracy. But truly an organization that had really democratic intent, but then had people responsible for carrying out a perspective. So there was that tension that went on within the organization. SNCC never became a democratic centralist organization. It was always democratic; so in that sense, I would agree that there was a tension in the organization [between floaters and hard-liners]."

The Grounding of Women's Liberation in Civil Rights

"Within the antiracist struggle there are different forms of struggle that go on, and I think it was [Jim] Forman, and I was in that group, and some others were in that group, that formulated [the idea that] everybody who was in the antiracist movement was an antiracist, but some thought that advancing the black struggle [meant] accommodating yourself to the powers that be, and some [believed in] resisting the powers that be. So who are your allies? Do you go after the Congresspeople, or do you go after the working class?

"This is what led me to become concerned about the treatment of women in the organization, of how do you deal with the different strains of oppression? So we went into the question of the women's movement already trained to think of the complexity of social phenomena. So that's why when we came up with the race, class, and gender framework, it was based upon our own experiences, but we had been primed to think in that way because of coming out of the left wing of SNCC.

"I don't think that women ran SNCC, but I do think women had a much more important role in SNCC than they did in other civil rights organizations. And certainly at the grassroots level, women played a prominent, if not dominant, role in the southern movement. That's absolutely true, but still what I think [Sellers] may not fully appreciate [is] the fact that you still have the outer and public face of SNCC, [which] was very much male-dominated, particularly in its latter stages when the charismatic chairman became the public face of the organization. But in the inner functioning of SNCC, there was more female participation. I agree and I disagree with some of the stuff [Casey Hayden and Mary King] have said, because I ended up being one of the founding members of SNCC Black Women's Liberation Committee. There were problems within SNCC in terms of gender relations and the expectations. There were also problems within SNCC of whether they saw the particular problems that women faced in society at large as key issues to take up in the course of antiracist struggle. Most people said no. And if you were to ask people at that time, they would have said, 'Well, the racial struggle is more important than the gender struggle.'

"Where I do think we made some inroads is the very fact that people now are looking back on it from a more gender-conscious position, and that's what I think is happening personally with Cleve [Sellers]. Compared with SCLC and CORE, the women in SNCC played much more important roles. They ran meetings. They made up agendas, and in some cases they were field organizers. So they did many more things, but that does not mean that some of the gender relations of the fifties and sixties did not influence SNCC. They certainly did, and I know that Stokely's statement about women's position in the struggle being prone is an indication not so much of Stokely's real view, the view that women were nothing, but more that he exhibited a lack of consciousness of the significance of the subject of women's oppression to the point where he felt he could joke about it. I felt he was joking about it. I really did.

"He felt he could joke about it because of the lack of consciousness, so unlike others who would say that that is an indication of the sexism in SNCC, it's, I think it's what I just said. If you [ask] women, 'Do you believe that women should be granted equal pay for equal work?' And 'Do you support women's right to choice in terms of reproductive rights?' most women will say yes. But if you say 'Do you believe in feminism?' [they say no].

"It seems that it's always posed in terms of male versus female, whereas we are usually talking about women's liberation, black women's liberation, which took into account race, class, and gender.

Which is why we eventually became socialists, and this was not a socialism in which we had read all of Marx. It was very much a socialism in which we wanted the working class to be the leading class because it was more democratic, and that would mean that we would have the government favor the poor and working people rather than the rich. It was that form of socialism. We saw that in some socialist countries [there was free education] and child care for women and free health care; that was a great form of socialism. We were very close to what was happening in Cuba, and we really believed that that was a better way of life. Ideologically, we only came to Marxism later."

What SNCC and the Antiracist Struggle Won

"What did we win? I think this is the question we started out with. Our main accomplishment was the overthrow of the Jim Crow system; we destroyed the legal basis for U.S. apartheid and opened the door to struggle for real equality. What today has been left over? I think left over is the fact that the U.S. government is not perfect as relates to its international [project]. There is a big core of people who recognize that from their youth and the antiwar movement around Vietnam. I think there's a big core of consciousness around racism that didn't exist in the 1950s and around women that didn't exist in those days. And at the same time I agree with you, but those are two separate questions. The question of the seeds of today's right-wing fanatics being raised in the sixties and seventies I agree with, mostly in the seventies.

"The seeds of [the Right] were there, but they weren't contending at that time with a more progressive view of these other questions: that racism existed from the beginning of the founding of the United States and has had a tremendous impact on the development of the U.S. culture as well as the economic and social and political status of black people in this country. We are contending with those who try to say, 'No, it's just the badness of black people that was the cause of their not getting ahead' or their stupidity or ignorance, etc. Now the problem is that those right-wing forces have taken over institutionally in the universities, in the federal courts, and in the Congress as a whole. But we have to remember what broke it before was a mass mobilization of people. Not so much in Congress and in relying on Congress, but the mass mobilization of people who finally got to the point where they said, 'No more.' And I think it's getting a little bit better to that point now where people are quite shocked by the level of corruption and greed in the Republican Congress and the level of actual illegal behavior not just against the masses of people, but against the Democrats on the part of the Republicans."

The Role of Young People in Sixties Movements

"I think there were reasons why the youth were part of the vanguard movements of the sixties. One, of course, the obvious one with the antiwar movement, was the draft and the fact that so many young people were being taken away. In terms of the civil rights movement, the other thing I think caused the mass movements, ironically, was the very fact that because blacks had been excluded from the political process meant that they had to go around the political process and find new ways to struggle in order to put pressure on the government.

"People have to remember that even though we talk about a mass movement and we talk about civil rights, it still was a minority, a vast minority of people who actually participated in those projects, and we still have some of those projects similar to that in terms of young people building houses for the poor or going on certain public-service projects. I know of certain bus projects, freedom rides that people have around immigration, for example. Now, they've never blossomed and been a part of a larger movement, but there are certainly a lot of local struggles going on around a whole slew of issues that bring people out into the streets. Now, what is significant, I think, is that none of these have taken national form at this particular time.

"The second important point is it might not be the students who are the leaders of this new mass movement. There is a lot that has happened in terms of the student movement to make it a movement that isn't likely to be as progressive as the one before. Number one, all of the money that it takes to go to school now. The lack of resources and the decaying education system mean that those who are going to school are more of an elite element in terms of society than those from before.

"The second thing about the students of today is there is less money in terms of scholarships and loans, so that most students now owe ten, twenty, thirty, forty thousand dollars or more when they get out of school. And, therefore, the whole burden of having to pay that money back [locks them] more into the system already than I think we were, back in the day, in terms of those kinds of responsibilities."

Frances Beal marches for Angela Davis (Beal is holding the sign on the left). (Photo courtesy of Frances Beal)

CASEY HAYDEN

Casey Reevaluating Her Original Critique of SNCC's Sexism

"Black women were very strong in SNCC. Ella Baker was our senior adviser. Diane Nash and Prathia Hall come immediately to mind as iconic leaders. And in local communities it was the women who did the cooking and housing and mothering of young SNCC workers. Among ordinary female SNCC staff, women were almost uniformly prominent, steady, solid, hardworking. Women were relational, among themselves, and with the men, and did much of the day-to-day grind that kept it all rolling. As any organizer knows, those two elements are key. And the SNCC style itself, I have often contended, was rather feminine, or, a preferred term, womanist: humane, patient, antiauthoritarian, an open system. In this context, it was the running itself, rather than who ran it, that mattered, because no one was really running it. Cleve [Sellers] is right that the critique was off the mark. It was correct in that its examples of male dominance in positions of authority were accurate and reflected the majority culture, but it was superficial."

The Relationship Between
Civil Rights and Black Power

"SNCC and CORE [Congress of Racial Equality] were originally radically nonviolent, as reflected in the Montgomery bus boycott, the sit-ins, Freedom Rides, Selma march. Radical nonviolence was not exactly integrationist. It was a methodology which was applicable to any situation. It aimed to redeem the situation and everyone in it through the power of truth or love or noncooperation with evil. SNCC and SCLC [Southern Christian Leadership Conference], which grew out of the nonviolent movement, were antisegregation organizations. (I can't speak to CORE, which I wasn't in and which had a different origin.) I think one wants to distinguish antisegregation from integration. Integration was never the intent of the movement as I understood it, if integration meant, as it seems to mean sometimes today, that blacks would be scooped up into the melting pot and lose their racial identity. SNCC was always predominantly black, and black led. Whites were welcomed but were adjuncts, in service, really. I would say that within SNCC there was a desire to drop race in personal relationships, at least in the beginning, but only within these clearly defined boundaries. So Black Power was not as much a rupture as it might appear. It was my observation that Black Power proper was rooted in and developed organically in the movement from the need to foster African American self-love and self-acceptance and cultural autonomy. I can't speak to its later development, as I wasn't there."

Gender Politics in SNCC and SDS

"Gender politics in SDS and SNCC were quite different. Black women were stronger, more vocal, more directly involved in all aspects of the organization in SNCC than were white women in SDS. I spoke to the gender in SNCC in your question about Cleve's comment. SDS was a very different kind of organization than SNCC, more intellectual, competitive, out of a student government or classroom or debate model, with elements of the European 'Left.' White women were relational and hardworking, like the black women, and in that respect were very important in SDS. The predominant style, the guys' style, was not the women's style. I remember typing the whole SDS mailing list onto these little addressograph stencils in the SDS office in the summer of 1961, while the guys talked strategy. I can recall getting so bored with a C. Wright Mills study group in our apartment in Ann Arbor that I'd invite the women up from our social action center basement to the living room for tea, where we'd talk about our lives in an early version of a consciousness-raising group. Many women have commented on [this] issue. See Helen Garvy's *SDS: Rebels with a Cause*. . . . Later, in community organizing, however, where those skills of relating and day-to-day work and human interaction are key, women blossomed. Later gender politics in SNCC, after the [1966] 'Sex and Caste' memo, were quite complex, but I wasn't there. Again, see Garvy."

KENNETH JOHNSON

The Largely Unknown Baton Rouge Bus Boycott

"What happened was that compromise was reached that all seats would be available to all passengers whether they were colored, and we were colored then, or white, except that no blacks could sit in the front seats. They were reserved for white only, and no whites could sit in the back seats. That was reserved for blacks only. That was not a very good compromise, in my view. It was not an elimination of total segregation. So it was compromise and didn't really hit the national news, and I think that's what caused it to not become well-known that Baton Rouge was the first one.

"[The Baton Rouge action was] completely ignored by comparison to Greensboro. The *New York Times* covered it, and I have those reports, and the *Washington Post* covered it, and so did some other newspapers, but it was not a big deal. And the documentary written by the guy who was on National Public Radio called *Eyes on the Prize* completely ignored ours.

"And our sit-in was the first sit-in to reach the Supreme Court, and we had a very famous lawyer who helped on that case. His name was Thurgood Marshall. But that's the way it was: The people who wrote the history simply didn't know what they were writing, and that includes all of the historians who wrote it."

Nonviolence as Philosophy or Strategic Necessity

"I can't speak for anybody else, but I can speak for myself. The nonviolent approach I never, ever completely bought into. For me, it was a strategy: We were outnumbered, and we would have been wiped out. It was a complete strategy for me.

"When we were sitting at the lunch counter on March 28, 1960, I had fear of not being able to defend myself if somebody attacked me, and people came up with all sorts of objects. They got those display racks to strike us with, and I could see them in the mirror coming up, and I had to keep telling myself, 'Do not . . . do not fight back.' That was the greatest thing because I wanted to fight back, I wanted to turn around and give them a good rap, but I knew I couldn't because that would have been inconsistent with the strategy that we had to take for the greater cause. So with me it was a practical matter.

"We would have been wiped out in our cause. You see, the media, the newspaper, the TV, the radio, and everybody were harshly against us. We were called rebels. I recall we went from Baton Rouge to New Orleans. We drove down for a rally, and we were the people to rally and to speak at a rally they had for us in Dillard University in New Orleans. Klansmen were standing beside the road hooting at us. They were broadcasting that the rebels were passing this way. And we just kept on going, and as we were traveling, we knew that we might be killed at any moment, but that was all right because we had in our hearts a greater cause in mind than our lives and ourselves.

"We were still outnumbered, vastly. We didn't make any gunpowder in '65, we didn't make gunpowder in '60 or in '65, nor do we make any now. And until such time as we make the gunpowder, then we've got to keep the strategic efforts involved. What happened to the Native Americans when they resisted? They had bows and arrows and these outlaws, so-called Americans, all immigrants, of course, had gunpowder, and look what happened. They were rounded up, and those who were not killed, they were shipped out west, given a pile of rocks and a barrel of whiskey."

Black Youth Culture Today

"I wish that there was some magic that we could get [the young] involved, and I had thought about it many, many days and hours to try and see how could that be done, and I haven't come up with the way in which this could be done, but old people, middle-aged people, middle-class people are too invested in the status quo to want to change. We used to say in the sixties that anybody over age thirty should not be trusted because they were too invested in the status quo.

"I think we were correct, and that would be especially true today, and the black middle class is in that category also. So we were called fools and idiots and rebels and all sorts of things in the sixties because of what we stood for. Now, when I came out of the army, I was hired by the Justice Department, Civil Rights Division, and I went to work, and within a few days they made me head of

Birmingham, Alabama, which was the hottest spot in the nation. And then they promoted me the next year to head of all of Georgia, and that's when I met Dr. [Ralph] Abernathy and all of those people in that office, and they were committed people, youngsters all around, and we don't have that today. Now how could that be regenerated?

Kenneth L. Johnson. (Photo courtesy of Kenneth Johnson/Ben Agger)

We believed that there were causes in life greater than the ones today.

"Rap is very destructive. I don't like it at all. I don't like rap music. Not that there's any hatred against it, just that it's sending the wrong message. It's sending the antimessage of there's a cause in life greater than one and this cause is freedom. It does not go to what I was taught by my parents and what I was taught by my parents: number one—respect yourself; then respect others and your elders. Stay in school and stay out of trouble with the racist law, and the law is racist, and you're not going to get a fair chance in it, so you don't do anything that would give them any cause to put you in that criminal justice system. So that's what I did; I believed that, and you can proceed that way. They told me that and I believed that. Who's around now to tell black youngsters that? Usually the father is not in the home, and look at all of the unwed mothers. We are twice that of whites. Whites can afford it because the system, white supremacists ruling this country, will protect them. They will not protect young people of color. So we still have to stay out of trouble with the racist folks. We still have to go to school and stay there, and we still have to respect our elders. That message is not being sent out, so I hope that your book will send some of that out. Now if you put that in there, I'm making by a voice identification that you are white.

"Okay. Now if you say what Bill Cosby said or what I've just said, the whole sky is going to fall on you. So what you've got to say is that there is a code greater than myself and accept it.

"We blacks, or those of us that listen to that rap, or grew up listening to that rap culture, are there because racism had something to do with it, proving [the relevance of] economic structure. But being born and raised in Mississippi, I had racism, too, but the big advantage I had, Mom and Dad were there. And I mentioned about the unwed mothers giving birth. I don't have anything against that. Don't marry if you don't want to marry. Have a kid when you get ready to have a kid. But those fathers out there dumping babies in the womb and walking away is not acceptable. And the rap culture promotes that and other bad things. Because you were born poor and raised poor doesn't mean that you have to be poor in the spirit or poor in the heart. Now I realize that I had a unique situation. I had my cousin, the dean of the law school at Southern. I've known him all my life, and his brother was a practitioner in LA. A great, great defense counsel named Gerald. My oldest brother is named for him, and parents, my uncles, my aunts, and everybody were around, and we had a few hundred acres of land with water on it, rivers, lakes. And we were independent, went fishing, every kid doesn't have that, white or black, but I had that. And so the thrust of racism did not quite kill me because I was protected by this cocoon that I was raised in. And you got a chance to get educated and then to practice in the Justice Department. But then every kid doesn't have what I had, so it was a matter of accidental birth that I got what I had."

TOMMY ANDERSON (NOW JAJA NKRUMAH)

My Father's Role in Eugene's Civil Rights and Black Power Movements

"Let me tell you, your father was a very influential person in terms of supporting and encouraging African American students in particular, and all students in general, encouraging us to continue to struggle for change in this society. In Oregon and under the table, he would give us suggestions and direction, but certain things he could not say publicly. He could not come out and say, 'Hey, you know you guys are almost right.' Not because he didn't think [armed struggle] was necessary, but he thought it was a losing battle.

"And he wasn't a coward. He boldly would tell us, and this is under the table, 'Hey, you guys are young punks, and you're going to lose. You don't know anything about what you're up against. You're going to lose. Understand that. I understand your spirit, and I understand what you're trying to do. You're trying to bring about a change, but you don't have enough guns or ammunition. Okay?'

"That's the way he would talk to us, but he would also say that he encouraged us to continue some of the positive programs like our breakfast program in Eugene. Like our free food program, like our free clothing program. These are programs that he felt could

win the support and the admiration of the masses of people. Like
our liberation school."

[Editor's note: I remember skipping school for a few days in high
school to attend the trial of Tommy's brother, Howard, who was
tried on trumped-up charges for assaulting a police officer. I recall
Howard being acquitted after a vigorous defense by a sympathetic
progressive attorney who, like my dad, gave up time for radical
causes.]

"I was never convicted of anything. But see my brother, Howard,
he would take most of the hits because he was really the leader
and they felt if they could destroy him, destroy his credibility, and
even physically destroy him, if they could have killed him, they
would have done it."

"And what was unique about the Black Panther Party chapter in
Eugene is that most of the members were from a particular area,
from Compton. We all knew each other prior to Oregon. We were in
elementary school together. We were in junior high school together,
high school together. So we were drawing our friends from this
area [in Los Angeles] to come to Eugene, not as Panthers, but to
get an education. We were all students at the U of O, at Lane Community College.

"And this was really before our radical [turn]. This was before we
were really conscious of what was happening to poor people in
general, and black people in particular, throughout the country.

"We were more interested in what was happening in the Eugene
community because what we discovered is that there were whites
in Eugene who suffered from the same kinds of oppression and
had the same issues as blacks and Latinos in the inner city.

"If they were poor, they were uneducated, the chance of them
going to the University of Oregon was very, very slim. Once in the
university, when they find out that the[y] were from Springfield or
one of the poor communities, they were not totally accepted unless
they faked it and acted like they were from a different class background. But those whites who were from poor backgrounds were
candidates for supporting the Black Panther Party, even though
racism still kept many of them from totally supporting black issues, but in terms of understanding what was happening to them,
it was very, very interesting how they were able to gravitate toward
a movement of people who were concerned about injustices in the
society and therefore brought about another organization that focused on poor whites, which was the Peace and Freedom Party.

"One of the things that made the Eugene chapter of the Black
Panther Party successful in forming working relationships with

whites is that we looked at society [in terms of] class issues. Like issues of rich and poor, issues of poor people as opposed to a black nationalist position of just black people."

The Relationship Between the Eugene Panthers and Weatherman

"It was a really healthy relationship. Politically, we both believed in armed struggle. We believed in tearing everything down; that's just one of our programs. We also believe in educating the masses and having different kinds of programs, but militarily we thought that engaging in armed struggle, strategic guerrilla warfare, could force the government to make some major changes, where the government's position was not going to change."

On the Panthers' Revolutionary Vision (or Hallucination)

"And we felt that the only way you can make them change is to snatch them out. We believed that Eldridge Cleaver was going to be in the White House and we were going to run everybody out, paint it red, black, and green, and yellow, and orange, the rainbow colors, and just redistribute the land. Today I look back at it and I say, 'Wow man. You guys must have had some LSD! How did you think that that was going to happen?'

"But we were getting our reality confused with other realities in other countries like Vietnam, like North Korea, like Cuba, and we thought that we could bring about that kind of change here.

"I thought that it was not only possible but probable. I believed it. But fortunately we had great speakers who had more analytical skills, like your dad, like Dr. Art Pearl. I mean these guys were telling us, on a daily basis, 'Hey, man. I understand how bad you want a change, and you might look at me like I'm a professor and I'm all comfortable, so therefore I don't want a change. I want a change, too. But through your little .22 pistol with five bullets, it's not going to happen. Okay? 'Cause these guys have M-16s with unlimited supplies of ammunition, and when one of them shoots you, what are you going to do? Go to the doctor, go to his doctor, and say, "Fix me"?'

"I remember [your dad] bringing to our attention how the capitalist system was making money in Eugene off of us. Because every time they would arrest us, they would say, 'Okay, the bail is $10,000.' So the community would raise, your dad and other people like Dr. Stephen Deutsch and Dr. Pearl, they were going in their pockets and they would pay. They would help raise the bail money, but every time they would do that, the state would make a profit.

"Now because of the population and the consciousness of the population, you can't get too far ahead of the masses, and that's one of the things that your dad would lecture on to the students. 'Hey, you can't get so far ahead of the masses of the people that you turn around and you don't even know where they are. You have to stay in contact. You have to move fast enough but slow enough where they can see you and you can set examples.'

Stokely's Influence on the Young Anderson

"Stokely Carmichael was the one who convinced me to get involved in the movement. Prior to that I didn't understand it, I didn't know, I didn't support it. I was saying, 'Hey, look, I'm here to get a degree. I don't want to hear anything about Black Power, white power. or any other kind of power. . . . I just want to go to school and get my degree and go back to my community and get me a job and work.' That was my consciousness, but sitting down, the day he came [to Eugene in 1967], my brother looked at Stokely, because they knew each other from the SNCC and from working in the South.

"And he said to Stokely, 'Can you really explain to my brother why we should have Black Power and why we should be involved in this struggle?' And Stokely sat down with me for about twenty minutes, just the two of us, and the way that he would ask me questions, he used the technique of asking a question to where you would discover the answer and you would know for yourself.

"And he just sat down and he talked to me, and after that meeting I was a changed person. I was convinced that there was more to it, that there was more to just going to the university, getting a degree, and going on doing an individual solo kind of thing."

Anderson's Roots in Hardscrabble Compton, California

"Of course, before going to the University of Oregon, I was a thug. I was in LA, and I was on a destruction course. I was a well-dressed gangster.

"I was a ghetto gangster, and thought that that was it and my brother—may God be pleased with him—he forced me out of Compton, took me to Eugene, and here I am in almost a foreign country.

"And he had the support of other professors like Art Pearl, like your dad, there were about five, Stephen Deutsch. About five professors who would allow us to take their courses, to really work with us, and to give us a passing grade, because academically we were to the curb. We were tore up. We didn't have the skills. And they understood that, and as a result I was able to graduate from the University of Oregon with two degrees.

"When I was coming up, most of the police were white, most of the businesses in the community were owned by nonblacks, but we didn't know that because we were still in a majority. There was never any straight Klan coming off into our community. At the time, Compton was a petit bourgeois community. My parents both worked, they owned businesses, they didn't drink, they didn't use drugs, they didn't do any of that. They were good Christian people.

"We were raised in a different reality than had my father lived in the South, where you would hear rumors of such-and-such being raped and hanged, where the GI came back from Vietnam and they found him in another state in his uniform hanging from a tree. These kinds of things, it didn't happen in Compton, so our awareness of the struggle was slightly different."

The Need for Socialism Today

"We have to have [serious economic restructuring, even socialism]. Two years ago I took a sabbatical and I revisited Oregon. And I worked in the mills and the woodworking industry, and I worked with young whites. Everybody was white but me, and I listened to their conversations, and I watched their behavior, and trust me, you're talking about an oppressed group of people. Whites are in trouble economically.

"And these are not whites who are going out drinking a beer with the money or trying to buy their little toys like a boat and a pickup truck. I mean, these people are young whites who are married, who got two kids, and they're bringing their check home, and when they do [the] arithmetic, they don't have enough money.

"They don't have it, and they're watching the TVs and they're seeing these commercials about what they should have to feel happy, and they're not happy. A lot of the whites are tired, but they haven't put their finger on it exactly or they're in denial in terms of who is oppressing them.

"They're in denial. Like those people I was telling you about in Grant's Pass. I'd be at all kinds of work there like short-order cook, working in the mills, and I'm working with people who [are] scared; they're in denial of what is really happening to them economically. Their families are falling apart because, you know, Sam or George or Alfred is not making enough money.

"And that's what caused whites in the South during the Civil War [to take up arms]. It wasn't about slavery; it was about economics. They would make a product and send it to the North, and the North was getting rich. And the South was saying, 'Hey, wait a minute. A few people are getting rich, but hey, these guys got all the political power, they got all the economic power, and they're in control, and we don't like it. We would rather break away and have our own little thing.' And that is where I see us today. Once they can come face-to-face with that fear, they're going to switch up.

"[The Greens] have the solution, and it's based on fear. They fear [that] 'oh, my God. These guys are going to wreck the planet, and we are all going to die!' The ozone layer, the trees, the oceans, they're messing it up to the point where it's not about color, it's about *Homo sapiens*. Us, as living, thinking human beings are going to go off. We're going to be off the lifeline.

"And it's because of these people who don't have the courage to say, 'Stop the pollution! Let's not cut down another tree. Why are you destroying the Amazon?' That Green Party, they've got a platform.

"And I'm not going to go join them tomorrow. Only because I have a different agenda today, but in all honesty, they are more in line with bringing about some meaningful changes, and that whole fear factor is there. The whole fear factor of 'Look what we're doing to our planet.'"

JOSÉ ANGEL GUTIÉRREZ

Chicano Radicalism's Roots in Backward South Texas

"South Texas was a fiefdom or perhaps an internal colony of agribusiness in the 1960s. Education, particularly postsecondary, was for the children of Anglos, not Chicanos. If we managed to graduate from high school, our higher education was to attend a junior college, which some of us did. There were no public senior colleges or research universities nearby. The closest research institution was in Austin and in Houston, some two hundred to four hundred miles away for south Texans. The only public college was Texas Arts and Industries in Kingsville. The Chicano generation of activists for the late 1960s and 1970s gathered there and graduated from there. We were naïve and politically inexperienced. We had no clue how the world worked or could be made to work for us, much less make a world. I had the limited *Cristal* (*Cristal* is Spanish for Crystal City, my hometown) experiment as a background.

At Texas A&I is where I first heard, read, and studied political writings of national Chicano leaders such as César Chávez and Reies López Tijerina. I had my first meetings and collaboration with Anglo liberals and blacks. It was at A&I where I first read Marx, Lenin, Weber, Mills, and learned about Fidel Castro, Haight Ashbury and the hippies, Mao Tse-tung, Frantz Fanon, Gustavo Gutiérrez, Camilo Torres, and the Nation of Islam. I studied the Mexican Revolution and its leadership. During my teen years, it was *pachucos* that were the counterculture movement in *Cristal* and the Texas Rangers that were the enemy. Our only allies were ourselves.

"I moved on to St. Mary's University, a Catholic school in San Antonio, for a master's degree in 1967. There I had instructors that made copies available of the Port Huron Statement, the Weather Underground activities, speeches of Martin Luther King Jr., Elijah Muhammad and Malcolm X, Huey Newton, and Stokely Carmichael. They volunteered their time to engage some of us in a reading circle of these figures and their events.

"We traveled at our expense to the locations of these figures and activities: Atlanta, Albuquerque, Keene, California, Denver, Chicago, Austin, and Los Angeles. We decided to form the Mexican American Youth Organization. We were now at a different level and engaged with repressive governments, locally and nationally, but still naïve and inexperienced."

Raza's Relationships with the New Left

"We met with and negotiated working collaborations with SNCC, some Austin-based SDSers and Weather Underground rebels, Socialist Workers Party members, primarily Latinos, American Indian Movement [AIM], Puerto Rican *Independistas* in Chicago, along with the Blackstone Rangers and the Nation of Islam. We traveled as MAYO to Cuba, China, Lebanon, Canada, Mexico, Colombia, and El Salvador to seek contacts and expand our network of information. We became involved with student movements in Mexico and collaborated with many *teatros*/guerrilla theater groups in Latin America. We formed a political party, La Raza Unida [RUP], in January 1970 that by 1972 had organizing efforts and candidates in seventeen other states plus the District of Columbia. We had in the Texas RUP some Anglo and black militants as organizers and candidates in San Antonio, Fort Worth, Dallas, and Denison. Other state party RUPers had similar relations with other groups, namely the Peace and Freedom Party in California, AIM in

South Dakota, Young Lords in Chicago, Black Panthers in northern California, and Quebec separatists in Canada."

Women in the Chicana/Chicano Movement

"Chicanas have long complained about their triple oppression and ownership. My grandmother Refugio Casas Fuentes put it best: 'We suffer as women, being poor and Mexican here (meaning U.S.) and in Mexico. We are the property of our fathers, then husbands, then children. We are free only when we are old and alone.' Chicanas in PASO [Political Association of Spanish-Speaking Organizations], MAYO, and RUP were always complaining about the dual tensions they faced: Chicano nationalism trumping feminist demands; supporting Chicano leaders by menial work, not shared leadership. I think they were right. I always saw women doing the work and never getting credit; being involved in everything, yet not seen as leaders; and seldom listened to by men.

"Once MAYO morphed into the RUP in the early 1970s, Chicanas moved into leadership roles with party work across the country. They also became candidates and learned to garner resources and mobilize voters. By the mid-1970s, women as leaders were no longer an issue in the Chicano movement. The demand for Chicano studies, beginning with the *Plan de Santa Barbara*, also opened the doors for Chicanas to rise as intellectual workers and get their own voice."

Gringo

"When I stated we must eliminate the gringo system in south Texas economically, politically, and socially in 1968, the media headlined that I wanted to kill the gringo. I have lived with that headline since. The new reactionary Right has revived the quote and made me once again the demon. I am unrepentant."

ROXANNE DUNBAR-ORTIZ

The Radicalism of Martin Luther King Jr.

"I didn't think it at the time, but I now think that MLK was on the verge of becoming a revolutionary leader for the poor and working-class majority in the U.S. He had turned anti-imperialist, not simply against the Vietnam War, and his Poor People's Campaign was having amazing success in organizing poor whites in the South and white working-class people everywhere (as well as Native Americans, Latinos, Asians), young and old. I think he came to see himself as having been called to lead a revolution. I think he is the most dangerous person the United States has ever encountered, because of his message and his mass base and apparent incorruptibility or ambition. His death was the death of the possibility of revolution at that time. Now, though, we must know that it destroyed something more than a man and an opportunity for revolution, but the very possibility for a revolutionary leader to arise among us. We have to figure out other ways."

DAVID GILBERT

Pan-Africanism and Civil Rights

"I believe that post–World War II decolonization of Africa was the key context for the reemergence of the civil rights movement, and then that independent African nations became a model for Black Power. (Richard Wright wrote a book of that title, based on Africa, in the 1950s.) And yes, many blacks in the northern ghettos wanted to fight back. Both these trends were brilliantly synthesized and articulated by Malcolm X, who laid the basis for the Panthers, Republic of New Africa, and other revolutionary nationalist organizations of the late sixties."

Participatory Democracy Within Capitalism?

"Slavery and genocide of Native Americans form the very foundation of this country. Economic issues are central, and the U.S. can only be understood as an international economy, and a completely rapacious one at that. 'Participatory democracy,' while very important, did not adequately grasp those realities. (In 1967, I coauthored the first SDS pamphlet to name the system as 'U.S. imperialism.') But if one is consistent and thoroughgoing about it, participatory democracy cannot be achieved within capitalism."

In the following chapter, I examine the future. All of the discussants acknowledge that young people today are mostly politically dormant, and we all wonder what might change that. Barack Obama's presidency may spark youthful activism, just as John Kennedy's presidency ignited the social movements of the sixties. My radical colleagues speculate about whether we can or should try to relive the sixties, carrying forward its imagination and energy. This raises questions about how to teach the sixties, how to relate to our children, how to nourish their politics and social values. Of course, this is much the challenge our parents faced when we were young once. Much of this discussion is framed by the last forty years, when, with only a few interruptions, the Right has held the White House and dominated the political agenda.

๕๑ Eight ๖๑

We Were Young Once:
Our Children and the Next Left

*Times filled with tragedy are also times of greatness and wonder,
times that really matter and times truly worth living through. Whatever the future holds and as satisfying as my life is today, I miss
the sixties and always will.*

—Tom Hayden

I conclude my discussions of the interviews by examining the implications of the sixties for the future, especially for younger people born after, sometimes long after, the baby boom ended. What
lessons can be learned? How should the sixties be told and written about? Why are young people not mobilized against the war in
Iraq, and why are they not activist in the ways that Hayden's generation was? Here I explore continuities and discontinuities between that time forty years ago and the present world as we think
through where we go from here. Although I found all fourteen respondents to be highly pragmatic and forward-looking, all of them,
and I include myself in this, were somewhat stymied by the dominance of evangeloconservatives led by George W. Bush. That is
precisely why I am writing this book: I want to rediscover the sixties as a contested decade, neither Aquarian nor demonic. The sixties, especially the early sixties of Port Huron and civil rights, were
remarkably progressive periods in American history. And this new
history, in both North and South, was forged in large part by
young people stimulated by their college reading to take democracy into the streets, creating a legacy of activism and empathy
with which we are still contending.

The few exceptions today are interesting. A former high school student, Pat Korte, and former Students for a Democratic Society (SDS) founder Al Haber and other notable anti–Iraq war activists have re-formed SDS, and they issue a newsletter called *Next Left Notes*. This organization is primarily for young people. For graying radicals like me, there is an "adult" counterpart organization that we can join—MDS, or Movement for a Democratic Society.

The stirring Barack Obama victory gives us graying radicals renewed hope; it reminds us of the New Frontier, with Camelot opening into the New Left. Things are moving again. Anything seems possible. Only time will tell whether Obama is, like John Kennedy was, a centrist or whether he carries the torch of the Port Huron Statement.

SETTING THE STAGE: APATHY AND ACTIVISM AMONG HAYDEN'S YOUTH

The kids are alright.
—Todd Gitlin

Forty years ago, young people such as Tom Hayden changed the world, even if their legacy is defined as much by political defeat as by important victories, among them civil rights legislation. Other examples of this youthful activism are the four young black men who attempted to desegregate the Greensboro, North Carolina, lunch counter in 1960, launching the Student Non-Violent Coordinating Committee (SNCC) and the civil rights movement. And the three young men murdered near Philadelphia, Mississippi, during Freedom Summer drew national attention to the gestapo-like Klan and thus broadened the civil rights movement beyond the South. The iPod generation has much to learn from Hayden and his ilk, although by virtue of electronic prostheses, this generation can achieve global connection and build cyber-community in ways that the Port Huron generation would have envied.

Christopher Lasch (1979), during the 1970s, described the existence in the United States of a "culture of narcissism," identifying consumerism, materialism, and individualism as outcomes of the decade that had just ended. The activism of the sixties had run aground and turned toward cultural expressions and exhibitions, alcohol and drug ecstasy, and self-absorption. This self-orientation lacked mooring in the New Left politics of everyday life, in the public sphere, or in community. It is facile to blame postsixties young people as if they have substantive alternatives, especially given the power of the Right to control the political agenda, the Evangelical church to set a social and personal agenda, and the media and cultural producers to promote false needs and divert people from reality and toward "reality television."

In our interviews, Dick Flacks laments the loss of sixties radicalism among his college students, who by contrast appear apathetic. Part of this is surely because kids today are not worried about being drafted and going to fight in Iraq, Afghanistan, or, perhaps, Iran in the near future. It is also partly because young people today inhabit a "media culture" in which instantaneous cultural and interpersonal messaging diverts them from political awareness and activism. They are constantly being entertained via television, gaming, and the Internet. They seek connection (via texting, e-mailing, posting), but they do not enjoy community of the kind exemplified in early SDS and the civil rights movement. Or perhaps their community is just different, and we cannot yet recognize this.

Just as the sixties do not lend themselves to a smooth narrative, building to a clear denouement, so the early twenty-first century resists the sort of analysis I have been offering. As we just noticed

Anti–Iraq war demonstration in Washington, DC, 2007. (AP Photo/Jose Luis Magana)

with the rebirth of SDS, some American college kids *do* protest the Iraq war, and even use old-fashioned vehicles such as marches with placards. For the most part, these protests have been bi-coastal and not in the "heartland," the so-called red states, although even that political geography oversimplifies. Obama's victory began to redraw that map as red states turned blue—perhaps becoming purple.

Nevertheless, kids live in a global village that allows them to be anywhere/anytime, to communicate rapidly, to acquire instant information, to reach a vast audience. They could (and some do) become activist "netrooters" who use means such as MoveOn.org to educate and organize. The Internet certainly changes the political calculus by giving users unprecedented access and reach.

The Internet might have been the perfect vehicle for sixties screeds calling for social change, if the users had had access to a computer. But, and this is what Flacks and I have been debating, one's posting can quickly become submerged in the huge amount of Web flotsam and jetsam. Blogs are a dime a dozen, so many that no one can keep up with them except by "bookmarking" a few favorites. A new form of Internet activism is called "hacktivism," using the Internet to further radical causes and to destabilize major social institutions, blending hacking (breaking into computer networks, usually illegally) and activism.

The Internet, the engine of a laptop capitalism, has begun to play a role in helping us remember and in determining what we remember. Probably every baby boomer with access to the Internet has had the experience of an unbidden e-mail from a long-lost friend or acquaintance who googled us. "Do you remember me? We were in elementary school together. I became a belly dancer and got married, but it did not last." (That was a real one sent to me by a very nice girl.) She continues: "I saw your name on a college reading list; I'm going back to get my master's degree. I wondered if it was the same Ben Agger. If so, please write back."

I teach my students about the sixties using this vehicle of searching for identity within generation and history. I try to stir them by telling them that I attended a Grateful Dead concert in 1968 for which the admission was $2.50. Ancient history! I recently taught a graduate student in Texas who happened to attend my high school in Oregon many years after me. Talking with her sparked memories, and I went online and found an announcement of that concert in the University of Oregon student paper, *The Daily Emerald*. And I forgot—this is my point here—that the concert was sponsored by SDS. Thus, my past, which I thought I remembered accurately, has been enriched and corrected using the

Grateful Dead concert, Eugene, Oregon, 1968, sponsored by SDS. (Courtesy of the Oregon Daily Emerald; *used by permission)*

Internet, not in a startling way but in stitching together the self I was and have become, which is always a work in progress.

And then there is the larger issue of the decline of discourse, particularly of books. I have already suggested that the "academization" of discourse dooms much writing to obscurity. Ex–New Left professors intend their writings to be read by a few hundred, not a few hundred thousand, let alone millions. Academia is not the only problem. Commercial publishers want books with short sentences that pander to television-accustomed taste. Finally, people, especially the young, spend much less time reading than they did before television and the Internet.

Young people today, even if they do not orient to traditional pulp discourse, e-mail, instant message, text, and post. They write and read, but in ways unrecognizable to their sixties parents. They seek connection, even if they do not always attain community. They compose themselves on the screen, searching for uncoerced instantaneity, the management of impressions they create, and a laconic discourse that can be produced and consumed quickly.

By "uncoerced instantaneity," I mean that they can make electronic connections rapidly, potentially in real time, but they can be selective about when, and to whom, they respond. Thus, young people with cells glued to their ear listen for and leave voice mail or they text. Gone is voice-to-voice contact, except as an infrequent aside, after sufficient vetting of voice mail and texts has been conducted. This fumbling toward connection reflects lack of self-confidence and fear of commitment. In the "old" days, they would have had to pick up the phone and risk getting a parent! Or they could have composed a letter or note. Or they could have just walked up to their friend's door and hoped that someone was home.

By "impression management," I mean Erving Goffman's (1959) term for the ways in which modern selves have front-stage and backstage lives. They read from social scripts but conceal the real "me," much as Sigmund Freud and George Herbert Mead, the founder of symbolic interactionism, recognized. Self-concealment and role-playing are ever necessary when people are equivalent to the impressions they make, when everything is about marketing and spin. The self is a commodity judged by its wrapping. There is caprice involved, too, as young people realize that they can try on and take off various possible selves, given the postmodern plasticity of self-presentation in this Internet era. Laptop capitalism promotes the use of "aliases," concealments. However, Goffman was writing in a modern or modernist stage of capitalism in which there was still a backstage, a more or less firm substratum of the self and of identity that could be concealed under a mask, but to which the actor/self could return after the performance was over. Today, it is not clear that young people (and some older people) possess a stable foundation of identity from which they then depart as they reinvent themselves using electronic aliases.

These unorthodox but frenzied literary lives lead to "composition" created and consumed hurriedly. The issue is not bad grammar but thinness of communication. Anyone who has spent time in a chat room recognizes that one-liners substitute for sentences with conditional clauses, let alone paragraphs, let alone full pages. "BTW" and "LOL" stand for deeper sentiments and more complex constructions. Kids deploy the available electronically mediated discourse, which speeds up and flattens out writing into, in effect, text bytes. Thus, connection may be fleeting. The ground shifts with every text message or MySpace posting.

Today, every ground is in the middle. Postmodern cynicism and irony abound, even if people do not name their disaffection postmodern or trace it to Friedrich Nietzsche through Jacques Derrida and Michel Foucault. Aversion to politics is a reaction to real events and deep disenchantment, including the denouement of the sixties: The Chicago police opened skulls in plain view of the world's media; Richard Nixon used "plumbers" to flush out the opposition's secrets and fix the election; Ronald Reagan was simple-minded; Bill Clinton had sex with an intern and then denied that it was sex; George W. Bush trumped the rest by appealing to Americans' fear of the Other.

I have often told my students that 1969 was the last good year, but in saying that, I misrepresent what really happened: It was the next-to-last year of a profoundly significant decade. It was also the year I left the United States, only to return twelve years later a changed person. I can only guess what I would have become had I stayed. I might have remained a small-town boy, without a more cosmopolitan vantage. Returning to the United States in 1981 was dizzying: I had missed more than a decade of American experience and was already a young adult. I have never returned to Eugene, even though I planned to do so many times. I was overwhelmed by the experience of disconnection. My sixties seemed buried in the past, in adolescence, never to reemerge. It took me another twenty-five years to figure out that I needed to settle accounts.

Although the sixties fascinate me because I sense that we are on the verge of reliving them, with Nixon/Bush and Vietnam/Iraq, and perhaps Obama/Kennedy or Hayden, I am equally interested in how my generation's distinctive experiences of those times formed us and differentiated us from our parents and succeeding generations. We are more egalitarian, less officious, perhaps too

Antidraft rally in Eugene,
late 1960s. (Photo cour-
tesy of Fred Tepfer)

driven. We have strengths such as vision and commitment, and we
also have weaknesses, such as an inflated sense of our own destiny. One might call this being "sixties on the inside," an identity
forged in the simultaneity of personal growth and political turmoil,
which defined our lives then.

This image is from the fall of 1968, my sixteenth year. It was an
antiwar rally in downtown Eugene. The young man with the micro-
phone, a high school classmate of mine, was said to have burned
his draft card publicly a few minutes after this photo was taken,
one of the first young men in Eugene to do so. Lots of kids did not
have long hair, and they dressed conservatively, much as Hayden
did during the Columbia uprising. Nevertheless, photography
challenges memory, which distorts the past into unequivocal images that by simplifying, exaggerate.

The experience of political upheaval as it affects the self is not
uniquely American. Indeed, given our relatively stable political system, we may be strangers to coup and conspiracy by comparison
with other less settled nations. But our worlds were rocked by Dallas, Memphis, and Los Angeles, and by the reportage from Vietnam, in ways that changed us forever, making us skeptical about
authority and official accounts of events. Virtually no one in my
age group who watched the 1968 Democratic National Convention
remained inured to the abuses of authority. We were all against
the cops and Daley even if, until then, we may not have been active in the movement.

There were many such instances when daily life was punctuated
by terrible news that signaled life changes, including an embrace
of radical politics. Just as the New Left began deep in the 1950s

FBI "missing" poster of three civil rights workers, who later turned up dead, Mississippi, 1964. (Bettmann/Corbis)

around issues of civil rights for black people in the American South, with the formation of the Southern Christian Leadership Conference (SCLC) in 1957 and SNCC three years later, so the right-wing counter-revolution began in the South. It was led by the Klan's nightriders and police deathly opposed to the end of segregation, which was slavery continued by other means. I was twelve when I heard the terrible news that three civil rights workers had been murdered and their bodies buried in rural Mississippi, near a town called Philadelphia, during the SNCC-sponsored Summer Project, or Freedom Summer, in 1964 (McAdam 1988). James Chaney, Andrew Goodman, and Michael Schwerner, a black and two Jews, were between twenty and twenty-four when they died. I remember that my father gave up his 1952 Chevrolet to two of his graduate students who were driving down from Eugene to work in Mississippi. We stood on the front lawn and waved good-bye.

The Summer Project was brought home vividly to us as my dad's students, Sandy Watts and Suzanne Maxson, traveled to Mississippi during that fateful summer of 1964. They wrote back about their experiences, and their remarks were published in Eugene's Congress of Racial Equality (CORE) newsletter, reprinted here. Their remarks are preceded by a description of the Selma-to-Montgomery march written by a University of Oregon student. These incredible documents, prepared with an old-fashioned typewriter and mimeographed for the local CORE chapter members, capture the texture of the times, and they bear firsthand witness to these earth-shattering events in the South.

The southern civil rights movement was certainly accelerated by the sympathy of the Kennedy brothers for the cause of civil rights. Jack Kennedy's death was devastating to black Americans, who recognized in him a significant supporter, if not a soul brother. Part of my story about the sixties involves reading, long after the fact, about theories of the Kennedy assassination. I do not love a conspiracy so much as I want to understand how things could be so murky for so long. November 22 looms large in any account not only of the sixties but also of the formation of baby boomers' identities.

My children endured such a day several years ago when, on a Tuesday, we learned that suicide bombers had crashed hijacked planes into the World Trade Center and the Pentagon. After dropping off my kids at school, I was driving away and I heard radio talk reporting the first sketchy details. A private plane had gone in . . . no, it was commercial. . . . The fires were being broadcast on CNN. Not until I got to work an hour later did I realize that America was falling apart again, this time in real time. The Kennedy assassination was conveyed by ticker tape, which one can view in the Sixth

6.

* * * * * * * * * * * * * * * * * * *

<u>March to Montgomery</u>: <u>Impressions of a U. of C. Student</u>

The following is an excerpt from a letter I wrote to a friend describing my trip to Alabama. Whereas it perhaps does not capture the "whole" of my experience in the South or every detail of the March, I hope it is an adequate summary. That the demonstration succeeded in once again making the nation face squarely the magnitude of the Negro Revolution — the nation and particularly Alabamians — and the urgent need for immediate solution, cannot be denied. How long it will be before hopes become realities and the quest after equal opportunity is fulfilled are questions which trouble us all. The Selma-Montgomery travail did make a significant inroad upon the hard core of American racism; I hope that the added impetus given the movement by the march in Alabama will result ultimately, and soon, in that hard core being shattered completely.

——— Gretchen Klippel

"...I called 'the only Unitarian minister in Birmingham' (no one knew his name) who had given refuge to Carl Nelson from Eugene a week earlier. However, the man was so frightened he would not give me his name as, he explained, he couldn't be sure I was who I said I was. I told him that I couldn't be sure he was who he said he was either but that I'd come a long way and had been told to call him for advice. His advice was that I remain in Birmingham that night, making it quite emphatic that driving to Montgomery alone and without a place to stay might prove to be disasterous. If I was sincere, he went on to say, I could meet him and the group at the Airport Hotel at 5:45 a.m. and drive with them. I took his advice and stayed at the Airport Hotel but the next morning, since his directions for finding the church had been very poor, I became lost and ended up driving to Montgomery alone.... I, of course, encountered no difficulties along the way but was overjoyed when I finally spotted a group of people gathering in front of a church outside the city. Judging by the mixture of Negro and white people, their attire and such, I assumed them to be marchers. I pulled over, was joined by a minister from New Jersey and five young girls, and was directed to the school grounds where people were gathering and from where the march was to proceed. Since there was no one there from Oregon (or at least I found no one) I "attached" myself to some people from the University of Colorado — who had in turn joined with some students from Tougaloo College in Tougaloo, Mississippi. Our seriousness of purpose and reasons for being there made us fast friends in a hurry.

"'Governor George,' of course, managed to detain the fast-growing crowd for nearly three hours before allowing us on city streets. Nothing could dampen people's spirits, however. He only made it possible for more to join in. Rumour had it at one time that there were 55 planes, private and chartered, circling the Montgomery airport trying to land at one point that morning. I can well believe it. Anyway, when things began to move I judged from the number of people in front of me (I could not see the front of the line some six blocks ahead) and behind me (I couldn't see the end of the line either) that I must have been somewhere in the middle. Seeing airial photographs of the gathering in the <u>Birmingham Post-Herald</u> later, I find I was nearly at the front. The line was two miles long; there were some 35,000 marchers involved.

"The beginning of our trek took us through the Negro community on the southwest side of Montgomery which was just like I had heard it would be—run down shanties and less than desireable living conditions. But only the living conditions could be described as shabby and poor — the people lining the March route were jubilant and, indeed, "rich" in spirit. Of course, we sang...

(continued, next page.)

Floor Museum. "President Kennedy has been shot in Dallas." I remember hearing on my parents' shortwave radio that Kennedy was planning a trip to Dallas in November. I do not know why I remember that. But it is another piece in the puzzle of self-assemblage.

Recently, our family returned by train from a trip to Canada and to Buffalo, New York. Our kids had just become Canadian citizens; like me, they are also American. We wanted our kids to have a

7.

March to Montgomery (continued)

and those who were too old to march with us—or too young—or sick—or had the
responsibility of looking after a family--sang and clapped along with us....

"As we neared the downtown area the number of federal troopers who had been
standing guard at every intersection along the way increased as the number of
white people increased. Most of the white on-lookers just stood and stared in
awed silence — some glowering with hatred and others just standing there amazed.
There were only a handful of hecklers who stood at one corner making obscene
gestures and calling us names. It only aroused a chuckle from the marchers--
possibly even a bit of pity. There was a confederate flag hanging from one
hotel window; a man stood on the curb and waved another. From the windows of the
Alabama Bible Society fluttered a huge photograph and banner proclaiming that
Martin Luther King was a communist. It just made Alabama and Governor Wallace
look all the more inane. ...everyone had congregated and settled in front of
the capitol building — from which flies the Alabama state flag and a confederate
flag but no American flag.... (King) is truly an admirable human being; he is a
clear-thinking individual, acutely aware of all facets of the dilemma both
black and white. He is an eloquent speaker and firm in his belief that need
for Negro civil rights cannot wait.... During the course of these three hours,
Wallace did not come out. It is said that he sat in the capitol building
peering out from between the slats in some Venetian blinds. What a picture!
The steps of the building were guarded by a double row of green-helmeted Alabama
"special" guardsmen.

"After the speeches were over, there was some bit of confusion in trying
to direct people to busses which would transport them to specific destinations
(airport, train station, etc.) The people I had been with in the demonstration
dispersed immediately following so I fell to making inquiries as to how I might
find a ride to St. Jude's where the march had started and where I had left my
car. Somehow I was misinformed and went to the wrong place — a baseball field
parking lot some seven blocks from the capitol. About one hundred others had
similarly been misguided so we started back to the capitol building where we
should have remained in the first place — only to have our way blocked at every
intersection by four burly, helmeted Alabama state troopers and two state patrol
cars. They informed us we could not go back to the capitol THAT way (or those
ways.) It was aggravating but we obliged and marched 10 blocks beyond and
around and back to our sought after place of departure.

"When back at St. Jude's I asked directions to the Birmingham highway
since they were urging everyone to leave Montgomery with the utmost haste, and
was piloted some twenty miles northward by a Negro boy. Looking back I'm even
more grateful for his having taken the trouble to help me out of town — knowing
now, as I didn't then, of the slaying of Mrs. Luizzo from Detroit."

* *

WORDS from SANDRA WATTS and SUZANNE MAXSON in MISSISSIPPI

For those persons interested in the Mississippi movement, particularly
anyone planning to go there, Suzanne recommends these books:
    SNCC: The New Abolitionists — Howard Zinn.
    Freedom Ride — James Peck.
    Our Faces, Our Voices — Lillian Smith.

(continued, next page.)

multinational identity and the possibilities and options that this
provides, and so I filed paperwork enabling them to derive their
Canadian citizenship from mine. Just before Christmas, we
learned that they were now also Canadian. And so we planned a
trip to show them their new country, as well as the border city,
Buffalo, where I had lived for over a decade after I returned to the
United States in the early 1980s.

8.

Sandra and Suzanne in Mississippi (continued)

    Our letters are greatly appreciated by both Sandra and Suzanne. For those who do not have their addresses:

        Sandra Watts   Suzanne Maxson
        Philadelphia Project   838 Lutz St.
        General Delivery   Canton, Mississippi
        Philadelphia, Mississippi

* * * * *

    Sandy is now working in Philadelphia, Neshoba County, Mississippi, one of the strong centers of the K.K.K. She is one of two civil rights workers there. She writes, "This project was not started until the middle of August due to the hostility encountered after the murder of the three civil rights workers here." The following are other excerpts from her letters.

    "There has been a SNCC Movement in Selma since 1962 and the workers were going along slow but sure in developing local leadership and working to an end of building up local people and working themselves out of a job. King, however, comes into a place and works on a National level and gets National support but in doing so he takes on all the work himself and disregards local leadership."

    "All these problems along with the voting bill make work down here very complicated and the problems very complex. We are all now trying to get together plans to deal with the problems of the voting bill. I imagine that if it goes through we will see white people down here registering Negroes and trying to control their votes. We must now try to undertake a very extensive educative program with the people down here."

    "It is seen now that it is not enough to get Negroes registered to vote. Far more important and serious problems are involved and the Movement is going to have to move into these areas and not settle for a main program of just voter registration."

    "For the first time since the Movement has been in Madison County — some three years ago — the Negro people got together---took over the whole program... in a County Convention and talked about what they would like to see done in their own communities. I think that we made a mistake when we first come into Mississippi.... Instead of creating programs and political parties we should have first brought the people together and out of their common need to see their immediate problems solved they would have developed their own vehicles for change."

    "There was also a young man — Negro — killed in Rankin County last week. His body was found by the railroad tracks near his home. He worked nights in Jackson and had a car almost exactly like one of the COFO workers who is working in Rankin County. The sheriff did not even talk to his folks and the body was embalmed by the county coroner five hours after it was found. There was no autopsy and the coroner's jury ruled that he died of "Unknown causes." His father later ordered an autopsy but the doctor who did it said he could not tell what had exactly killed him because the body had already been embalmed. However, the theory among most of the COFO workers is that his car was mistaken for the COFO worker's car or because someone thought that he was letting one of the workers drive his car. The FBI is not doing one thing in this case and neither is the sheriff's department. This is just one of the many killings that go on in Mississippi all the time and that nothing is done about."

(continued, next page.)

    On the way home from the train station in downtown Dallas next to Dealey Plaza, we turned left by the Texas School Book Depository. If Kennedy's motorcade had not taken the same left on that November day in 1963, we would not be talking about the sixties as history and identity. Indeed, some assassination conspiracy theorists contend that the motorcade route was changed at the last minute, exposing Kennedy to a rifleman's opportunities that did not

9.

<u>Sandra</u> <u>and</u> <u>Suzanne</u> <u>in</u> <u>Mississippi</u> (continued)

"We also had testing of the Civil Rights Law here last week without incident except for the one fact that no one got served or admitted to the white restaurants or library."

* * *

<u>Suzanne</u> is working in Canton, Rankin County, Mississippi. She describes her surroundings as she writes, "The office has heavy screening on the windows, a 2-way radio goes on all the time. Beside the phone are lists of who to call in emergencies. FBI, Justice Dept, Farmer, even Lyndon."

"COFO is not sponsoring a summer project but FDP (Freedom Democratic Party) is as is SCLC -- King's group. COFO wants to keep going as it is.... The problem is to organize in a grass roots way, then let the local people program what they want -- we function as aides not leaders. The messianic tendency of people who come in for a short time isn't too helpful in the long run. That is COFO's thinking. However the local people love the idea. Out here some are planting extra large gardens to feed them."

"Today we all (the staff I work on) went to Jackson for the civil rights commission hearings. We ate in the canteen 3 whites 3 blacks. It was an integrated (for the occassion) restaurant. None of us ate -- its choking. Every time we ride together we get tense."

"Everything a Negro has must not be as nice--new as white."

"These Negroes still think the whites are human and will ultimately treat them right."

"You sit in a car as a cop passes and wish you were invisible so that the Negroes carrying you won't have trouble."

"...a horse which I ride. I have no other form of transportation sometimes.'

"I have a real good feeling going on about the people and have some hope. It seems like we do so little."

"The young man I work with has an interesting history. He started a school boycott, was kicked out and began working for CORE. He has spent about 4-5 months in jail -- once was put in front of a cop car and told to run. He ran about 5 miles, dodged off into the brush ran till he couldn't then went to sleep. One time a cop held a gun on him and told him he was going to kill him. Sears said the cop was scared to death. He was with the task force that looked for Chaney and friends.
"The spooky thing is that Sears isn't a phenomena. People I meet and work with can tell you longer lists. I think what impresses me is that Sears really believes cops and segregationists are human and will ultimately realize they are wrong. He thinks they'll have to be pressured but he thinks they are human. It just amazes me. I think they are brutes that don't think Negroes are human and feel nothing about depriving, beating or killing.

"As I say and hear said every day, WHY ARE PEOPLE SO MEAN?"

------ Freedom
S ----

CORE newsletter, Eugene, Oregon, 1965. (University of Oregon Libraries–Special Collections and University Archives)

exist along the first route. But others respond that the map, printed on the front page of a Dallas paper a few days before the presidential visit, was too small to be drawn to scale and that more precise details were given in text accounts of the planned route. Also interesting is the headline that "controversy" surrounded the Kennedy visit as he made his way to the hostile South.

I explained to my kids why they were passing over hallowed ground. My daughter picked up on the possibility of shots from the grassy knoll. I further explained—the real point here—that they became Canadians because I had left for Canada in 1969 because Lyndon Johnson escalated the Vietnam War, whereas Kennedy had probably wanted to pull out because, because, because. Not only did history intersect with my own biography but also that intersection affected the lives of my children, who could link their train trip to Canada with their passing in front of the School Book Depository. History came alive in the various selves we have become, surrounded, as we were, by the physical environments of Toronto, Dallas, the train station, and our return to suburban Arlington.

The connections are the interesting things—November 22, the motorcade route, Vietnam, Canada, my kids. Excavating identity through storytelling about events surrounding our earlier years yields not only the self—quite a find—but the elusive meaning of the events, which is never clear in the moment. Kennedy's assassination turned the sixties, and thus our lives, in a different direction, away from idealism and toward combat, ending with disappointment and even new lives abroad. This echoes an earlier discussion about America as a state of mind. Some of us, embittered by assassinations, racism, and an escalating war, not only turned away from America but also left it and augmented our identities with new identities as Canadians or Scandinavians, making this multiculturalism available for our children. This is one way of explaining why my kids got to go to Canada that summer and visit a Toronto bar frequented by draft dodgers, after which we drove the route Kennedy had taken when I was exactly my son's age—eleven—so many years ago.

But not all sixties people feel a need to retrace their steps. Perhaps they stayed home, lucked into a student deferment, established careers, and raised kids insensitive to politics. It is a demographic mistake to portray baby boomers as having been homogeneous during the sixties. In my high school, there were a few of us politicos, a cohort of hippies, and a vast majority of middle-class kids whose parents supported the war, at least until Tet, and led normal lives, with carpooling, football, and weekend parties. The clean-cut kids in the image reproduced here, taken from the 1968–1969 school year at my high school, appear to be conducting student government in an orderly way. And that was a year of unprecedented loss of equilibrium, with accompanying self- and social expressiveness.

Eugene was more liberal than most American towns, and there were professors' and professionals' kids mixed in. We boomers were a diverse lot for whom the sixties later became very different stories about Oedipus, grass, and concerts. The hard Left and

Student council meeting, South Eugene High School, 1968. (Photo courtesy of Fred Tepfer)

Right were galvanized about the war and civil rights, but many were in the amorphous middle, not particularly exercised about these issues until late in the decade.

The same could be said for Americans today. The war in Iraq, although unpopular, has not generated mass protests (on American shores) to match the Vietnam protests. Millions have rallied overseas, but Bush was oblivious; indeed, these "anti-American" protests may have hardened his resolve to stay the unilateral course. The young, although more likely to favor the Democrats, have not turned out to the polls in large numbers, at least until Obama. Even then, fewer voted than pollsters anticipated. Bush was viewed as incompetent, but he was reelected in 2004 because a slender majority of Americans apparently approved of his unyielding military leadership. His "war presidency" reinforced his macho/military image by comparison with that of the defeated John Kerry, who volunteered to fight in Vietnam and was a decorated veteran. The Swift boat scandal, where military veterans, with White House support and perhaps masterminding, tried to discredit Kerry's military record, was Orwellian: Kerry volunteered to fight in Vietnam and Bush avoided military service using family connections. But Bush talked tough, persuading the "silent majority" (again that term) that he would be uncompromising on terrorism, a manipulative political category designed to generate support for jingoistic policies.

An exemplary photographic image supposedly depicts John Kerry and "Hanoi Jane" Fonda (who slid from vixen to Viet Cong sympathizer) at a June 13, 1971, rally in Mineola, New York. They appear to be sharing the platform, suggesting political collusion between the two. Kerry and Fonda were both at this rally, but the Right doctored the picture to make it appear that they were together onstage. Kerry returned from the war believing that it was wrong, and he led a growing group of antiwar veterans who spoke out against Nixon's policies, a group that included Adrian Vaaler, from Eugene, who enters my story in a few paragraphs.

The Right diminished protesters during the Vietnam era by calling them "communists" and "pinkos." This had currency during the cold war. Today, the Others are "terrorists," hardly a valid theoretical category. As noted earlier, terror, the explosion of local random violence, is apparently different from military violence in that it is difficult to predict and resist. "Terror" as it is used today has a distinctly anti-American connotation. Terror is done "to" us, from the outside, by evil enemies. Our military interventions are "measured responses" spreading freedom and democracy. But cruise missiles smashing into buildings and homes are unpredictable violence—terror by another name. Terror is the killing of innocent civilians and children in the name of regime change. "Terrorist" is the name used by Americans to characterize their enemies, who are "othered" as evil.

This parallels the discursive construction of the Vietnamese "enemy" during that protracted war. Viet Cong and North Vietnamese regular forces were characterized as brutal and inhuman, as Japanese soldiers had been similarly portrayed during World War II. They were termed "gooks," objectifying them so that they could be killed without shame. Their military atrocities were magnified, whereas our My Lais were downplayed or ignored. Philip Caputo (1977) makes the point that terror and brutality were orders of the day during the guerrilla-style Vietnam War, which was fought at close quarters. War crimes are difficult to distinguish from war itself, as he discovered when he was court-martialed (but eventually acquitted) toward the end of his tour of duty in Vietnam.

Sometimes, the shoe was on the other foot. By 1969, radicals had objectified their enemies, especially police, as "pigs," as we saw earlier in our discussion of Weatherman. Weathermen termed working-class youth, whom they were trying to recruit, as "grease." And, of course, southern whites had called blacks "niggers" for decades. Everyone was objectifying everybody else in order to deplete their humanity. Discourse was very powerful then.

The silent majority accepted the Pentagon and White House portrayal of our Vietnam-era enemies, and the cold war Soviet Union, as subhuman. This helps explain why they remained silent for so long. The acquiescent majority was paralleled by those—their children, mainly—who were not particularly political but who liked to smoke dope and listen to the protest-oriented rock of the day. These kids were as apathetic as their parents, impervious to televised violence, and reluctant to join a mass political movement. For the most part, they did not become hippies, who led a whole lifestyle of anti-instrumentality, self-expression, and psychedelia. The stoned majority did not protest; it escaped, substituting grass for beer and sixties rock for the earlier music from Buddy Holly and Elvis Presley's era.

These kids were more likely to be liberal than their parents, especially on social issues such as civil rights and free speech. They did not want to go to Vietnam, and some enlisted in the National Guard to avoid it. Others received student deferments. But they were not joiners, and they found SDS rhetoric too strident. Everyday life for many Americans during the sixties was unmarred by eruptions of political conflict. They read about such events but were largely inured to them, especially if they lived in the suburbs and the Midwest. They were quick to try marijuana and attend rock concerts; in the language of the early twenty-first century, they "partied," but did not join or even vote for political parties.

Although I just said that many kids wanted to avoid Vietnam, some served, even some from Eugene. Those drafted may not have had escape routes such as Canada or conscientious-objector status.

Ten boys, all from South Eugene High School, were killed in Vietnam between 1965 and 1974, spanning the beginning and end of our involvement. The boys ranged in age from nineteen to twenty-seven, with most at the young end. It was discovered in 2008 that an eleventh boy had also been killed in action. Thus was the war brought home, for their families, friends, and classmates. Kreg Viestenz had been in Vietnam only a month before he was killed. (See Box 8.1.) Stories of the sixties are incomplete without memories of the dead. Given their age, these boys were innocents.

— ౭ం **Box 8.1   Kreg Viestenz, a Boy from My High School** ख —

Kreg was airborne qualified with the First Cavalry. The First Cav's historian reports that "PFC Kreg Arthur Viestenz, KIA on 18 September 1968, was assigned to C Troop, 1st Squadron, 9th Cavalry. The 1-9th CAV was the Air Cavalry Squadron for the 1st Cavalry Division (Airmobile) during the Vietnam War. Commonly referred to as the Cav of the Cav they performed reconnaissance missions for the division." They were primarily mobile airborne soldiers. Adrian Vaaler, a Vietnam vet from Eugene, remarked that "usually the Air Cav Troop provided transportation for soldiers. If that Air Cav Troop was the same as the one in my unit, they also used gunships for reconnaissance, or possibly Cobra gunships. We commonly called the First Cavalry Division (Airmobile) the First Air Cav Division. We usually avoided the official military designations for units."

Viestenz's official service records indicate that he was killed in Quang Tri, which is a province as well as a city near Hue. He was probably airlifted to an emergency military hospital at Long Binh, where he was declared dead. UH-1B Huey gunships, manufactured by Bell Helicopter, were the primary means of transporting soldiers into the field.

Kreg's brother, Kerry, provides rich detail about his brother's life and death. Given the circumstances of Kreg's death, this is a profile in courage. Kerry's moving words remind me that I was in school on the day that Kreg's death was announced over the loudspeaker, bringing the war home. They remind all of us that lives were ended just as they were getting started. Kreg Viestenz was courageous in battle and had a passion for golf. But the tragedy of Kreg is that we will never know what he would have become.

I remember when [Kreg] was sent to Fort Benning, GA, and I think also to Fort Bragg, NC, for additional training. Kreg did indeed enlist but not directly out of high school. He went to U of O for a couple terms and just was not sure why or for what end purpose he was going. I am not sure exactly what prompted him to enlist, but it was not a decision lightly taken. He was very dedicated to the cause in Vietnam as he understood it and said he preferred to enlist rather than be drafted.

A little background on our family life will give you some insight into Kreg. We grew up in an army family as our dad was an army officer. We were stationed in Fort Riley, KS; Germany; Oregon; and Fort Benning, GA. Much of our youth was living in army posts, but we were fortunate to have been assigned to Eugene, OR, for many years. Dad was the active commanding officer of the army reserve unit there for many years. Kreg went to grade school in Eugene from fourth grade, then to Wilson Junior High thru eighth grade. At this point we transferred to Fort Benning, GA, for two years and then came back to Eugene to finish Kreg's last two years of high school at South, where he graduated in June of 1967.

Kreg was always a good student and participated in many athletics. He discovered golf while we were in Fort Benning, and this became his passion. By the time he was sixteen, he was capable of shooting even par. Kreg played on South's golf team, which went undefeated in district matches his senior year. Although they faltered at state competition, the team was highly talented. He once caddied for a very successful woman pro golfer by the name of Clifford Ann Creed and considered going on the road to be a professional caddy. I know he dreamed of golf as a profession, but just out of high school there are so many other things of interest to do that he lost focus on his golf. I think he also figured he may be drafted if he did not go to college and get the student deferment. As I mentioned before, he was totally set against being drafted, and once he decided to enlist, he went in 100 percent. Kreg did not do things unless he was going to do them 100 percent. Kreg was fearless and a daredevil, so this often got him into trouble as he would push the boundaries of parental and school limits. Nothing serious or illegal, just adventuresome sort of trouble. Kreg was also very outgoing, with a great sense of humor, and made friends easily. He was two years ahead of me in school, and I looked up to him proudly. He was a great older brother who made sure the younger boys in the family were taken care of before his interests. Kreg was second oldest in the family of four boys, and he took the role of oldest brother when Kirk joined the navy right out of high school. All of us boys had our first name starting with a "K," Kirk, Kreg, Kerry, and Kirby. I am not sure that was for any particular reason, but it would sometimes drive my mom crazy trying to discipline us four and getting her K's mixed up.

I think you should also know that Kreg received the following service medals awarded posthumously: Army Commendation Medal, Purple Heart Medal, Air Medal, Good Conduct Medal, and Bronze Star Medal with "V" device. Others prior to his death include National Defense Service Medal, Vietnam Service Medal, Vietnam Campaign Ribbon, Combat Infantryman Badge, Parachutist Badge, Expert Badge with Rifle Bar, and Sharpshooter Badge with automatic rifle and machine gun Bars.

The Bronze Star Medal with "V" device is especially noteworthy, and I would like to share with you the reason for this medal as described on his award: award of the Bronze Star Medal for heroism. Reason: "For heroism, not involving participation in aerial flight, in connection with military operations against a hostile force in the Republic of Vietnam. Private First Class Viestenz distinguished himself by exceptionally valorous action on 18 September 1968, while serving as a rifleman with Company C, 1st Battalion (Airmobile), 5th Cavalry during a search and clear mission in Quang Tri Province, Republic of Vietnam. When his unit became heavily engaged with a large enemy force and his platoon leader was wounded, Private First Class Viestenz exposed himself to the intense hostile fire as he crossed an open area to aid his injured comrade. While he was administering first aid to the wounded soldier, Private First Class Viestenz was mortally wounded. His display of personal bravery and devotion to duty was in keeping with the highest tradition of the military service, and reflects great credit upon himself, his unit, and the United States Army."

According to one of his comrades at the scene, Kreg was shot across the midsection while attending to his platoon leader and medevaced out on a helicopter stretcher, where he died shortly thereafter.

I know very little about Kreg's experiences in Vietnam as he was not there too long.

I do remember much about my experiences. I remember clearly the day the army vehicle drove up to the house and the man came to the door. My mom must have known something was very wrong as she ran back to the bedroom as my dad answered the door. I stood within earshot as the man came in and told my dad of the death of Kreg. News traveled fast in the community, and I was shocked when I heard the announcement of his death over the PA system in my first-period class at South Eugene High. It was an unexpected announcement and kind of shook me into the reality of what had happened. My older brother, Kirk, immediately took a leave from the navy and came home. He was a great help to us as he took care of us younger boys while Dad tended to Mom. Kirk insisted that we view Kreg's body in the casket, and now I am glad he made us do that or I would still be hoping he was MIA [missing in action] rather than dead. I was hoping there had been a mistake, but seeing Kreg in the casket made it final for me. I still miss Kreg and wonder at what his future would have been had he lived.

On the day Viestenz died in combat, another soldier from Oregon was also killed in the same battle. In 2005, the local high school in Eugene erected a memorial commemorating their military service. The memorial was not without controversy. Some high school students argued that the memorial glorified war. There was school board discussion about whether all high school dead from every war should be honored. Eventually, the memorial was approved. Interestingly, the memorial was the idea of Adrian Vaaler, who returned to the United States opposed to the war. He notes: "I belonged to a group called Vietnam Veterans Against the

Plaque honoring Vietnam War dead from my high school, South Eugene, Oregon. (Photos courtesy of Fred Tepfer)

War (VVAW). We were the first veterans group in history to protest the war we participated in. The group organized in 1967 and still exists today. Its main claim to fame was a demonstration on the capitol steps called 'Dewey Canyon III.' Senator John Kerry was a leader of our group, and at that demonstration veterans threw their medals or ribbons over the barricades to protest the war."

Vaaler played "Taps" on his trumpet at the high school ceremony unveiling the granite memorial, which bears the simple inscription "We remember our friends, casualties of the Vietnam War." Taps was often heard throughout the decade and much later as we struggled not to forget. The master of ceremonies at the event, not a Vietnam vet, struck a sour note when he contrasted the brave dead with the cowards like me who went to Canada. He didn't realize that those who refused to serve were fighting their own wars. Clearly, time has not healed all wounds, and Vietnam is far from a settled issue in the hearts of Americans. The war may never end. In 2008, an eleventh name, that of James Golz, was chiseled onto the memorial. It was only recently discovered that he had attended South but had not graduated from there.

Vaaler addresses the differences between the Iraq war and the Vietnam War, especially the differences in their aftermaths. I have pointed to parallels between our wars "then" and "now," but there are differences as well.

It should be noted that we in-country vets were equated with the policy that sent us there; thus we were treated like dirt when we returned home. . . . We had no choice in deciding the government's war goals, so we were not supported by the people opposed to the war, like the men and women of today's armed forces. The distinction between policy and service is now clear in the current conflicts. Over the years I've discovered that Nam vets are about equally divided whether the war was wrong or we should have paved Vietnam all the way to Hanoi. Historically, former secretary of defense Robert McNamara discovered in the 1990s in conversations with Vietnam's leaders that we could have pulled out of Vietnam in the early sixties with the same result that occurred in 1975.

He makes an interesting point that many Vietnam-era vets were prowar and wished that we had "won" the war. Veterans, like citizens at large, took diverse and often divergent positions on the issues of the day. We must paint an accurate portrait of the baby boomers, many of whom were not sympathetic to the New Left and some of whom may have actually supported the Vietnam War, as their parents did, even as they smoked dope furtively. Others, like Viestenz, died in combat. By 1968, when he died, many U.S. soldiers opposed the war, recognizing its futility.

℃

This illustrates how we should not succumb to the temptation to blame or praise whole generations. We former activists may bemoan the fact that the "children of the children" do not seem very political, even though they (and we) helped get Obama elected, as I discuss in the following chapter. Today, it is a trope of baby boomers that anyone under thirty cannot be trusted. We graybeards write off the children of the children as potential activists, even hacktivists. Hayden is quoted in the *Los Angeles Times* on his viewing of a recent movie about Bobby Kennedy as saying: "If Bush dared to reinstate the draft, I feel absolutely certain it would be like the '60s again. Campuses would go out of control immediately." We return to this issue in the interviews, where the activists talk about the future and about the role of young people in social and political activism.

Hayden describes his students at Pitzer College as "politically subdued." He goes on to note that they are overwhelmed with their studies, part-time jobs, career planning. I agree with him up to a point: My students, even more utilitarian than Hayden's Pitzer students, would probably protest if they were faced with military conscription. However, missing from this portrait of parallels between then and now is "the movement," any movement, whether inspired by SDS or SCLC. In particular, there are no leaders of a "new" New Left, or perhaps next Left—kids like Hayden slightly older than those to whom he appealed—and there are no visions, manifestos, or action plans. Visions often turn into hallucinations, a postmodern irony perhaps. Yet the Port Huron Statement, *The Autobiography of Malcolm X* (Malcolm X 1965), and *The Feminine Mystique* (Friedan 2001 [1963]) played major roles in explaining the sources of people's alienation and in projecting images of a better society. Such "utopias" are missing today, either because no one thinks big and looks forward, or because books just do not matter in the way they used to (see Jacoby 1999, 2005). The decline of discourse into text messages and reality television makes it incredibly difficult to imagine the emergence of a next New Left, even if the draft were to threaten college kids with the interruption of their lives.

In the interviews quoted in the following pages, Hayden suggests that the Port Huron Statement did not start social change but summarized ongoing struggle; as such, the document became well-known after the fact. I agree with him that this is often the way in which manifestos insert themselves in history. Karl Marx and Friedrich Engels (2002), in *The Communist Manifesto,* suggested that intellectuals do not lead the insurgent working class so much as observe and then theorize its alienation, composing documents (call them manifestos) that explain the sources of this alienation, and then propose a utopia made possible by a combination of structural conduciveness and political will. And so the writing of Port Huron reflected the fact that young people were already agonizing over systemic sources of oppression and organizing to change them. The document was symptomatic in this sense. But eventually it inserted itself into the fray, considerably after 1962, I suspect, and began to make a political difference *because* it spoke to people already involved in struggle and helped them articulate themselves and strategies in new and elevating ways.

But for all of this to happen, one needs social movements, leaders who can write, and a popular culture in which books and ideas make a difference to people. Hayden suggests that such movements spring from emergencies, moments of acute agony brought about by state repression. Leaders emerge, perhaps from the universities. Writings can surprise us with their relevance. The "system" counteracts all of this by spinning emergency into business as usual (or by outright lying, as in Tonkin), tracking leaders using covert intelligence gathering, and taking advantage of a media culture in which books have little impact.

These are not arguments for lassitude. The fact that kids are politically subdued, in Hayden's terms, is an occasion for trying to politicize them without using the didactic techniques of "political education" (of the Maoist/Weather kind). Kids' postmodern irony can be challenged by teaching, lecturing, and writing that do not condescend but use the occasion of personal insecurity, which abounds today, to make general points about "the system." C. Wright Mills (1959) called these "sociologies." Young people love Obama because he is cool, a good beginning but not enough. My students, and perhaps Hayden's, too, worry about lucking into a job that becomes a career and yet having time left over from work in order to have a "life," which includes self-care and perhaps a family. A powerful social critique of the insecurities engendered by these precarious labor market circumstances is Barbara Ehrenreich's (2005) *Bait and Switch: The (Futile) Pursuit of the American Dream,* in which she describes her harrowing experience of trying to obtain a white-collar job after being fired. That kids are plugged into their iPods should not cause next Left leaders simply to abandon the possibility of mass movements, especially when we can look back forty short years to witness the opening of history to a small handful of smart and courageous college students.

In our discussions here, we talk about the future and especially the role of young people in social change. All of my respondents orient to young people and have positive views of their possible role in progressive social change—perhaps because all of my respondents were young once. All of them notice that young people are not for the most part politically involved, and they consider the reasons for this.

RICHARD FLACKS

The Youthful "Audacity of Hope" During the Sixties

"It is a puzzle that's still somewhat unsolved to my mind, why there was this tremendous burst of youth-based energy, really globally, in the late fifties and early sixties, why people who were very young, like we were at Port Huron, or, for a different kind of but parallel case, why a Bob Dylan could come along and think, 'I can remake American popular culture, I, a twenty-year-old,' which I think he had as a sort of fairly conscious understanding of what he was trying to do.

"Why the SNCC people could think that after a hundred years of oppression, they could break through segregation. And with a great deal of disdain for the wisdom of their elders, which was a common thread in all of this. Well, I think one answer is that the post–World War II era, the fifties, felt like a tremendous vacuum of political and cultural leadership from a dissenting point of view. Retrospectively, people have very effectively reconstructed the threads of a New Left to go back rather than forward. In other words, you can look at *Dissent* or *Liberation* or the *Monthly Review,* or what have you, and see how what came together among young people at Port Huron had this ten or fifteen years of buildup, which we were conscious of, but we didn't identify those threads as the Left. We didn't identify it as the Old Left. The Old Left, we thought, was obsolete and not worthy of attention. But someone like Dave Dellinger, these guys were not, or Miles Horton from Highlander, they weren't the Old Left; they were in some way models that had been ignored by the Old Left, or people with ideas that were largely ignored. I didn't mention C. Wright Mills, who's in a way the primary author of the Port Huron Statement in that sense, or Paul Goodman. So the Port Huron Statement isn't simply a work out of our heads."

The Iraq War and No Draft

"I'm just sort of ruminating on how there are probably a significant number of even conservative Republicans who are uneasy about the prospect of their party. The only thing they can hope for is that the Democrats won't find the right formula for sweeping. For example, I don't know what your experience is in Texas, but I'm pretty disturbed by the political apathy of most students now.

"One would have thought this war would have activated people. Well, they don't live in the kind of two-party system that you and I might still imagine exists. The majority of students at UC–Santa Barbara [UCSB] identify as Democrats, but they don't know why. They don't have strong reasons for it, other than women who understand Republicans are against abortion rights and are very traditional, but in terms of broader social understandings, they don't have much reason to get excited, and Kerry's certainly not exciting them. That doesn't mean they can't be excited. If you could convince students that if Bush is reelected we're going to have the draft back, I think that would mobilize people like crazy right now.

"I can tell you why the draft was important in mobilizing [the young during the sixties]; it moved the student movement from a minority expression into a majority expression. In fact, the energy of Port Huron, the SDS, and the identification of white kids with the South, with the southern movement, and the whole counter-culture kind of expression in the first part of the sixties had very little to do directly with the draft or the war. It was deeper; it had something to do with what I've written about. I wrote a book on youth and social change, it's way out of print now, in 1971, and my argument there, which was not all that original, was that young people increasingly experienced a real disconnect between official, institutional values and structures which were rooted in the Protestant ethic and a vaguer but more liberating set of possibilities around hedonism and self-expression and antiauthority, feelings that were derived from popular culture and coming from the consumer society, and coming also from families and the way family upbringing was being restructured. And that disconnect is a lot of what the culture war is still about, but in a way one of the big victories of the sixties was that the Protestant rigidities of American institutions were largely swept away, so the average kid now coming into college doesn't experience his parents as out-of-date, patriarchal, antihedonistic people. If anything, they may experience their parents as overly irresponsible.

"When I came out here and saw this tremendous antiauthority energy that was here, it was far more passionate than at the University of Chicago, where the typical political interests were more traditional, not so culturally expressed. I realized that the kids at UCSB who were attracted to protest and the counterculture were coming from conservative backgrounds, not the liberal backgrounds that I was used to seeing in the New Left. They were coming from homes where their parents were alcoholics but were professing to be Christians, that kind of thing. They were coming from homes where their fathers were either in the military or in the defense industries, in a war situation. It wasn't just the draft; it was the contradiction between what their parents claimed to be for and what was really going on in the world. They could see it in some ways; they could hear it in the music. I don't know that we should even be thinking about reviving something about the sixties. If you're saying, could we have a new period in which a kind of reform spirit was in the air? [The answer is] maybe.

"That's why I said the simplest way to see that happen is to raise the draft as the issue. One of my parting shots to my classes here was, 'As you go to think about who you're going to support in the upcoming election, I would like to see young people asking both candidates what they think about the draft.' I said, 'I can't tell you standing here that John Kerry, who I might end up voting for, is opposed to the draft. I don't know that, but it certainly would be a hot question to ask.' I'm trying to figure out right now how to raise that question in the campaign. I'm sure Kerry would rather not, and I don't know if Bush would. Students know that there are actually bills in Congress to restore the draft. This is already in people's awareness, and so whatever the draft did in the sixties, it would unify the student body now to have that as a real threat. Yes, I do feel that."

Radicalizing Kids Today

"It's too broad to talk about the 'kids.' There are really alright kids who are highly engaged activists, who are better informed than most of us in the sixties (because they really absorb a great deal of information and ideas online), and each year I work with some who

are ready to work full-time in some organizing role in some movement scene. The great mass of white kids are . . . 'willfully clue-
less,' and these are most likely to 'radicalize' only if their bubble is
burst. But that was true in the sixties, too. I don't really care if
'kids radicalize'—I am interested in helping those who want to contribute to democratic change find ways to do it on campus and in
the world beyond. It would help if more faculty who identify as
Leftists would actually teach ways for students to be better informed and to find radical vocations. What would it mean to 'radicalize' just now? Abandon electoral politics, or support third parties? That would be unfortunate. Instead, we political theory types
have to help people see how direct action and movement interre-
late with electoral politics. And we have to start teaching about alternative social possibilities so that radical hope can be vitalized.

"The most important dynamic already happening in line with
your hope here is the mass immigrant rights movement in California that has led to a real leftward shift in our politics. It isn't about
who is presidential candidate (though Obama will be helpful perhaps in these terms) but how organizing is carrying on. I doubt we
need ERAP [Economic Research and Action Project]—we have a
myriad of organizational efforts already happening. In my home
county a widespread organizing effort is going on right now in
Latino and working-class communities with real payoffs at the
polls and in policy. Living wage campaigns, and some of the labor-
initiated organizing, are what's happening. Help students learn
about what is going on in these ways and how they can plug in!
Democratic Party policies will follow from mass movement and
electoral participation rather than precede it. And, of course, the
Left formations have to have programmatic and visionary material
to offer!"

TODD GITLIN

Gitlin's Pragmatic Aims for the
Contemporary American Left

"I'm willing right now to do anything possible to establish the preconditions of small 'd' democratic politics, and those preconditions
begin and end right now with defeating George Bush. If we do defeat George Bush, then there's a political infrastructure to build
up. Maybe I'm not New Left anymore in the following sense—that
I'm willing to leave to individuals and grouplets and tendencies
and transitory movements the conduct of personal life, the affir-

mation of culture, the staking out of identity. I want to let people tend to themselves. You know, I have my way of doing it. I don't insist that other people do it my way.

"But I do think that I am a sort of vulgar materialist about what I expect from politics. I expect more equality, or what I hope for is more equality, the wherewithal of a materially decent life for people, meaning health care, meaning living wages, etc. I don't demand of politics anything more than that, domestically. Internationally, I think necessarily we should be multilateralist, environmentalist, diplomatic, less militarist. We could talk about what that would mean, but in other words, I'm now drawing a conventional boundary between politics and culture, and thinking that the work of culture is not politics, and the work of politics is not culture.

"I would put it this way: I'm impressed by the irrational core of the human being, and so I think that there are desires that are satisfied when people do destructive things. And in America the destructive streaks are not just on the part of the guys who do the bombing, and John Ashcroft and his pals, but also those who like them, or love them, or feel that they represent them. There is a dialectic of mutual attachment between the tyrant and the staff, or the tyrant and the fans. This is to me the big truth about the human condition that makes me more modest about the political possibilities than I was in the sixties."

TOM HAYDEN

Contemporary Radical Social Movements

"[To restructure the distribution of wealth,] you need a social movement that creates an effective threat to the status quo. Second, responsive political leadership brought to the podium by the social movements. Third, the majority coalition reflected in the election of politicians that are responsive to the program, in other words, a movement to rescue the government from the clutches of those who would have it decay, wither away. And you need a committed government to intervene in the market.

"[Social movements] are here. They were there in the sixties and people didn't notice it, except for Mills. He was the only intellectual apparently who noticed it at the time. I'm saying they're here, and if Bush is reelected, their presence will be even more apparent. Currently, their presence is blotted out a little bit because the presidential campaign is absorbing most of the energy for very understandable reasons. The global justice movement and the anti-

Iraq war movement are real movements. The fact that there were a million women in Washington [for the March for Women's Lives in 2005] shows that that is a real movement.

"The civil disobedience by gay and lesbian couples on behalf of marriage, right where my friend Harvey Milk was gunned down just [thirty] years ago, is a sign of a real movement.

"The environmentalists have been buried momentarily under their hopes for the Kerry presidency and so forth, but there is a real environmental movement. Also, because these movements have been relatively successful in securing public support, they don't appear so vividly to outside sources. Some of them may differ with the conventional way of shaking things tactically, but most of their goals are accepted by half or more of the American people.

"I think what pulls movements together is the presence of an enemy. You can't desire an enemy or select an enemy, but, for example, a second term of Bush and the revival of the idea that the U.S. should have an empire or be the policemen of the world, that would pull the movements together.

"There's plenty of that going on, and what's lacking is the dynamics that unify. The presidential campaign could unify.

"The draft could unify. But I think there's sufficient intellectual work being done. I speak a fair amount to audiences, young and old, and the question I hear over and over is whether there is any hope for winning, rather than 'What is the big picture?' They haven't seen a big picture, but they don't see how to overcome what's in their office or neighborhood, and so on. Going back to Marx, *The Communist Manifesto* was written, when was it, 1848?

"Port Huron was written at a time of insurgency. That was the character of the age. Apathy was over and insurgency had come. Between '62 and '68 there was mobile insurgency. There's a parallel there with the time in which *The Communist Manifesto* was written, I think. But people don't take much time to analyze what the social movements were. There was a rising in Ireland; it was crushed. They know all about that one; they don't know much about the others. But that's the parallel—that these manifestos became useful to people who were trying to make sense of these insurgencies and all this chaos.

"And then the other thing that's misunderstood about Marx. I think you can find an article I wrote, the only article I think I've ever written on Marx, recently; it's on my Web site somewhere, but there's a lot of parallels between the World Social Forums and the Working Men's Association that Marx and Engels collaborated on. But one of the things that the more ideological Left misses is that the reform that Marx was focusing on was not communist revolution; it was the eight-hour day. I think without Marx and Engels, I'm not sure we would have had the eight-hour day."

MARK RUDD

Restoring the Draft and
Galvanizing the Young Today

"I'm a big supporter of the draft. I hope we can have a draft. Absolutely. I think about this a lot because I talk with young people, and my own experience is that youth have a tremendous energy and get a lot of things accomplished that older people can't. They'll take more risks; they'll put more time in. We've got jobs, mortgages, and kids in college, blah, blah, blah. So I'm a big supporter of the youth movement; I'm always looking for the youth movement.

"Sure, a draft would be helpful, but I think it's going to happen without a draft. I think it's going to happen with young, very young people now, seeing this stupid, harmful war, and becom[ing] radicalized. I think there will be a time, as in the sixties, when young people realize that it's cool to rebel. That's the essential cultural fact that they have to come to, that the coolest possible thing you can do is be a rebel."

Awakening People Politically

"I think that apoliticality is gonna go, I don't know how: a global war on terrorism that lasts two, three generations, more terror attacks, more environmental disasters, price of gas going up. I pray for the price of gas to go up to fifty dollars or seventy-five dollars or one hundred dollars.

"People will wake up. They're rational—just the rationality of thinking, 'Gosh, isn't there a way to organize the world so that Americans aren't hated everywhere?' I think that young people will one day wake up and say, 'I don't like this shit they're sellin' and we'll do our own shit, and it'll be rebellion.'

"The dreary e-mail battles [surrounding the re-formation of SDS and its counterpart 'adult' organization, MDS] were actually quite useful. SDS now knows not to get too intimately involved with us grayhairs, or at least to keep some distance. Young people should organize themselves; old people need to get our shit together. Please don't yoke yourselves to us too closely, because we'll probably bring you down. There is absolutely no doubt now that the generations need to keep organizationally separate for a while.

"One final lesson of the last few months: MDS has to figure out some way to tame the depressing tyranny of the verbose armchair listservers. These discussions go on and on endlessly, completely disconnected from actual organizing and real people's struggles. There must be a lot of angry frustrated old guys out there with lots of time on their hands. This situation is totally weird. It's as if the ego-driven ideological quibbling of SDS in 1969 has lain dormant all these years, only to reemerge like some long-sleeping deadly virus two generations later. For myself, I don't care who leads, who makes decisions; let's just do some work that needs doing."

ROXANNE DUNBAR-ORTIZ

Organizing or Agonizing

"The draft won't be reactivated. It's a transitional time for the military. Iraq and Afghanistan are vital training for counterinsurgency, which is the only kind of war to be fought in the future. Meanwhile, there is an endless supply of foreign volunteers who can thereby gain citizenship. Once they have it developed, there won't be a need for more troops. Anyway, they are not dumb enough to make the same mistake twice. But I do think that counter-recruitment, especially among the undocumented workers, which means having Spanish-speaking organizers, is extremely important. Also, to organize within the military. And in public middle schools and high schools. I think we need many organizers, much more than demonstrators. Mark Rudd says that we need to organize rather than simply express ourselves, and I agree. It's hard work, but there's no other way, face-to-face organizing. I don't agree that books can no longer have an impact or 'change the world.' Look at the effect of the Left Behind series, of *The Purpose-Driven Life* and other Evangelical books. We on the Left need to be writing radical, inspiring, provocative books. I've made that my main mission as a radical in the past decade: continuing. I think your book can be important and even change the world. Don't underestimate the power of the word."

Choosing Sides, Getting Strong

"I think the children of the white Right and self-righteous can become revolutionaries, especially those from the working class. I don't think they can become liberals. Why would they? It's so boring! There has to be some passion to attract young people. We need more black and white explanations of things, bad and good, right and wrong, justice and injustice, instead of all the grays and the on the one hand and on the other hand. It's difficult for young girls to get involved in feminism, because they don't yet have the accumulated experience to see the ways in which they are being oppressed, including by the fashions and icons presented to them. Back in the flare of the women's liberation movement, many young women did get involved, because it was new and cutting-edge and daring and, well, cool. That's probably not going to happen again. I see women in their late twenties and in their thirties becoming feminists all the time. I do think every young woman should be urged to take martial arts. I think parents should demand that it be taught in schools, in elementary schools. It's amazing what martial arts can do to make a girl know the power of her body in ways other than sexual activity. Other sports can achieve that, but they require too much innate skill, muscles, and height. A two-year-old can master martial arts."

CASEY HAYDEN

Progressive Movements and Bureaucracy

"I don't think it inevitable that progressive social movements become bureaucratized and top-down, but I do think it is a tendency of organizations. At a certain point it seems that organizations want to engage the powers they are against on the powers' own terms. Democratic organizations' means, their strategy and methodology, are at first the same as their ends (leadership as service, community, trust, internal democracy and equality, patience, fraternity, and so on). But these values tend to become less important than winning, and doing what it takes to win, on a more militant or military model. However, social movements are not organizations. They are a rising up and then a falling away of many, many, many people, for the most part inspired and courageous and, to some extent, doing their own thing. Social movements are mysterious and natural and have their own life and death, often organized and aided (or sometimes not so aided) by the organizations active inside them."

Young People and Political Cynicism

"Yes, political cynicism is rampant. We were idealists, and we thought that if folks understood the complete corruption of our system, they would rise up. Not so. Kids now know it's corrupt, and so they stay out of it.

"And of course part of the reason they stay out of it is because of the curtailment of civil liberties, and the fear that Homeland Security instills, even on the unconscious level. Confronting this fear can be the beginning of an uprising. It was for us.

"On the other hand, there is something to be said in times like these for 'Turn on. Tune in. Drop out.' That is, one can just go underground, outside the system, and do your own thing nonconfrontationally. In our funky downtown neighborhood with many young people moving in, we have an active neighborhood association, permaculture blossoms, folks ride bicycles (eschewing the oil problem), and we elected the most liberal congressman in DC. Generally, in my experience, the path to movements is through the heart, through believing in one's own life and sinking deeply into it. I tell young people, 'Whatever turns you on, go for it, find others like yourself, and find strength there.' I like where I am and I feel good here, and that's how I tell if the politics are right.

"The world today is as far away from my youth as I was from World War I: a different social, political, natural landscape; a different planet. The kids know it better than I do, and they will find their way, which may involve forms and strategies we can't conceive of now."

Progressive Optimism

"I'd guess Tom, and maybe Dick, are closer to them and can envision their expansion more easily than you. But being a half-full person is important, especially in the hard times, in isolation. I feel, from living where I live, with the younger folks in my neighborhood into the natural world, planting trees and creating bike paths and building cisterns and solar panels and fighting for low-income housing, that there is something good happening which will come to fruition. Something is happening everywhere. Texas is not solidly conservative, although much of what is happening may be somewhat hidden. There are cracks somewhere. One must seek out the good, the hope, and live inside it. Democratic social movements arise when the time is ripe, when enough people feel constrained by the laws/mores/powers/patterns/belief systems and forces that be, and find each other, and feel powerful with each other. It will happen again.

"All social movements and organizations appear over-the-top when viewed through the media, from the outside. It is in the interest of the moneyed classes to have it so, and they control the media. Power analysis of the media helps people understand this, as does bringing real people together."

Contemporary Feminism

"I believe the women's movement is alive and well in my relationships with my women friends.

"Feminism viewed as gender equality, as choice of gender role, is necessary, but a traditional gender role choice is not necessarily conservative. It was my choice, as long as I could afford it. I had my daughter at home in 1971 in the Bay Area, with friends in attendance, and a midwife, helping create the home birth movement, taking birth back from the paternal medical establishment. Many women today are resisting cesareans, which are made-to-order for the medical establishment, and even second-birth cesareans. We are nursing babies now, not true in the fifties, and fighting for the right to do so publicly. Women are home schooling, or even unschooling, on the pattern of our own freedom schools, and banding together in groups to support each other. And these few examples are only in the areas of birthing, education choices. Assuming power relationships in the home are egalitarian, the choice of a traditional feminine role can be antipaternalistic, liberating, holistic, and groundbreaking. One can view the kinds of options I suggest as an expansion and deepening of the feminist movement, rather than as oppositional."

DAVID GILBERT

Hope and Recognizing the Costs of Empire

"I think the key to getting young people involved is to find ways to make real the hope that humane social change is a possibility. One aspect may be to link the various issues that have mobilized people—antiglobalization, antiwar, environment, criminal justice, the race and class lessons of Katrina, immigration—both to feel the much larger, joint constituencies for change and also to illustrate the nature of the system as a whole. Another aspect is to find ways to build sustainable organizing campaigns, such as antirecruitment, to involve new people, and to make a visible difference even if only on a local level.

"There are very real material interests that link people in the U.S. to the system—mainly the benefits accrued from empire, and the advantages to the majority from white supremacy. That's what makes so many people vulnerable to the media and political hype. But ultimately the empire, while extremely beneficial for the super-rich, proves much too costly for much of the working class—and also alienated us from our basic humanity. Most would be far better off in a more humane and sustainable society, but such changes against power feel impossible ('You can't fight city hall'). So people settle for the more immediate little benefits from the system. What we have to do is point out the ways people here pay the costs of empire and at the same time the ways they can be inspired to feel there is a realistic hope for a more humane future, which comes from linking up with the world's majority, the most oppressed."

CARL OGLESBY

On Teachers, Teach-ins, and the Future

"Every Friday a group of mainly townspeople, but with a sprinkling of students, would get together at a certain corner in downtown Amherst[, Massachusetts] with a bunch of signs and stand there and [protest] the war, and people in their cars and their trucks would drive by and honk and they would be friendly. And then when the group had been there for an hour or so, it would break up and go back to where we came from. I don't know if that's still going on. I went a couple of times, but then it got too cold, and I didn't feel like doing it. There may have been a few teachers in the group, but I don't know where the teachers are at. I think the teachers don't know what to do. The teach-ins [during the sixties], what was crucial to their impact is that they were something new. By this time there have been teach-ins on everything. It has become a 'ho-hum' technique. It doesn't bother anybody anymore. Oh, a teach-in, oh, okay. And without that quality of newness, without that quality of daringness, it can't be what it used to be."

In my final chapter, I return to my own experience of the sixties as I summarize my narrative, which emphasizes a political sixties and refuses nostalgia. I explore why I cannot get rid of the sixties—why they are in me and in many of my generation. I do not want to turn back the clock; rather, with all of the activists interviewed for this book, I want to move forward, whatever that might mean. Given the parallels between right-wing repression and xenophobia during the Nixon and Bush eras, restoring the sixties as a progressive moment is a beginning. This restoration may be fraught as post-

Frances Beal supports Obama. (Photo courtesy of Frances Beal)

boomers such as Obama are embraced by old-time activists such as Reverend Jeremiah Wright, Bill Ayers, and Frances Beal. These radical dinosaurs remind the Right what is at stake in the election of a black Democrat who carefully distances himself from those times but whose life and candidacy are born of them. Relationships between the generations, as all parents know, are never easy. This is a good time to revisit the past, telling stories that remind the young that parents were once children.

ॐ Nine ॐ

My Sixties at Fiftysomething

The hell with facts! We need stories!
—Ken Kesey

And so, for me at least, the sixties will never end, even as I settle my score with the impact of certain key public events on me while I was struggling to become my own person. The sixties will not end because, as Sigmund Freud (1989) demonstrated, the inner child never ceases to call out from a certain compartment within the "adult" self, staking its claim to attention, nourishment, and gratification. Freud recognized that we are never entirely adult, if by that we mean free of the past. Even when we leave aside the question of the unconscious, it is enough to notice that we are forever forgetting things that happened to us, and that we authored, in our haste to live life in the present. This is at once necessary to go forward and amnesiac, refusing to learn from past mistakes and relive earlier enthusiasms. Read this way, Port Huron was a children's manifesto, a fantasy of insatiable kids who wanted freedom, happiness, justice, and truth—goals of democratic theory as important as one can imagine.

The vision of the young Port Huron campers turned into hallucination not because the Weatherbureau issued the wrong political forecast, or indulged its own will to power, but because the Right had become so powerful by decade's end. The cost was millions of Vietnamese dead, the ruination of American inner cities and black people's lives, too many dead Kennedys and civil rights leaders. It was not youthful vision that caused these outcomes but the agendas of obstinate elders, almost always male, who would not listen or flex. Richard Nixon, J. Edgar Hoover, William Westmoreland, and Robert McNamara are the real villains of the sixties, not the Weathermen, who immediately learned from the townhouse explosion that violence without political strategy would amount to suicide. And it was Nixon who opened the way for Ronald Reagan and the George Bushes.

But, as I have said, the Left was often too much like the Right. Leftists, especially the young males, were possessed by a demon that Friedrich Nietzsche (1910) called "the will to power." We have learned from Mark Rudd that even Kent State was complex, involving Weather-like provocation; it was not a simple morality play. The Right imprinted itself on everything, including the young Left, which, in its hubris, imagined that it could bring about a revolution. I have identified a tendency of the late sixties Left, both white and black, to become like its enemy, the Right that controlled state power and the means of domestic repression. Weatherman and Black Panthers tried to fight fire with fire, which was never the way to go, given both overwhelming odds and the tendency for the "revolutionary" Left, in its militancy, to resemble the Right. Perhaps it is enough to say that the Right and Left were dichotomous thinkers and that they viewed truth as absolute.

IN MEMORIAM

John Kennedy (d. 1963)
Medgar Evers (d. 1963)
Carol Denise McNair (d. 1963)
Cynthia Wesley (d. 1963)
Carole Robertson (d. 1963)
Addie Mae Collins (d. 1963)
Michael Schwerner (d. 1964)
Andrew Goodman (d. 1964)
James Chaney (d. 1964)
Malcolm X (d. 1965)
Jimmy Lee Jackson (d. 1965)
James J. Reeb (d. 1965)
Robert Collins (d. 1965)
Vernon Dahmer (d. 1966)
Carl Louvring (d. 1967)
Arthur Erwin (d. 1967)
James Cartwright (d. 1967)
William Muir (d. 1967)
Dennis Mickelson (d. 1967)
William Beckwith (d. 1968)
Kreg Viestenz (d. 1968)

James Golz (d. 1968)
Robert Kennedy (d. 1968)
Martin Luther King Jr. (d. 1968)
Samuel Hammond (d. 1968)
Delano Middleton (d. 1968)
Henry Smith (d. 1968)
Fred Hampton (d. 1969)
James Rector (d. 1969)
Carlton Gray (d. 1970)
Ted Gold (d. 1970)
Terry Robbins (d. 1970)
Diana Oughton (d. 1970)
Allison Krause (d. 1970)
Jeffrey Miller (d. 1970)
Sandra Scheuer (d. 1970)
William Schroeder (d. 1970)
Robert Fassnacht (d. 1970)
William Andrews (d. 1974)
Edward O'Grady (d. 1981)
Waverly Brown (d. 1981)
Peter Paige (d. 1981)

I cannot get rid of the sixties because these deaths, plus those of millions of Vietnamese and poor Americans too obscure for public viewing, overshadow the progressive activism of the time. Indeed, in many of these cases, activism got the people killed. Or got them drafted. Or put them in the wrong place at the wrong time. The list includes Leftists who blew themselves up trying to blow up others and some of their victims. We find desperation and danger even a decade after the sixties ended. Bad judgment and bad luck abounded. The 1981 Brinks robbery that resulted in the death of two police officers and a Brinks guard, and the resulting long-term imprisonment of Kathy Boudin and the life sentence of Dave Gilbert, is certainly a legacy of the sixties; there were only losers. The issue is not blame, but the length to which radicals went in the Klan/FBI/police state that became America. Becky Thompson offers a poem capturing the experience of visiting David in prison:

Comstock Correctional Upstate New York
for David Gilbert*

on my first visit ice packs my tire treads
my car spins around to head home in the snow
parking lot divides: *visitors* and *corrections*
I drive around in circles, car pacing
the guards see my first time eyes
search my bag and body, smiling
my underwire bra the threat they enjoy fondling,
passing it from one guard to the next
a series of doors slam shut
each metal clink I feel smaller
bathroom walls smell of steel gurneys
vending machines spit out Hormel's chili
the numbers assigned press us together
rows of women with lipstick holding infants with ribbons
I stare at the door where the prisoners emerge
privacy between visitors an invisible line
you enter the room, stride gentle, palms open,
your hard-earned blue tee under prison shirt grey
yellow formica table stockades our legs
your hands, Jewish dancing, eyes as big as the clock
I start in with questions, you talk fast, I scribble,
no tape recorder allowed, I chronicle long hand
my questions review the drama of Black Power
armed struggle, you explain, *another word for defense*
my pacifist leanings collide with your logic:
they shot Hampton in his bed, assassinated Malcolm
I couldn't keep running for white cover in college
underground life teetered our judgments
my body stays tense with secretary's function
each inmate who enters you hold with your eyes
tender man in this dungeon, life sentence, I am sinking

you see me falling, ask: *are you breathing?*
you reach across distance, a light brush on my arm
your touch sends electricity I had reserved just for women
my twenty years lesbian falling into your body,
interview shifts from subject to belonging
I leave before count, thirty-five pages in hand
officers' cajoling, a cover for terror
they unlock and lock the maze to the outside,
a part of me stays, slipped inside your skin.

* David Gilbert, a member of the Weather Underground in the late 1960s and 1970s, was sentenced to life in prison for his involvement in the 1981 Brinks robbery. He continues to do antiracist work in prison.

Death continues, but so do protests. My vantage from conservative Texas can obscure regional and political variation. At my university near Dallas, the Reserve Officers' Training Corps used to shoot off its cannons in order to announce its presence. But in Eugene, there is opposition to Bush's war. And Barack Obama swept the bicoastal states and even former Dixie states such as Virginia and Florida. Following are images of political installation art from the present-day University of Oregon campus. Each red flag stands for three U.S. dead in the war; each white flag represents six Iraqis killed. This time, progressive Eugeneans are keeping track of the casualties. The Vietnam dead haunt these sites— poppy fields of protest. These fields are only a few miles away from the high school memorial to my dead classmates.

The sixties are in me and indirectly in my children, who share my insubordinate temperament and, I hope, my joie de vivre. Tom Hayden and the others come across as joyful, not only as hardened organizers but as optimistic and exuberant citizens. We all spoke truth to power and still do so. Who has not had an inflexible and vindictive teacher or boss? It is in the nature of bossdom that

Flags commemorating Iraqi war dead, University of Oregon campus. (Photos courtesy of Fred Tepfer)

subordinates are treated miserably; it is the rare authority figure who demonstrates empathy and behaves democratically. Bureaucracies, especially schools, kill the spirit. The authoritarian classroom is the embryo of fascism.

Children who animated the sixties and carry it forward as graying boomers now chastise their kids for being on the sidelines. Yet the children of the children are apparently on the move. Barack Obama's campaign for president depended heavily on the support of under-thirties, many of whom are coming to politics for the first time. They used social networking tools such as MySpace to raise money, organize meetings, chat politically.

Is Obama New Left? I want to hear the cadences and coda of the Port Huron Statement in his transformational politics, but I am not certain about this. He says little about social class. His supporters are mainly kids and latte liberals; the white working class is not yet persuaded. Perhaps his centrism is necessary in these times. Given my own background and biases, I am not yet willing to give up the boundary between Right and Left; the middle always seemed like dangerous ground. Hayden writes that he supports the supporters of Obama, those who yearn for radical change. Like me, he is not yet convinced that Obama inherits the mantle of the Port Huron SDS leadership or SNCC. It is clear that Obama speaks to black people, who have not had a real hero since Martin Luther King.

I asked the movement leaders how they view the Obama phenomenon, especially as former sixties movement activists. Here are their responses.

TODD GITLIN

"Obama's campaign was a movement campaign, an insurgency—in large measure the product of a popular mobilization, passionate and well organized, cross-demographic, the best of amateur politics harnessed to professional party intelligence. It was an insurgency dressed up as conventional politics, undertaken by a politician who started his self-education as a community organizer. Obama adroitly combined, or blurred, the prevailing outrage against Bush with postpartisan appeal and thereby staked out a big Democratic tent and a mandate for—what? An amalgam with a progressive tilt. Postsixties pragmatism fired by the energy of new, younger, and darker-skinned voters.

"So now a door opens, but what's on the other side? Plenty of pitfalls that don't need itemizing, starting with an imperative to rescue a sinking economy. And political opportunities. If Obama kicks in economic improvements quickly, he gets to build an enduring majority. Green energy and comprehensive health care and an Iraq phaseout are his other imperatives. If he manages those well, progressives can be encouraged that he can change the games in the Middle East and Iran. If he doesn't, he's self-limiting, another sad story. Either way, we'll continue to be frustrated, no doubt."

ROXANNE DUNBAR-ORTIZ

"I am amazed and joyful that an African American man could be elected president of the United States. It signals the sea change that has taken place during the past half-century since the Supreme Court desegregation decision. I think many of us on the Left, including myself, underestimated the change in consciousness and behavior that could lead to such a result. And not just any black person; rather, Barack Hussein Obama, whose African father was Muslim and whose stepfather who raised him was Indonesian Muslim. Yet the man's charisma and compassion struck a human chord, breaking through race hatred and distrust of Muslims. Furthermore, the primary campaign also clearly revealed

Roxanne Dunbar-Ortiz. (Photo courtesy of Roxanne Dunbar-Ortiz)

that a woman, Hillary Clinton, could be elected president. And parallel with the presidential race during 2008, capitalism was crumbling, revealing the intricate man-made mechanisms that keep it going long after its irrelevance to human well-being. Socialism is even being discussed openly. The planets appear to be aligned for an extraordinary window of opportunity to begin the toppling of the empire and the U.S. state as we know it.

"So in the short term, I think those of us working for social justice and the end of U.S. warmaking are obliged to adjust to the new realities of race, gender, and class in the United States today and put class war and antimilitarism at the top of our agendas.

"Don't get me wrong: Barack Obama is no Evo Morales, the other head of state to be a first, as the indigenous president of an American state, Bolivia, in 2006. Evo came to power on the shoulders of a mass movement that was built on decades of struggles."

MARK RUDD

"I am more optimistic now than at any time in my life due to the collapse of the rule of the free-market militarists who were in power since 1981. In retrospect, it seems to have been necessary to pass through a terrible right-wing consolidation in order to remind the American people that we have responsibility to each other and to the planet. We've been reminded that the government is the embodiment of the collective and that certain problems can best be solved using its resources; also that international law is a much more effective way of solving global problems than violence (war). President Obama may prove to be a leader on the level of Lincoln or Mandela.

"As Leftists, our job is to help bring into existence mass popular movements to push Obama and the government toward rational decisions such as investing in green energy, universal health care, shrinking the military budget. In so doing, consciousness of possibilities will grow. We won't be creating socialism, but we'll be waking up younger people (and reminding ourselves) to the idea that what they do can make a difference, an idea that was squelched during the last thirty years. It's back again now—time to get to work."

FRANCES BEAL

"The election of Barack Obama is a great advance for the progressive movement. On the most basic level, the fact that a country that had been inundated with racist messages about Willie Horton and welfare queens and the black criminal elements for decades was able to overcome its prejudices and vote for change is a remarkable phenomenon. It is clear that Obama is not a revolutionary; in fact, he is clear about his role of saving capitalism from the consequences of an unregulated finance and banking system, corporate greed, and mismanagement. But his attempt to return to a more equitable distribution of the nation's resources and to reestablish bourgeois democratic rule at home and in foreign policy has already opened up avenues for progressive reform and for the Left.

"Moreover, his campaign identified, organized, and activated an already existing broad democratic coalition, including labor, civil rights and civil liberties groups, youth, women, people of color, environmentalists, and an antiwar constituency that has pushed the right-wing extremists to the fringe of political discourse. Most importantly, this new coalition has severely damaged the GOP's racist southern strategy and its explicit racial appeals, and has started to isolate the Democratic Party's right wing, which had conceded to this onslaught. The extent to which the Left is able to participate in this political motion, while at the same time holding Barack Obama accountable to a peace and justice agenda, is the extent to which we move closer to a more democratic society and a more peaceful global existence."

CASEY HAYDEN

"I didn't believe he'd be elected, and it took a while to sink in, but I finally got it, and I cried and danced, glued to the TV, through the inauguration. I love this guy and view him as our proud legacy, the child of our shared youth. It's amazing to remember how much sacrifice it took to do this one simple, decent thing. I don't know how much he can actually accomplish, given the karma of this country, but he intends to, and does, open a world of new possibilities. May the common good be the common will."

TOM HAYDEN

"My paramount concern was to prevent a Republican victory in November. Even though it seems to be a Democratic year, no one can say which Democratic [candidate] can defeat, say, John McCain, the full-throated advocate of 'winning' the Iraq war. At stake are many issues beyond Iraq, not least the appointment of the next generation of federal judges.

"I will vote without hesitation for the Democratic nominee, if only to stop the neoconservative usurpation of power that began in Florida in 2000.

"One must choose candidates based on the issues for which they stand, the spirit they invoke, and the people they are able to mobilize. As for issues, the differences between Obama and Clinton on Iraq are difficult to pin down. Obama was against the Iraq war five years ago and favors a more rapid pullout of combat troops than Clinton. But both would replace combat troops with an American counterinsurgency force of tens of thousands, potentially turning Iraq into Central America in the 1970s. Obama seems more supportive of diplomacy than Clinton, but he supports military intervention in Pakistan's tribal areas. Edwards favors a more rapid pullout from Iraq but is unlikely to prevail.

"On Iraq, the antiwar movement has helped turn a public majority against the war, a historic achievement. But the movement alone lacks much capacity to forge anything beyond the slogan of 'Bring the troops home.' Our most achievable goal is a strong voter mandate for peace in November, the election of more congressional Democrats, and spreading public awareness of the dangers of counterinsurgency. The election of a Democratic president is a necessary condition for ending the war, but sadly not a sufficient one.

"So the choice remains.

"I do not like the Hillary haters in our midst. As president, her court appointees alone would represent a relief from the present rigging of the courts and marginal improvements for working people. On Iraq, I believe she could be pushed to withdraw. She is a centrist, and it will be up to social movements to alter the center.

"Nor do I like the role being played by President Bill Clinton, who is telling lies about Iraq and Obama that are unbecoming of a former president.

"Neither do I agree with Gloria Steinem's divisive claim that the gender barrier is greater than the racial one. Who wants to measure slavery against the Inquisition? In the case at hand, who among us would argue that the barriers against Hillary Clinton are greater than those facing Barack Obama? What is compelling is that most black women support Obama.

"I respect John Edwards's campaign and the role he has played in driving the Democratic Party toward a progressive agenda. At this point, however, I cannot foresee a primary he will win.

"That leaves Barack Obama. I have been devastated by too many tragedies and betrayals over the past forty years to ever again deposit so much hope in any single individual, no matter how charismatic or brilliant. But today I see across the generational divide the spirit, excitement, energy, and creativity of a new generation bidding to displace the old ways. Obama's moment is their moment, and I pray that they succeed without the sufferings and betrayals my generation went through. There really is no comparison between the Obama generation and those who would come to power with Hillary Clinton, and I suspect she knows it. The people she would take into her administration may have been reformers and idealists in their youth, but they seem to seek now a return to their establishment positions of power. They are the sorts of people young Hillary Clinton herself would have scorned at Wellesley. If history is any guide, the new 'best and brightest' of the Obama generation will unleash a new cycle of activism, reform, and fresh thinking before they follow pragmatism to its dead end.

"Many ordinary Americans will take a transformative step down the long road to the Rainbow Covenant if Obama wins. For at least a brief moment, people around the world—from the shantytowns to the sweatshops, even to the restless rich of the sixties generation—will look up from the treadmills of their shrunken lives to the possibilities of what life still might be. Environmental justice and global economic hope would dawn as possibilities.

"Is Barack the one we have been waiting for? Or is it the other way around? Are we the people we have been waiting for? Barack Obama is giving voice and space to an awakening beyond his wildest expectations, a social force that may lead him far beyond his modest policy agenda. Such movements in the past led the Kennedys and Franklin Roosevelt to achievements they never contemplated. (As Gandhi once said of India's liberation movement: 'There go my people. I must follow them, for I am their leader.')

"We are in a precious moment where caution must yield to courage. It is better to fail at the quest for greatness than to accept our planet's future as only a reliving of the past.

"So I endorse the movement that Barack Obama has inspired and will support his candidacy in the inevitable storms ahead."

RICHARD FLACKS

"Barack Obama was born at the moment that SNCC was beginning and sit-ins and Freedom Rides were in full flower. A few months after his birth, SDS met at Port Huron. It is sometimes forgotten that the founding visions of both groups included the coming into being of a majority electoral coalition that would link unions, the civil rights movement, political and religious liberals in a Democratic Party freed of its Dixiecrat wing. At the same time, both groups implemented a ground-up, community-based organizing process that would enable the voiceless to be heard, that would use direct action as well as the ballot to foster participatory democracy. The strategy of fusing electoral and movement activism was largely frustrated as the sixties wore on. But versions of it have been practiced in the decades since at the local level. While the USA was supposedly moving to the Right, a decidedly leftward shift was going on in cities and towns, regions, and states as veterans of the sixties, partnering with succeeding generations of organizers, fostered new social movements and electoral coalitions at the grass roots. Barack Obama was part of this process. Michelle Obama explained his presidential campaign as a project. She declared, 'Barack is not a politician first and foremost. He's a community activist exploring the viability of politics to make change.'

"His election validates some of the hopes of the founding period of the New Left. In his campaign, he frequently asserted that electing a president was insufficient for change, that movement from the bottom up was essential. His campaign organization at the local level was consciously modeled on methods derived from the organizing tradition. Now we have a chance to test out the potentials for democratic reform in the interplay between grassroots movement and national government. On the one hand, there are the tens of thousands who became activists in the campaign and who are now on the lists of 'Obama for America.' Can some semblance of a democratic grassroots organizing structure emerge out of this new formation? And how will it relate to the vast network of established national, state, and local organizations progressives have built since the sixties? Those who want to fulfill the better legacy of the sixties now need to be occupied with the question of what we need to do as activists on the ground, rather than what he will do in the White House. For he knows, as do we, that the ground is where the people's history is made."

In our interviews conducted during the Bush presidency, Gitlin argued that the New Left was a fleeting moment, implying that it matters little whether Obama is the next Hayden. On the evidence of the Right's consolidation in the meantime, he certainly has a point. However, Gitlin's comments here, made after Obama's election, suggest otherwise. He recognizes that Obama's was a "movement campaign." And the children were involved. We sixties activists will need to wait and see whether our American regime change is an opening to a new world, perhaps even resembling the world out-

President Barack Obama, Secretary of State Hillary Clinton, and former president Bill Clinton march with a crowd to the Edmund Pettus Bridge to commemorate the 1965 "Bloody Sunday" voting rights march on March 4, 2007, in Selma, Alabama. (Photo by Scott Olson/Getty Images)

Selma-to-Montgomery voting rights march, March 21–25, 1965. (Library of Congress)

lined in the Port Huron Statement. I don't underestimate the ability of the Right to regroup and thwart progressive agendas. If Obama opens the political process, another New Frontier, perhaps we can finally put the sixties to rest. Something tells me that Obama will do good but that we will continue to need stories about courage and self-sacrifice such as the ones told here. Obama would be the first to admit that his presidency stands on the shoulders of civil rights workers who stared down the Klan and police. On March 4, 2007, during the presidential primary, Obama and Hillary Clinton gathered in Selma, Alabama, in order to reenact the beginning of the tumultuous march from Selma to Montgomery.

Linking arms with former civil rights leaders and activists, they crossed the Edmund Pettus Bridge, which in 1965 separated the old segregated world from the new integrated world, a tipping point of the sixties. Similarly, five of the students who desegregated Little Rock public schools in 1957 were invited to Obama's inaugural, closing the circle among generations of people affected by the civil rights movement.

Obama's election demonstrates that we need to live in the moment, avoiding nostalgia. All progressives believe that the best is yet to come. "The sixties" are too often compartmentalized and then briefly resurrected on the anniversary of the Kennedy and King assassinations or of the death of another boomer rock star. Or they can be passed down through oral histories such as this one as we tell our children and students stories about our enthusiasms and disappointments. Why the Cuban missile crisis was so frightening, why the first Kennedy's death rocked the world, followed by Bobby's, why music spoke to us and expressed our hopes, why Vietnam was so close to home as well as far away—these are the things our youngsters need to hear, especially because their own worlds are full of confusion. Then is now. And the lessons we take from the sixties, notably about the power of the people, can be applied today. That apathy appears to have replaced activism is not a permanent condition, especially if we tell the sixties well. But we need to hurry: The kids who were in their teens and twenties during Port Huron, Montgomery, and Chicago are now in their fifties, sixties, and beyond. They are us—the children having become parents and grandparents and having their own stories to tell. These are stories of risks taken, opportunities missed, hearts broken, and great excitement generated. They are stories in which efficacy and emergency coexist, with Lyndon Johnson's decision not to seek a second term followed by Chicago and Nixon's repression.

The sixties were caught on film and in images, as I have demonstrated throughout this book. These images tell a story, often better than words can. The children of the children relate to these images better than to texts, even though stories told to them and music played for them spike their imagination. This book has been about connections and parallels, between then and now, between movements, across generations. Many of the players were very young, and young people today fill their shoes. Fred Hampton was twenty-one when he was killed in 1969. Cleveland Sellers's son, Bakari Sellers, was elected to the South Carolina state house at the tender age of twenty-two. He is now a law student and worked in Obama's presidential campaign. Both Hampton and the younger Sellers are charismatic and passionate, even as there are stylistic and rhetorical differences between the two. Bakari worked for Obama, but he also works to commemorate the 1968 Orangeburg events, when state police killed three young black activists attempting to desegregate a bowling alley. Bakari's dad, Cleveland, now president of Voorhees College in South Carolina, was shot in the incident. Fred Hampton and Bakari Sellers are bookends of the sixties.

Bakari working for Obama can be found on YouTube. In the same video, Cleve talks about how the Orangeburg massacre has not been sufficiently investigated and commemorated: http://www.youtube.com/watch?v=zhCPKCa9bdE. And then on YouTube, Fred Hampton can be discovered at his most eloquent: http://www.youtube.com/watch?v=HSO6bqlq494. Fred's words are angry; he and Bakari's dad were militants. Barack and Bakari are buttoned-down radicals; they are smooth and eloquent. I must not be the first to notice the striking physical and sartorial resemblance of Barack and Malcolm X, suggesting that radicalism can be silky smooth as well as incendiary. Here are some of Hampton's words, taken from the death struggles of the late sixties. Barack and Bakari would not exist if Hampton and the elder Sellers had not lived the lives they did. Watching these videos, we can easily see how the young would be ignited by Hampton, Obama, and both Sellers men.

> If you ever think of me, and if you think about me, niggers, and if you ain't gonna do no revolutionary act, forget about me. I don't want myself on your mind if you're not going to work for the people. Like we always said, if you're asked to make a commitment at the age of twenty, and you say I don't want to make a commitment only because of the single reason that I'm too young to die, I want to live a little bit longer. What you did is, you're dead already. You have to understand that people have to pay the price for peace. If you dare to struggle, you dare to win. If you dare not to struggle, then, god damn it, you don't deserve to win. Let me say peace to you if you're willing to fight for it. Let me say in the spirit of liberation, I've been gone for a little while, at least my body's been gone for a little while, but I'm back now. And I believe that I'm back to stay. I believe that I'm going to do my job. And I believe that I was born not to die in a car wreck. . . . I don't believe I'm going to die because I got a bad heart. I don't believe I'm going to die because of lung cancer. I believe that I'm going to be able to die doing the things I was born for. I believe that I'm going to be able to die high off the people. I believe that I will be able to die as a revolutionary in the international revolutionary proletarian struggle. And I hope that each one of you will be able to die

in the international proletarian revolutionary struggle. Or you'll be able to live in it. And I think that struggle is going to come. Why don't you live for the people? Why don't you struggle for the people? Why don't you die for the people?

I close this book with a series of images that portray the causes and effects of my own life. For most of us, the images are what we remember. Everyone recalls the famed Zapruder film, an amateur movie of the assassination taken by a bystander on that fateful day in Dallas, has been dissected frame by frame. Frame 239 shows Kennedy clutching his throat after being hit by a bullet, just a few frames from the fatal head shot. He might have survived had this been the only bullet to find its mark.

Recently, another color film of Kennedy's motorcade was discovered. Like the Zapruder film, it was shot by an amateur, George Jefferies. He captures what might be the last best moment of the sixties. Neither of the Kennedys, nor America, knew what was about to hit them. Everything changed in an instant. Moments after the assassination, Lyndon Johnson, a Texan, was sworn in as the next U.S. president. Ignoring the growing reservations that Kennedy had

President Lyndon Johnson bowing out of the presidential race (on television), March 31, 1968. (AP Photo)

had, Johnson rapidly escalated the war in Vietnam. Here is an image of Johnson addressing the nation on March 31, 1968, when he announced that he would not seek another term as president. He was driven out of office by antiwar protesters. And he realized that the war was unwinnable. This was only a few months after the surprise Tet Offensive showed that the U.S. forces were vulnerable. Although Johnson left office, he was followed in the presidency by Richard Nixon, who continued the war.

Fifteen days before Johnson withdrew from the presidential race, Bobby Kennedy announced his candidacy for president. This was the same day as the My Lai massacre. Although members of his family were terrified that he, too, would be assassinated, he wanted to end the war. Perhaps Johnson withdrew because he could not best Bobby, who tugged at the nation's heartstrings given what had happened in Dallas five years earlier. When I heard the news that Bobby had declared, we were at the Oregon coast on spring break, staying in Yachats, a town lying on the starkly beautiful and desolate Pacific coast. We walked the beach that evening, wondering about the future.

It was impossible for me, given my age and the times, to glimpse my future in the distance, where ocean met sky. I could not recognize in that moment how history was opening and events were

Yachats, Oregon beach. (Photo courtesy of Caroline Imbert/Ben Agger)

changing me. The footprints in the sand were quickly covered over. I have not returned to Yachats, but I was prodded to remember by a French woman who sought her identity in Eugene—the opposite direction from me. The Internet led me back to that night when I viewed "Carrie in Eugene," a moving evocation of Eugene through the enchanted eyes of a French woman named Caroline. You can find her work at http://www.youtube.com/watch?v=XUXnmgjr8aQ and at http://www.youtube.com/watch?v=88Bn90-foGM.

Things went south quickly as Bobby visited Eugene in late May during the Oregon Democratic primary and a few days later was assassinated in Los Angeles. Martin Luther King had been gunned down two months earlier. My father, in despair, moved our family to Canada in 1969.

Not only did I leave the United States. I also decamped the sixties, along with many other foot soldiers of the New Left. I retreated from politics to "theory"—an academic life—and to running, along with other personal pursuits, including love and, eventually, family. Was I running away? Or toward? I theorized running as a non-Cartesian merger of mind and body, a connection to mother earth. I was looking for America. My texts were Robert Pirsig's (1974) *Zen and the Art of Motorcycle Maintenance: An Inquiry into Values*, a book everyone read, and a less well-known classic called *Meditations from the Breakdown Lane: Running Across America*, James Shapiro's (1982) chronicle of his solo run across the country. A totally apolitical book written by an ex-radical was really very political: Like me, Shapiro was looking for "home" within, an existentialist reaction to the end of the movement. His final words: "The bear went over the mountain to see what he could see. And what did he learn? That everywhere there is sky, everywhere there is ground. At every moment, everywhere, we are home."

Feminism developed its personal politics by addressing home, family, body, sexuality. I developed my politics through exercise. Mark Wetmore, the University of Colorado track and distance coach, borrowing from Tom Wolfe, talks of an Edge City of extreme physical exertion—running not into oblivion but into meaning. Few young people seek Edge City these days, whether in running or working. They are not to blame; Edge City—another name for utopia—has been malled over. We of the sixties still search for community, albeit in ways and places uncharted during those original times.

After twelve years in Canada, I returned to the United States to work at a university in Buffalo, where I lived from 1981 to 1994. Buffalo is a city with no illusions. It is working-class and proud of it. This is the home of the original chicken wings, one of economically depressed Buffalo's claims to fame. Having run out of food, the cook threw together what he had on hand, including chicken wings, celery, Tabasco sauce, and blue cheese dressing. It is appropriate that hardscrabble Buffalo's signature dish uses the least expensive part of the chicken. Buffalo was the nation's eighth largest city in the late nineteenth century, and it had a thriving steel industry when I arrived. But "deindustrialization" laid off tens of thousands of employees from major companies such as Bethlehem Steel in Lackawanna, New York. By the time I left Buffalo in 1994, the biggest employer was the state university.

Buffalo was the site of significant antiwar protests during the sixties, and the State University of New York at Buffalo had an active SDS chapter. The Panthers were also on the scene.

I do not believe in fate or destiny. Things ebb and flow. Yet people can change the direction of the swift river of history and also of their own lives. In this spirit I report that I left Buffalo in 1994 to move to the scene of the crime—Dallas, Texas. Although urban Texans may maintain that Texas is in the "New South," the decapitation of a black man dragged behind a pickup truck in Jasper, Texas, in 1998 suggests otherwise. The telling of that story suggests a different sequence of images—the Greensboro sit-ins, James Meredith's courageous stand, Bull Connor's attack dogs, the murder of the three civil rights workers, King's killing in Memphis.

Anchor Bar, Buffalo, New York, home of chicken wings. (Photo courtesy of Wikimedia Commons)

The weather is sunny in Texas. Interesting architecture abounds, as the postmodern flourishes on the Dallas skyline demonstrate. But I cannot drive by downtown Dallas without looking out at the Book Depository, the grassy knoll, the triple underpass, and the route to Parkland Hospital, realizing that I am who I am—and where I am, living in Dallas—because of the events that transpired there long ago. It is precisely the embedding of history that helps me connect where I was during those important years to the person I have become. Hayden, now almost seventy, jokes that I will soon have to call this project "the sixties at fifty," given the breakneck speed with which the years melt away. These images of the sixties provoke archaeological chipping away as we try to make the past present. Where were we when? And what did it mean to us? We recover ourselves as we recover what happened in that decade or more of our shared experience. We must neither varnish our mistakes nor pretend that we did not take sides. Only by allowing this remembrance to take place, willing to revisit the conflicts of the past and our own complicity in them, can we bring that decade forward. This storytelling is important political work as we try to teach the children well.

Casey Hayden reflects on what it took for young people to try to change the world, and she stays in touch with the "New Left" within her still. Our time in Texas links our stories, as do our basic values. Bluebonnet fields, strawberry fields. Her moving words are a place to close this book.

Dallas, Texas, skyline. (iStockPhoto)

My daughter Rose said to me, "My question about the movement is how all these people got so empowered to do all these things. It's about the inside." I've tried to speak to that question with my story. That story, which has come full circle, ends in apparent separation from my brothers and sisters in struggle, my movement family. On the inside, however, that separation does not obtain. On the inside, in my bones, I am still with them all. This isn't fluffy or sentimental. It's a visceral thing, earned by doing what was common to us all. What we did was pretty simple, as we knew at the time. What we did was, we put our bodies on the line.

We embodied, not as an abstraction, but actually, the struggle and the stress, the ambiguities and the paradoxes, of creating new social realities. Giving ourselves completely, we were as lambs. The unity we achieved transcends any political differences we might have had in the past as well as the distance between us now in space and time. We were many minds but one heart. It is my own heart, and nothing can separate me from all it contains: the triumphs and the tragedies, the exhaustion and the camaraderie, the laughter and the freedom and the love and the anger, our courage and anguish, our arrogance and humility, the splendor and tears and youth. . . .

Suddenly, and unbidden, as I wrote the words above, the bluebonnet fields of my Texas childhood appeared with perfect clarity in my mind's eye. Blanketing the low hills, spread among the live oak trees, as far as I can see they gently lie, beautiful and vanished, the fields of blue.

The sixties were our lives. Now they are memories, stories, books. They stay alive by being told and written, but they necessarily lose something—the immediacy of lived experience. But as we have seen throughout this account, the immediate events and experiences were never clear; it took decades for people to figure them out, and even then there are many disagreements about what happened and about its significance. Even after much research, I am not sure I have all the facts straight. Memory is not to be trusted, as the New Year's Eve party demonstrates.

Acknowledging that there are many truths does not mean there is no truth. Gary Mack, the curator at the Sixth Floor Museum in Dallas, makes the intriguing point that we could resolve the issue of a single shooter or multiple shooters if only people who were present and who took photos during the assassination would dig through their files and bring their evidence forward. Even if they did not capture the shooting directly, they could help resolve the issue of whether Lee Harvey Oswald acted alone. Their photos, taken from their viewing vantage, are, in effect, stories. The stories can help us get to the truth, which, although elusive, is attainable if we put our heads together.

This is my book, although it stands on the memories of others. It is time for others to write their sixties. My sixties are these sixties, the sixties I have told. I have left out a lot. I have forgotten much.

I plan to return to Eugene soon when my son and I travel there to run in a road race. Writing this book helped me realize that I never left. Yet little will seem familiar to me. But in the haze of exhaustion and free association that running provokes, I may look over at him and see myself when I was a teenager and stalking the same streets, and I will wonder what he is seeing. Perhaps he will be imagining what it must have been like for me to grow up in the shadow of the bomb, to protest the war, and to come of age at a Eugene McCarthy benefit concert. This is the way that father and son inhabit the same world and feel connected. One day he may read this book and want to write his own book about the events that formed him. He may tell his children about the time we spent together looking for America.

References

Adorno, Theodor W. 1974. *Minima Moralia: Reflections from Damaged Life.* London: Verso.

Agger, Ben. 1992. *The Discourse of Domination: From the Frankfurt School to Postmodernism.* Evanston, IL: Northwestern University Press.

———. 1993. *Gender, Culture, and Power: Toward a Feminist Postmodern Critical Theory.* Westport, CT: Praeger.

———. 2002. *Postponing the Postmodern: Sociological Practices, Selves, and Theories.* Lanham, MD: Rowman & Littlefield.

Ayers, William. 2001. *Fugitive Days.* Boston: Beacon Press.

Bernstein, Basil. 1975. *Class, Codes, and Control.* New York: Schocken Books.

Bloom, Allan. 1987. *The Closing of the American Mind.* New York: Simon & Schuster.

Breines, Wini. 1982. *Community and Organization in the New Left, 1962–1968.* New York: Praeger.

Caputo, Philip. 1977. *A Rumor of War.* New York: Ballantine Books.

Debord, Guy. 1983. *Society of the Spectacle.* Detroit: Red and Black.

Debray, Regis. 1967. *Revolution in the Revolution? Armed Struggle and Political Struggle in Latin America.* New York: Monthly Review Press.

———. 2007. *Praised Be Our Lords: A Political Education.* London: Verso.

D'Souza, Dinesh. 2007. *The Enemy at Home: The Cultural Left and Its Responsibility for 9/11.* New York: Doubleday Books.

Dunbar-Ortiz, Roxanne. 2002. *Outlaw Woman: A Memoir of the War Years, 1960–1975.* San Francisco: City Lights Publishers.

Dutschke, Rudi, Gretchen Dutschke-Klotz, Helmut Gollwitzer, and Jürgen Miermeister. 1980. *Mein langer Marsch: Reden, Schriften, und Tagebücher aus zwanzig Jahren.* Reinbek bei Hamburg: Rowohlt.

Ehrenreich, Barbara. 2005. *Bait and Switch: The (Futile) Pursuit of the American Dream.* New York: Metropolitan Books.

Ellis, Richard J. 2000. *The Dark Side of the Left: Illiberal Egalitarianism in America.* Lawrence: University Press of Kansas.

Fish, Stanley. 2008. *Save the World on Your Own Time.* New York: Oxford University Press.

Freire, Paulo. 1970. *Pedagogy of the Oppressed.* New York: Seabury.

Freud, Sigmund. 1989. *The Ego and the Id.* New York: Norton.

Friedan, Betty. 2001 [1963]. *The Feminine Mystique.* New York: Norton.

Frith, Simon. 1978. *The Sociology of Rock.* London: Constable.

Garvy, Helen. 2007. *SDS: Rebels with a Cause*. Los Gatos, CA: Shire.

Gitlin, Todd. 1987. *The Sixties: Years of Hope, Days of Rage*. New York: Bantam Books.

Goffman, Erving. 1959. *The Presentation of Self in Everyday Life*. New York: Doubleday.

Goodman, Paul. 1960. *Growing Up Absurd: Problems of Youth in the Organized Society*. New York: Vintage.

Grossberg, Lawrence. 1997. *Dancing in Spite of Myself: Essays on Popular Culture*. Durham, NC: Duke University Press.

Gutiérrez, José Angel. 1998. *The Making of a Chicano Militant: Lessons from Cristal*. Madison: University of Wisconsin Press.

Habermas, Jürgen. 1971. *Toward a Rational Society: Student Protest, Science, and Politics*. Boston: Beacon Press.

———. 1987. *The Philosophical Discourse of Modernity*. Cambridge: Massachusetts Institute of Technology Press.

Harrington, Michael. 1962. *The Other America: Poverty in the United States*. New York: Macmillan.

Hayden, Tom. 1988. *Reunion: A Memoir*. New York: Random House.

———. 2001. *Irish on the Inside: In Search of the Soul of Irish America*. New York: Verso.

Hofstadter, Richard. 1963. *Anti-intellectualism in American Life*. New York: Knopf.

Hogan, Wesley C. 2007. *Many Minds, One Heart: SNCC's Dream of a New America*. Chapel Hill: University of North Carolina Press.

Horowitz, David. 2006. *The Professors: The 101 Most Dangerous Academics in America*. Washington, DC: Regnery.

Illich, Ivan. 1972. *Deschooling Society*. New York: Harper & Row.

Jackson, Thomas F. 2007. *From Civil Rights to Human Rights: Martin Luther King Jr. and the Struggle for Economic Justice*. Philadelphia: University of Pennsylvania Press.

Jacoby, Russell. 1987. *The Last Intellectuals: American Culture in the Age of Academe*. New York: Basic Books.

———. 1999. *The End of Utopia: Politics and Culture in an Age of Apathy*. New York: Basic Books.

———. 2005. *Picture Imperfect: Utopian Thought for an Anti-utopian Age*. New York: Columbia University Press.

Jay, Martin. 1973. *The Dialectical Imagination: A History of the Frankfurt School and the Institute for Social Research, 1923–1950*. Boston: Little, Brown.

Kann, Mark E. 2005. *Punishment, Prisons, and Patriarchy: Liberty and Power in the Early American Republic*. New York: New York University Press.

Lasch, Christopher. 1979. *The Culture of Narcissism: American Life in an Age of Diminishing Expectations*. New York: Norton.

Lemert, Charles. 1997. *Postmodernism Is Not What You Think*. Malden, MA: Blackwell.

Malcolm X. 1965. *Autobiography of Malcolm X*. New York: Ballantine Books.

Marcuse, Herbert. 1969. *An Essay on Liberation*. Boston: Beacon Press.

Marx, Karl, and Friedrich Engels. 2002. *The Communist Manifesto*. London: Penguin.

McAdam, Doug. 1988. *Freedom Summer*. New York: Oxford University Press.

McLuhan, Marshall. 1989. *The Global Village: Transformation in World Life in the Twenty-First Century.* New York: Oxford University Press.

Metzler, Ken. 2001. *Confrontation: The Destruction of a College President.* Eugene: University of Oregon Press.

Miller, James. 1987. *"Democracy Is in the Streets": From Port Huron to the Siege of Chicago.* New York: Simon & Schuster.

Mills, C. Wright. 1959. *The Sociological Imagination.* New York: Oxford University Press.

Naison, Mark. 2002. *White Boy.* Philadelphia: Temple University Press.

Neill, A. S. 1977. *Summerhill: A Radical Approach to Child Rearing.* New York: Pocket Books.

"Never Again Will They Fight Alone." 1970. www.sunrisedancer.com/radical reader/library/weatherman/weatherman45.asp.

Nietzsche, Friedrich. 1910. *The Will to Power: An Attempted Transvaluation of All Values.* 2nd ed. Edinburgh: T. N. Foulis.

Oglesby, Carl. 2008. *Ravens in the Storm: A Personal History of the 1960s Antiwar Movement.* New York: Scribner.

Pirsig, Robert M. 1974. *Zen and the Art of Motorcycle Maintenance: An Inquiry into Values.* New York: Morrow.

Port Huron Statement of the SDS. 1962. www.martinrealm.org/documents/radical/sixties1.html.

Power, Thomas. 1971. *Diana: The Making of a Terrorist.* New York: Houghton Mifflin.

Rudd, Mark. 2009. *Underground: My Life in SDS and the Underground.* New York: HarperCollins.

Sale, Kirkpatrick. 1973. *SDS.* New York: Random House.

Sellers, Cleveland. 1990. *River of No Return: The Autobiography of a Black Militant and the Life and Death of SNCC.* Oxford: University Press of Mississippi.

Shapiro, James E. 1982. *Meditations from the Breakdown Lane: Running Across America.* New York: Random House.

Stone, Robert. 2007. *Prime Green: Remembering the Sixties.* New York: Ecco Press.

Varon, Jeremy. 2004. *Bringing the War Home: The Weather Underground, Red Army Faction, and Revolutionary Violence in the Sixties and Seventies.* Berkeley and Los Angeles: University of California Press.

Weather Underground. 1974. *Prairie Fire: The Politics of Revolutionary Anti-imperialism.* San Francisco: Communications Co.

Weber, Max. 1958. *From Max Weber: Essays in Sociology.* New York: Oxford University Press.

———. 2009. *The Protestant Ethic and the Spirit of Capitalism, with Other Writings on the Rise of the West.* 4th ed. New York: Oxford University Press.

Wells, Tom. 1994. *The War Within: America's Battle over Vietnam.* Berkeley and Los Angeles: University of California Press.

"You Don't Need a Weatherman to Know Which Way the Wind Blows." 1969. www.martinrealm.org/documents/radical/sixties1.html.

Index

About the Author

Ben Agger, author of many books, is professor of sociology and humanities at the University of Texas–Arlington, where he edits the journal *Fast Capitalism*. His most recent books are *Critical Social Theories*, 2nd ed. (Paradigm Publishers 2006) and *Fast Families, Virtual Children* (Paradigm Publishers 2007).